BORN IN OUR HEARTS

BORN IN OUR HEARTS

Stories of Adoption

Filis Casey and
Marisa Catalina Casey

Health Communications, Inc.
Deerfield Beach, Florida

www.hcibooks.com

Library of Congress Cataloging-in-Publication Data is available
from the Library of Congress

ISBN 0-7573-0129-0

Publisher: Health Communications, Inc.
            3201 S.W. 15th Street
            Deerfield Beach, FL 33442–8190

Cover and inside book design by Lawna Patterson Oldfield
Cover photo ©PhotoDisc

Not flesh of my flesh,
Nor bone of my bone,
But still miraculously
My own.
Never forget
For a single minute,
That you weren't born
Under my heart,
But in it.

Author Unknown

CONTENTS

CHAPTER ONE
Letting Go

CHAPTER TWO
Facing Loss and Gaining Hope

CHAPTER THREE
Embracing Our Differences

CHAPTER FOUR
Adopting the Older Child

CHAPTER FIVE
Embarking on the Lone Journey

CHAPTER SIX
Experiencing Fatherhood

CHAPTER SEVEN
Becoming Brothers and Sisters

CHAPTER EIGHT
Grandparenting an Adopted Child

CHAPTER NINE
Encountering Shadows of the Past

ACKNOWLEDGMENTS

First and foremost, thank you to all of the families who have so willingly shared your personal stories and everyday miracles for this book. Because you shared a part of your life with us, the narratives in this volume have the capacity to inspire others and allow readers to experience what connects us all: love and family. While each story is a distinct looking glass into lives that have been brightened by adoption, each single prism of light cannot speak for adoption alone; it is only through gathering of these beams of light together that this collective voice will ring true.

Among the special people I wish to thank is my husband, Bob, who has survived the roller coaster of our lives and assisted me throughout these last thirty-four years together. His invaluable advice on this book exemplifies what a true partner he is. Thank you to my daughter, Sarah, and my son, Matthew, for their love, understanding and encouragement from the early stages of this project and beyond.

To my coauthor, co-conspirator, and daughter, Marisa: you have blessed, enriched and expanded our family's world and I'm so happy that we undertook this adventure together. It truly has brought us closer together and allowed our relationship to flourish and I am so grateful for that. Thank you for sharing your life with ours.

Thanks to Stephi and John Meyer, lifelong friends who served as great models and whose inspiration and help made this book possible.

To Peter Vegso, for taking the initial interest in the concept and for making this book possible.

To Bonnie Delongchamp, my right-hand woman, who has always provided constant encouragement and has made this book a labor of love. Her generous soul, can-do attitude, organizational skills, personal commitment and hard work continue to support me in countless ways.

Thank you to Daniel Gould Levine, for expert editing of many of the stories in the volume, the book is richer because of your many hours of reading and editing suggestions.

To Allison Janse, for her discriminating editing and making the project go so smoothly. I especially appreciate your personal interest in this book. To Anthea Stephens, for her initial organization and involvement. To Rita Guatstella, for her poetic words and involvement over the years. To Ana Douglass, for hours of reading and valuable suggestions. To Kim Weiss, for doing such a good job in supporting this book. To Jaimie Adler, for her enthusiasm and persistence in getting us noticed.

In addition we'd like to thank all of you who made the effort to submit your heartwarming tales for possible inclusion in the book. While we were not able to use all the stories, we were touched by each and every submission. We ask for your understanding and hope there will be additional volumes for future publication.

Finally, special thanks to the Alliance for Children staff: Ruth Rich, Vivian Cone, Robert Lamarche, Bonnie Delongchamp, Camille Conte, Ana McDonnell, Renee Lubowich, Martha Lamb, Jill Greblick, Chris Jenkins, Nancy Morin, Yunfen Shih, Shannon Shaper, Anna Johnson, Bonnie Elbaum, Xiaozeng Wu and Weihang Chen for their dedication, patience and for believing in our cause as they work everyday to help connect children with families in which they can flourish.

INTRODUCTION

The inspiration for this book began over thirty years ago when, as a young lawyer, I started The Alliance for Children, the first international adoption agency in Massachusetts. Over the years, we've placed nearly five thousand children, ranging in age from infants to preteens. They come from as far away as China, Russia and Latin America, and as near as around the block or the next town. The walls of our office are covered with their smiling faces. Their stories, and those of their parents and other family members, are a rich narrative from which we take pleasure and solace daily.

Over the years, I've seen the attitudes toward adoption, especially international adoption, change for the better. People are more open to it, more willing to consider a child of another race and another culture. Yet classic misconceptions still exist: Families formed through adoption are somehow second best, or parents who adopt a child from another culture or race are saints, or that all children adopted internationally have emotional problems. I've always marveled at the persistence of these tired concepts, which are at such variance with the wondrous exhilaration of having your child placed in your arms for the first time. There is a reason that people who've adopted once often adopt again and again! And it's why, after having our two beautiful biological children, Matthew and Sarah, my husband and I adopted our third child, our wonderful Marisa, from an orphanage in Colombia. As a woman who's experienced both forms of motherhood, I can tell you that adoption is its own unique joy.

Adoption, in particular, helps us learn the truth that our children—however they come to us—are unique individuals.

This book presents the diverse voices of many who have been touched by adoption in the United States. Each story is a distinct looking glass into life that has been brightened by the experience of adoption. Yet, each tiny prism of light cannot speak for adoption alone. What you'll find here is the trepidation and triumph of families adopting internationally, the struggle and sacrifice of single parents, the pride of grandparents, the glee and jealousy of siblings, and the stories of courageous birth mothers and adoptive parents made whole by having a child "born in their hearts." The stories may touch on the various aspects of adoption, but the experiences lived and the emotions felt are universal to all human beings who have been touched by love, hope and the joy of family.

The goal of this book is to speak openly to anyone who is considering bringing a child into his or her life. Through these voices, adoption emerges as the joyful, frightening, tender, confusing, exhilarating, deliberate, serendipitous experience it is, and in many cases as a divine occurrence of fate. Adoption is also a magical process, a journey that transforms individuals who come together and rejoice in making a family.

As a young (only) child, growing up in Middle Village in Clifton, New Jersey, a garden-apartment complex filled with young families, I remember Rhoda, our next-door neighbor, telling my mother that she was planning to adopt a child. I cried and begged my mother to also adopt so I would have a brother or sister, but it was not to be.

Law school graduation led to my looking for a happy part of the law. Meeting a neighbor who had recently adopted, and who experienced a great deal of frustration and lack of resources in international adoption, motivated me to found an international adoption agency.

As the mother of two biological children, I did not initially intend to adopt a child. But as I watched children join their adoptive families and saw pictures daily of children who needed families, I started thinking of becoming an adoptive parent.

My husband was delighted with the idea. He had been interested in adoption ever since he escorted a baby from Bogotá, Colombia, and found that he had bonded to the child in the twenty-four hours he spent bringing her from the orphanage to the waiting family in Massachusetts. No problem convincing him.

Our two children were nine and eleven years old at the time we discussed adopting a child. Our son Matthew's major concern was whether a baby would mean that we would no longer be able to travel. Our daughter Sarah was delighted with the idea of a younger sister. We soon began the adoption process.

In time a one-inch-square, black-and-white photo of a little girl arrived at the agency. She had been selected by the orphanage in Colombia to be our child. She had a short boyish haircut that we later found out was a result of a bout of lice. She was nearly three years old with beautiful, huge green eyes and lips like a cupid's bow. So began our journey to bring Marisa into our family and into our hearts.

We created a book about our family and sent some photos to Bogotá so she could have a preview of her new family. After several months of waiting, my husband and I traveled to Bogotá to meet our daughter. After working at the agency for seven years and helping lots of families, I had no idea how emotional the meeting would be when my time came. I was excited and nervous, and then I understood all the emotions of parents who had gone through this process before me.

The day we arrived at the orphanage was three days after Marisa's third birthday. I will never forget the moment when a beautiful child was brought into the room at the orphanage where we waited. Her hair was carefully curled, and she wore black patent leather shoes, white lace ankle socks and a navy and white dress with an apron. She was clutching a picture of her sister Sarah in her right hand.

My heart leapt, my husband and I squeezed each other's hands as our friend, the orphanage director, asked Marisa a question (which we later learned was "Do you know who these people are?") to which she answered, "*Sí, Mami y Popi.*" This moment and this child exceeded all of our expectations.

I had prepared myself for a year for this moment. At certain times I was so worried about adding another child to our family. Could I handle number three with my busy work schedule? How would a child who had spent the first three years of her life in an orphanage and in foster care adapt to a new life in our home? What would the adjustment be like? Would she be frightened or sad? How would we communicate? Were we too old? Were we too naïve?

Right from the beginning, we found a child who was trusting, independent, able to adjust to us, talkative, and a bit spoiled. At our first meal together in Bogotá, we told her she would need to eat her lunch before enjoying a chocolate coin placed before her. She then promptly listed (in Spanish) every person she no longer liked (including us) because she was not getting her way.

Julia, a friend and the agency translator, accompanied us to Colombia and spoke Spanish as her first language. When Marisa met her she said, "My mother thinks she speaks Spanish. You really speak Spanish." Despite the initial language barrier, it is amazing how many things worked out the way they should, the way we hoped they would.

♥   ♥   ♥

Adoption was a normal state of affairs in our family's universe. Living in our family meant late-night phone conversations in

"Spanglish" and visitors from various foreign countries. With a mother who is the executive director of an international adoption agency, the idea of adopting was not strange or out of this world for our family. Being so closely connected with the adoption agency even after Marisa's adoption gave us a constant reminder of how special our family story is. Adoption has immensely enriched our family. We know that we are very fortunate to have found each other.

Marisa came to the Casey household as a bright Spanish-speaking three-year-old. There were no secrets in our home, and we tried to be as open as possible, yet that did not mean that understanding each other came so easily. During Marisa's high school years, her experiences were similar to other teenage children, but they were coupled with adoption questions, such as, "Why was I given up for adoption?" and "Where do I really fit in?" During these years, there were many discussions, and our relationship was not always smooth sailing. After Marisa entered college, perhaps because of some distance from each other, we all reflected upon our situation and became better able to communicate with each other. Then we truly began to recognize and appreciate our differences. By virtue of living in a home where adoption was an integral part of everyday life, the idea evolved to work together on this book, sharing different perspectives and stories about adoption. Working as a mother-daughter team, with the generous help of so many others, we found compelling stories of families and individuals who were touched by adoption, stories as unique as our own.

Our family is connected to other families who have adopted— other families that know what it's like to explain to doctors about not having a complete medical history, or what it's like to face family tree projects in school where there are so many empty branches. We all learned from each other and from our common experience. With these lessons fresh in our minds, we set out to collect stories of others who were affected by adoption. We hope this book offers comfort and information and a sense of belonging to a larger community.

At its core this book is about family. Many stories are about hope and determination, while others describe hardship and are bittersweet. Some relate emotion, others facts. Yet, in its own way, each story is a love story.

When I talk with adoptive families, so many of them say with pride, "This child is just perfect for our family," or "This child makes our family feel complete." We wonder how that happens so frequently. We also feel exactly the same way.

CHAPTER ONE

Letting Go

Roots and Wings

Marisa Catalina Casey

I f I think real hard, I can see the couch. I can feel Ximena's hand enveloping mine, leading me into the office where they were. All I knew was that this was the day—the day I was going away with these new people.

I can see their expressions in my head. They were shy, but they tried to hide it. They tried to show they were strong so I would be strong. They wanted desperately for me to like them, for me to call them Mommy and Daddy, and for me to smile and accept them because they had decided to accept me.

I can't feel now how I felt then. I can't remember the thoughts running through my head. At that age, my native language flowed freely and naturally through my brain like a fish through water. Now, I stumble on my words, searching my mental images for the Spanish textbook page about forming the subjunctive. Each night, I long to dream in Spanish.

They stood up. They held a box—a blue box with a cellophane window. Through the transparent plastic I could make out the face of my first doll, the first toy I wouldn't have to share with any other children. I wasn't shy. I didn't hide behind the orphanage director, Ximena, the only person in the room to whom I had any connection. I just stood, and when Ximena asked me, *"¿Catalina, sabes quienes son estas personas?"* (Catalina, do you know who these people are?), I answered, *"Sí. Mami y Popi."* They smiled confidently. I was theirs.

I can't recall the name I gave my doll, nor the name that came in the package, but I do remember her car seat and bowl. The bowl was wooden with a wooden spoon. The wood was smooth, and I used to love running my tiny fingers over the concave curve. Once, I took a red crayon and colored in the wood. I don't know why, but the bowl was never the same after that day.

I would lose the chair and the bowl for long periods of time without really noticing it, until one day I would wake up and feel the need to find the set again. Maybe I had dreamt about Colombia, or maybe I wanted to see if they were how I remembered them . . . if the blue checkered cloth of the car seat was as bright as I had imagined, or if the red crayon had rubbed off of the wood yet. I never found the doll.

On the plane from Bogotá, I wore soft, purple corduroy overalls and a white shirt with some kind of print on it. I had been given a brand-new dress from the orphanage to wear when I met my parents. It was white with small dark blue dots on it, complete with a blue apron and ruffles. I wore white tights, a white shawl and tiny, black, patent leather dress shoes. My hair had been cut and curled in preparation.

My brother had always wanted a little brother. When my photograph arrived in the mail, he thought his wish had finally come true. Months before my parents' trip, the orphanage sent my passport picture to my new family. They thought I was a boy based on my short hair and my birth name being Francis. My light brown hair was slicked back, and my huge green eyes popped out of the black-and-white photograph. I did not smile. In the photograph I have a bewildered look on my face, as if I really were face-to-face with these new people I would call my family, as if I knew that they would have the same frowning brow and wondering eyes when they looked at my picture.

I was a new person the day I met them. I carried my doll around with me all day long. I kept her strapped in her car seat while I carried her, as if she would fall out or run away from me given the chance. I protected her with my arms folded across the white ribbon seat belt. She was mine.

I refused to wear my seat belt on the plane, and the Colombian flight attendant pleaded with me to cooperate so that the plane could take off. I wouldn't budge. Finally, in a moment of desperation, I allowed myself to be bribed by Julia's lollipop. Julia was a friend of my mother's who had been instrumental in making the connection with Ximena and my orphanage. Julia's lollipop wasn't just any lollipop; it was a huge rainbow spiral with the colors all swirling and melting into one another. Red into orange, orange into yellow, yellow into green and green into blue. The lollipop was as big as my head.

Logan International Airport in Boston was crowded. I lay sleeping in my father's arms, wearing my new, soft, purple overalls and sucking on my perfectly curved left index finger. I don't remember when I started doing this, nor when I stopped, but occasionally, I bend my finger and stick it into my mouth to see how it feels, to see if it will give me any comfort—as if I knew the secret power my finger possessed back in Colombia when I was a child. Now, as an adult, I find no comfort in sucking on my finger. My index finger is too large to fit comfortably into my mouth, and whenever I try, my finger ends up with teeth marks on it, and the taste in my mouth is of iron or sweat or lunch or toothpaste.

That first night is a blur—so many new people and new places, a new language I would learn to speak, an old language I would forget. Finally, I had a room of my own, complete with a big bed and a closet full of little dresses, pants and shirts. We hung up the old dress in my new closet and then I paused to survey my new clothing. *"Bonita, bonita, bonita"* (beautiful, beautiful, beautiful), I said while looking through my new dresses, passing pastel pinks and greens and yellows.

"Fea!" (ugly) I shouted when I reached the blue and white dress from Colombia. Thus began my love-hate relationship with my past.

♥ ♥ ♥

My transition to life in the United States included changing my name from Francis Catalina Cuartas to Marisa Catalina Casey; my introduction to my new big brother, Matthew, and my new big sister, Sarah; my induction into various preschools and kindergartens where I learned English; and finally my "naturalization."

I hated my middle name until junior high school. I refused to sign my full name, opting for the more impersonal and safer "Marisa C. Casey." I rejected my past both subtly and overtly until my journey at the age of twelve back to Colombia and back to my orphanage. During that same year I began Spanish-language classes. I felt a particular familiarity and facility with the language. I didn't have many problems with the accent, and I recognized certain words in my books. I felt this same familiarity on my trip back to Colombia.

My parents and I did not stay very long on our visit to Bogotá. I have hazy memories of visiting my orphanage and having people I didn't know recognize me. I even saw a picture of myself on the wall. My adoptive parents had sent it to the orphanage to show them how I had grown. That trip I had enough of a taste of my birth city to want to return there again. I can recall the smell of the air and the benign sense of well-being I felt playing at a *finca* in the countryside with children my age. Yet I knew I was different. I still feel different.

During sophomore year of college, while discussing in a writing class a personal essay of mine dealing with adoption, I was stunned to see a fellow student write the following comment on the bottom of my paper: "You don't look adopted." To this day I don't know what she meant, exactly. Did I not look Latin American? Do adopted children somehow look different to her? I like to think it was just naïveté, yet I often feel like I am defending myself and my Latin American background and Latina-ness. I was born in Colombia but I grew up in the United States, speaking English and watching cable television. I am a member of my own unique subculture, born to Colombian and Spanish birth parents but being raised in a white, middle-class family in a predominantly white, middle-class suburb of Boston.

The summer before my senior year of high school I worked in an orphanage in Cuenca, Ecuador, where I confronted many of these issues. I will never forget the children at El Tadeo Torres that I cared for, especially one little boy named José. The first day I met him, José took me by the hand and led me outside to the backyard of the orphanage. He tripped several times walking through the overgrown weeds as we passed the surreal vision of rusting orange and blue metal structures. The circle of little wooden *barquitos* each rotating on the same axis looked like a spider, each boat making the same spine-tingling creak from rain and old age. On that first day, like I would on so many other days, I lifted José onto the decaying seat of one of the little boats and helped him adjust his heavy boots under the seat in front of him, the same clumsy boots which imprisoned the feet that would kick and refuse to be still when I changed his soiled clothing.

José had permanent bumps on his head as a result of his birth father's repeated brutality. He had to have multiple surgeries to correct the damage, but some wounds wouldn't heal. I suspect he didn't remember much of his early life. I don't remember much about my life before I was adopted. I don't remember the other children who were in the orphanage or foster care with me. As I looked at the children whom I cared for that summer, I wondered if they, too, would forget one another if they were adopted. I wondered if any of them were destined to leave, if they would have the luck that I had to find a family but also to be able to return, or if they would simply stay where they were. Forever.

In addition to severe mental and physical problems, José, like all of the other children at this particular orphanage, had emotional problems too. On a bad day, he threw tantrums for no apparent reason. On a good day, he smiled and sang and laughed. Many people couldn't see the real José beyond his tantrums and his mixed-up language.

For six weeks, I peeled off urine-soaked pants and put on clean ones. For six weeks, I worked on deciphering his speech and restraining him while he tried to kick and punch me in an attempt to break free from my arms. In those six weeks, I discovered my strengths and my limits.

On one of my last days at the orphanage, José took me by the hand, as he always did, and then he clearly said, "Maritza." At that moment, I realized the most important thing I could ever realize about myself: my own worth. Here was a child who could not pronounce his own name, nor could he remember where his bed was, yet he remembered and spoke my name. I discovered many things that summer, but the most important of all was that both physical and emotional borders can be transcended and each person has the capacity within themselves to do so.

Three years after leaving, I returned to El Tadeo Torres. I was happy to see that I recognized only two children, and they recognized me: Carlos and Janira, brother and sister. All of the other children I had cared for that summer, including sweet José, had been adopted or had returned to their birth families. The happiest news was that Carlos and Janira were in the process of being adopted together into a family. Often, I think about them and all of those children. I wonder how they are doing, where they are and who is loving them now.

♥ ♥ ♥

Throughout my years in high school and college, I had the good fortune to travel to a number of Latin American countries. Each unique adventure taught me something new about myself, my heritage, and the opportunities that I have and may take for granted in my life in the United States. A physical journey is not necessary for these lessons to be learned or taught, but immersing myself in the culture of these various countries was my own personal catalyst.

Over my life I have questioned my identity as a person who was internationally and transracially adopted. I've listened to others talk about family resemblance, not knowing if someone else on this planet shares my green eyes. I have watched births on television, wondering what mine was like. I have explained to my doctor that I don't know my medical history, worrying that I am missing vital information. Knowing these experiences are common for adoptees gives me comfort. I am no longer bitter or angry that my path may be more difficult than others or fraught with detours or missing signposts. I used to think that growing up meant being independent enough to leave my family. Now I am beginning to realize that the return to family defines maturity, that there isn't a family dynamic more true or real than any other, and that family is what you make it. Adoption is special because parents who adopt know this. The children they adopt will learn this over time. At this point in my life, I am happy for the bumps in the road that have shaped me into a person who deeply cares for and appreciates my family, my community and my world.

An expression that has always stuck with me is as follows: "There are two things a parent can give to their child. One is roots and the other is wings." Not knowing my birth family or the details of my first three years used to make me feel like I didn't have roots. I have since realized that I have wings because my adoptive family has nurtured me and created an environment in which I could grow and learn, and which has enabled me to grow my own roots and sow my own seeds wherever I like.

I hope the lessons I have learned from my trips to Ecuador and other countries in Latin America stay with me throughout my life. As I write this in early 2004, I will have another opportunity later this year to explore my birth country when I return to Bogotá for my orphanage's twenty-fifth anniversary, ten years after my first trip back and twenty years after I was adopted. I hope to look back at all of my experiences in Latin America and beyond and know not only that one person can make a difference, but that one person must make a difference if we are to live and thrive with one another. I wish to pass this knowledge along to my children and somehow to all adopted children. Each of us has the power to change the life of a child.

Thinking About the Birth Mother

Anonymous

My oldest daughter will be four in July. She was born in Ecuador, and my husband and I adopted her when she was an infant. We know almost nothing about her birth parents, the people who gave her life. Those people are an integral part of her story, and she loves to hear that story. She also loves her little sister's story, the story of how she was born to us. She recognizes that these stories are very different—except the part where "Mommy and Daddy were so happy to have their little girl and love her with all of their hearts."

My adopted daughter has brought only joy to my life, but my happiness is shadowed by a sadness that I am certain awaits her when she is older and more cognizant. I am the parent of a child adopted from overseas, a child whose biological parentage is and is likely to remain a mystery. The sadness she may feel someday already sneaks up on me as I tell her and her sister their stories. There is a blank space in her story while her sister's story has so many rich details. That space is not empty, but we can't see what's there. She has a birth family: a mother and a father, grandparents, cousins, maybe siblings. But no amount of looking is likely to illuminate that space for my daughter.

I have started trying to come up with a composite story that is probably true about my daughter's birth parents. I have yet to share any of these possible scenarios with my daughter because I am not comfortable with the extent of my knowledge about the situation of the average person in Ecuador, and I am not yet comfortable with the idea of presenting my daughter with mere possibilities. Fortunately she doesn't need the details yet, and I have some time to work on them. I sometimes find myself feeling a little envious of the parents who adopted girls from China. While each birth family's situation is unique, China's one-child policy provides a heartbreaking shorthand explanation for so many infant girls becoming available for adoption.

When I think about my daughter's birth family and try to prepare for the "why" question that is sure to come, the explanation I always foresee giving is simply poverty, which seems to be a common if not universal factor in birth parents' decisions. Ecuador has no large, thriving middle class, and precious few people there are wealthy. Chances are pretty good that my daughter's birth parents were poor. If they had not been poor, maybe they would have decided to parent our daughter. Combine poverty with issues of abortion access, and the stigma of out-of-wedlock births in many poor, developing countries, and many women around the world have few options when faced with an unplanned pregnancy.

I live with the knowledge that I have the joy of parenting and loving this wonderful child because of the circumstances of her birth parents. The dilemma is agonizing: If the problem of world poverty had been solved five years ago, I might not have my daughter. If I had the power to turn back time and end the hunger and suffering caused by world poverty, knowing I would lose my daughter, would I do it? Could I do it?

I avoid thinking about this dilemma and focus instead on details and unanswerable questions. I wonder at what point in her pregnancy my daughter's birth mother made the decision not to parent her child. Did she know from the moment she discovered her pregnancy? Was the decision made only after her baby, my daughter, was born? Was the birth father involved in the decision? I wonder if they are together now, if they were ever together. I wonder about other siblings my daughter may have.

I also focus on the questions to which I know the answers. These questions and answers comfort me. For example, I know, because I am a parent, that my daughter's birth mother loves her. I know that she struggled over the decision, no matter when or how it was made. I know she remembers and thinks about her daughter. Even if she never looked into her baby's beautiful eyes, she remembers the child she carried. I can tell my daughter these things with complete confidence. I hope they comfort her too.

Of course, I find myself praying that searches by international adoptees will one day be easier and present greater likelihood of success. I hope that circumstances in countries like Ecuador change so birth parents are freer to identify themselves and open the search process. In any case, we will try to be sure my daughter understands that someday she may search, but that searching does not always mean finding.

For me, right now, almost as strong as my wish that my daughter will someday be able to find her birth mother is my longing to thank her. But I can't even do that. I've heard some adoptive parents say that they think a lot about their children's birth mothers on their children's birthdays. I do too, because that is the one day I can be certain she is thinking of our daughter. But I think of my daughter's birth mother almost every day, and I believe she thinks of my daughter, her baby, almost every day too. Every day I send a thank-you south—a thank-you and an apology. "I am so sorry for whatever it was that put you in the position you found yourself in almost four years ago. But please don't ask me if I would have changed it if I could, because I fear my answer will not be noble. You are in my heart, and I will do everything I can to ensure you are in my daughter's—our daughter's—as well."

Every birth mother's situation is different, yet every birth mother's story is the same. I once read an article written by a birth mother, and I found myself shifting the details. I imagine a young mestiza woman telling her tale. She has dark brown eyes, light brown skin and straight black hair falling down her back in a single braid. She looks like my daughter. She looks like her daughter. She cries softly as she recites her story. I am not stealing the story of the birth mother who wrote. I'm just borrowing it, because it is all I have.

♥

Dear Birth Mother

Joy Murphy

We always planned on adopting a child, although we planned on adopting only after having biological children. But things don't always work out the way we plan them. The pain and discouragement of repeated miscarriages and the uncertainty of our ability to conceive a child led us to reassess our plan. Considering the adoption process was actually an easy decision for us. People worried that I was trying to replace babies that we had lost. In reality, we were trying to build our family, in the only way that I knew we could. Things had come full circle for me. I was adopted.

We researched many programs and countries, read countless books and dreamed of what was to be our future as a family. As prepared as we were trying to be, fate had a hand in the path we would take next: to our adoption agency's information meeting, listening to a family that had just returned from Colombia. I remember leaning over to my husband, Steve, and whispering, "What do you think about Colombia?" The answer to my question was written on his face, and that was it for us. We were on our way to having all of our dreams come true. It would be seven months until our daughter would be placed in our arms—seven months until the best time of our life together would begin.

The emotional journey was a piece of this story I thought would be no problem for me. Growing up, I certainly had issues with my own adoption. Adolescence was a tough period for me. I felt alone and unsure of whom I was. I had fantasies of who I thought I might be, but no concrete evidence. Growing up, my parents had always told me that I was adopted. It was something they taught me to be proud of. However, it ended at that. I learned quickly that opening a conversation on the circumstances of my adoption and my wanting to know more about my birth parents would lead to my mother crying, and that was not something I was prepared to deal with. I think she was afraid of losing me. As a result, I kept most of my thoughts and insecurities to myself.

I had dreamed of the day that I would be of legal age to search for my birth family. When that day came, I did nothing. Years passed and along came the Internet. Beginning my search online would be an easier way to find information on my past. I would find myself beginning to search, dreaming of a reunion, only to have my own defense mechanisms stop me from going any further. One time I went so far as to return to my own adoption agency. I talked with the woman who did the intake report for my biological mother. She informed me that she was able to share some nonidentifying information in addition to what was contained in my original papers. I found out that I had a brother; he was two years younger, and also placed for adoption as a baby. I began to search for both of them. Again, defense mechanisms took over, and this search ended as quickly as it began. Someday I will find them; someday I will have the answers and connections that I have been craving for as long as I can remember. Someday, but not right now.

Even with all of this emotional "baggage," I felt that I was a strong person. I believed that adopting our own child would not have any effect on what I had dealt with in my past. If anything, I knew that beginning the adoption process would give me a new perspective on the adoption dynamic. I was finally beginning to see things through the eyes of my mother—something I had always tried to avoid (you know how mothers and daughters can be). Renee, our social worker, warned me that I might want to have some support in place for what I was about to experience. I thought she didn't know me very well. I knew I could handle it. Renee knew me a lot better than I did.

It began with a visit to the Department of Vital Statistics for copies of our own birth certificates. This apparently simple task involved an unexpectedly long wait, and we couldn't figure out why. I was secretly hoping they would slip up and give me my original birth certificate. That did not happen. What did happen was that they photocopied my husband's original birth certificate right away. Mine was a different story. They sat down at a desk, four feet from me, and began to handwrite the information gleaned from the original. I begged them to no avail to let me see the original. My husband left with our legal birth documents in hand, but I left with a broken spirit and a broken heart. I cried for the entire forty-five minutes going home.

Then came the "Dear Birth Mother" letter we were to write for our class at the adoption agency. I jumped all over it. Though it was just an exercise for most in our class, for me it was a way to say things to a "birth mother" that I wish I could have said to my own birth mother. My emotions were finally on paper. Everything I wanted to say, at last I had a chance to express. It felt great, such a weight off my shoulders. Then came the dreams followed by the nightmares. I dreamt of my childhood dog. My dog was my best friend growing up. She became old and ailing, struggling to hold on. On the way home from school one day, I stopped at the store for some juice. I returned home five minutes too late. She was gone. I didn't get to say good-bye. I wasn't just dreaming about losing my dog; I realized I never got to say good-bye to my birth mother. I was just a baby at the time.

My emotions began surfacing in that fashion. I started doubting what I was doing. I wondered what I had gotten myself into. I asked myself if I could love this child as much as I would love a biological child, which was a strange concept for me to consider. My mother loved me 100 percent. In her mind, there was no difference between an adopted child and a biological child. In fact, I had never known a "biological" bond. Yet I found myself asking these questions: *Would I know how to take care of the baby? Would we bond with the child of a stranger?* I was even worried about "breaking" her or doing or saying something that would hurt her emotionally.

One day, our phone rang. It was our social worker, Renee. After I had spent the past months nagging her through e-mail, she was calling to check up on us. Had we collected all of our documents and had them sealed at the Colombian Consulate? Had we assembled all of the documents that would make up the "dossier," which needed to be sent ASAP to the orphanage in Colombia? Finally, she announced that she had good news for us. It's a GIRL!!!! I couldn't believe my ears. Our family was at last beginning to take form. Even so, the wait was not over. Yet another month passed before we were cleared to travel to Colombia.

Finally, on a beautifully clear morning in Bogotá, on February 4, 2000, we were united with our daughter. From the moment the director of the orphanage placed her in my arms, all of my fears about becoming a mother melted away. From the very beginning, we were meant to be a family. All of the pain we had previously been through finally made sense. It was all worth it. We would have endured one hundred times the pain for the happiness we have been experiencing since that February morning. No longer am I dwelling on my own adoption experience, laden with self-pity. I am suddenly reflecting on my daughter's experience, both here and now and in the future. I am looking forward to the talks and feelings that we will share, and hopefully the support I can offer her all through life. All of a sudden it is not about me. It is about our beautiful two-year-old, about us. It is about our family and our future.

♥

Having Andrew

Andrea Mackowitz

May 14, 2002, was the most frightening day of my life. I found out for certain what I had already suspected: I was sixteen and pregnant. What was I supposed to do? How was I going to tell my parents? I had never been more scared. I put off breaking the news as long as I could. Finally I told my mom. Her reaction was what I expected, but she added, "We will get through this." The next day we both told my dad. Trying to digest the unsettling news was very stressful for us all. My mom and dad, who had been adopted, felt strongly that adoption was our only option. How could I care for a baby when I couldn't take care of myself?

First we spoke with an adoption attorney and agencies, deciding on an adoption agency in Wellesley, Massachusetts. Rob was the social worker for the agency, and my mom felt she made a good connection with him when she explained our situation. We all felt it was very important to find the most knowledgeable social worker. I trust my mom and her instincts, and of course she was right about Rob. He is one of the nicest people I have ever met in my life, and I was very comfortable with him. He is such a funny guy, and just talking with him and being around him made me feel better about everything.

Rob explained the process of adoption and the different ways to go about it, including closed and open adoptions. Without a doubt, I knew that I wanted to have an open adoption. I couldn't even imagine carrying a baby for nine months and never seeing him or her again. I told Rob the qualities I was looking for in prospective parents. He gave me three family profiles to look through. I studied the information very carefully. People told me that when I came across the right family, I would know it right away. They said I would have this gut feeling.

The emotions I felt after reading through Paula and Doug's profile were indescribable. I knew they were perfect, exactly what I was looking for. I believe that I could have looked at all the people in the world and still thought they were the right ones. They had so much in common with my own family, and they were everything I wanted for my child and more. I immediately called Rob and told him I wanted to meet with Paula and Doug.

The day arrived to meet them. My parents and I were very nervous, but I knew everything was going to work out. The moment I saw them, all my nervousness disappeared, and without even talking to them I was 100 percent positive they were the ones. After that meeting we stayed in contact until the baby was born, getting together many times and talking on the phone. I would call them to update them on what was going on in my life and what was happening at my doctor's appointments.

Every time I was with Rob, he asked me what I wanted for the future contact with the baby. Each time I told him that I did not know. I had no idea how I would feel once the baby was born. I was very confused about that aspect. About a month before the baby was born, I came up with a plan. I would like to see him at least three or four times during the first year. After that, it would be at least once a year. Having such a good relationship with Paula and Doug has made all of this very easy. They realized the importance of my being involved in the baby's life and agreed to what I wanted.

Once the baby, who I named Andrew, was born, I fell in love with him. I could not believe how much I loved him. I spent every minute with him in the hospital. I fed him, held him, and even changed his diapers. My family and friends came to visit us. He amazed them. Usually if a birth mother is placing her baby for adoption, the baby will leave the hospital and go straight to a foster home. But I wanted him to go home from the hospital with Paula and Doug.

I would be leaving the hospital on Monday. As Sunday evening came, I realized how much I did not want this day to end. I knew that tomorrow I would be leaving Andrew, and he would be going to live with his new family. I had no idea how upset I would be. I made it through Sunday night, but as soon as I woke up Monday, I felt terribly sad. I did not want to go home. I wanted to stay in the hospital as long as I could. When my mom woke up, I could tell how upset she was too. We did nothing but cry all day. My brother came in to visit the baby one last time, and even he was upset. My dad, who cried a lot too, remembering his own adoption, was there all day to help my mom and me. Even though I knew how much this was hurting him, he stayed strong to help us.

Rob arrived at the hospital around noon; Paula and Doug around four. It was the saddest day in my life. The worst part was walking down the hall to meet Paula and Doug and give Andrew to them. I was crying the whole way. We sat together with Paula and Doug and talked a little, but it was very hard. It was time to leave and time for me to hand Andrew to Paula.

I suddenly stopped crying once he was in Paula's arms. I knew that I was doing the right thing. I knew that going home with them would be much better for my baby than if he went home with me. I knew that I was doing the right thing. Rob told me that the birth mothers he had worked with before all came to a point where they realized they had done the right thing. I felt that immediately.

About five months have passed since that day, but I know in my heart that what I did was best—for Andrew and me. But even after leaving the hospital, it hadn't really hit me yet. A month later, when I went to court to terminate my parental rights to Andrew, I really felt it. It was such a scary place to be. In court, when I realized what I was doing, I broke down in tears. I had known all along that Andrew was going to be adopted by Paula and Doug, and that they would be his new parents, but finalizing the decision was so difficult. Going to court and terminating my rights would mean I could never have control of him. Legally, he would no longer be mine. I went into the courtroom in front of the judge, and my parental rights were ended. I could never take back what I had just done.

But in my heart I knew I did what was best. It was the hardest decision I have ever made, and probably the hardest decision I will ever make, but I know Andrew will be better off with Paula and Doug as his parents. They can give him all that he needs. Not only does he have two parents and a sister who love him very much, but also he has me and everyone else in my family to love him.

My house is filled with pictures of Andrew. From the hospital I brought home as much as I could to remind me of him. I have one of his blankets, one of his newborn shirts, and two of the hats he wore. As a child I never slept with blankets, but ever since the hospital I sleep with his blanket every night. I say "I love you" and kiss his picture every night before I go to bed. When I left the hospital, Paula and Doug gave me a necklace with his birthstone, a sapphire, embedded in a heart to wear and to remind me of him. I never take it off. I do not feel right if I don't have it on.

Going through this process was very difficult for my parents and me, but I have to say that I remained strong. I was so lucky to have support from all of my family and friends. People I did not even know that well came up to me and told me what a strong person I was, and that I was doing the right thing. Every time I heard that, I was reassured even more. Not everyone in this situation is as fortunate as I am to have the necessary support. I thank God for all this support.

Even though this whole situation didn't begin well, I feel the outcome was wonderful. All that I went through was worth it. To see Andrew and to know what a great life he will have makes me feel so happy. He deserves nothing but the best. I believe everything happens for a reason. Andrew was meant to be with Paula and Doug. Fate brought us all together. Not a day goes by that I don't think of him. Not a day will ever go by that I won't think of him. He is a part of me, and I will love him forever.

♥

The Intertwining of Lives:
An Adoption Story of Memory,
Journey and Acceptance

Ann Cohen, Donna Severy Laffan
and Debbi R. Swanstrom

Donna's Story: Beginnings

The 1960s, nineteen years old, small-town, rural Vermont and pregnant! *What do I do? Where do I go? Who do I tell?* I was certainly faced with a nightmare. I was the oldest of six children from an upstanding family in a small community, and I had no choice but to tell my parents, as scared as I was, that I was pregnant. Naturally, I heard: "How could you have let this happen?" "Who is the father, and is he going to marry you?" Marriage was not an option. My parents could not support me and a child, nor did they really want me to stay at home and have the baby. During those times, girls were sent away so parents could "save face," despite the fact that news always had a way of getting out anyway, so what did it matter? I was in no position to keep and raise a baby on my own; I had no money and was so young. How would I be able to provide the financial support and emotional stability that a newborn baby needs—and what about the

(EDITOR'S NOTE: *This story reflects the lives of three women—a birth mother, Donna; her adult daughter, Debbi, who sought her out after a quarter of a century; and Debbi's mother, Ann. Their voices are woven together in an attempt to reflect the complexity of what happens when a woman carries a memory for so long, when an adult child reaches out for clarification in life, and when a loving mother accepts and finds peace in her daughter's journey.*)

future? I was definitely not equipped to raise a child, financially or emotionally. Adoption seemed to be the answer. Have the baby and give it away to a couple that was not able to have their own children. I needed some place to go and someone to help me until the baby came.

I had a summer job working for a woman I'll call Mrs. H, who moved, or relocated her horseback riding school from New Jersey to Vermont for the summer. My parents and I talked with her, and she agreed to let me go back to New Jersey with her for the winter. Mrs. H would provide room and board, and I would continue working with the horses and do any domestic work that she and her family required. Mrs. H also had a sister who was willing to help me with my medical treatment by introducing me to her obstetrician. When Mrs. H packed up for the summer and moved back to New Jersey, so did I.

The next five and one-half months were busy, working on the farm, going to the doctor's office and meeting with the adoption agency. I was asked so many questions—questions regarding my family history, and as much as I could answer them, the history of the birth father's family. The months before I gave birth were perhaps the loneliest of my entire life. I did not have anyone I felt comfortable talking to, except the woman who managed my case at the adoption agency. She was my sounding board, and the question that kept popping up was whether I was making the right choice for me. I battled with myself constantly. Ultimately, I came to accept that giving my baby up was the right choice for me.

The day came, and I went to the hospital to give birth. The only thing I remember about the birth is that the nurses were rude. I was another pregnant teenager, and they had seen enough of that over the years. I don't know why, but I did not feel any compassion from them. The next thing I remember was waking up in a room all by myself and asking a nurse about the baby. She was not very helpful other than saying all went well; I'd had a girl, and she was healthy. I was in the hospital for a few days, and the only person who came to see me was my case manager. She asked if I had been down to the nursery, but I hadn't. I figured that because I was giving the baby up to a welcoming family, it was better not to see my baby girl. Yet, resting in the hospital bed, the only thing I could think about was my baby, so I pulled myself out of bed and walked down alone to peek through the window. I found her and looked and looked at her and went back to my room feeling so sad that I couldn't hold her and touch her. I had been advised that to actually hold her would be the wrong thing to do. I guess the going wisdom of the time was that suppressing my motherly instincts would help me cope in the end.

A Daughter's Journey

The toughest decision I have ever made in my life was also the best decision I've ever made. I was going to search for my birth mother. I was fortunate to have enough love and support from my family, which made me strong enough to set out on this journey. My name is Debbi, and I was born on January 25, 1969. I was adopted when I was two months old. Here is my story.

The thoughts were always there. You know the ones: *Who am I? Where do I come from? Who do I look like?* My parents, Ann and Bob, encouraged me to search for many years. They said, if for no other reason, that I should find out about my birth family's medical history. I have always been grateful for their acceptance, which I needed to make this journey. After so many years of being asked "Where did you ever get that blonde hair?" (my parents have jet-black hair), I finally mustered up enough courage to begin my search. It took many years of mental preparation before I could start. I knew that I needed to be prepared to find the worst, the best or something in between. I had some notes that the adoption agency gave to my parents when I was adopted. The notes said very little, only telling me the smallest tidbits of information about my birth mother and father: their height, weight, nationality, overall health—not much to go on.

I wrote my first letter to the adoption agency requesting my background information in 1993, but I didn't muster the courage to mail it until June 1994. My search had begun. I crossed my fingers and held my breath. In November I received a letter from the adoption agency: my "Adoption Background Information." It contained "everything" the agency knew about me, over four pages worth! I could barely grasp what I was reading, information every nonadopted person already knows. I finally knew my birth weight and length and my ethnic background, finally an explanation for the blonde hair. Best of all was all the information about my birth mother, my birth father and their families. It was all so incredible. I never thought I would know these "secret" parts of my life!

I digested that information for about eight months. In June 1995, I wrote my next letter to the agency—my search application. A lot of legal hoops needed to be jumped through, lots of letters to various government agencies to release records and information. The next five months were an agonizing waiting game. On November 14, 1995, I received a call from the adoption agency saying they had found my birth mother and that she was very interested in communicating with me! I was an emotional basket case. I was so happy that all I could do was cry.

Contact

I had decided to give my baby away, so I knew I needed to pick myself up and move on with my life, and move on I did. I finished college, and several years later I married a wonderful man. The years prior to my marriage were up and down. I even saw my baby's father a few times. I thought about my baby often, but probably not as often as I did after I was married. I told Bruce, my husband, about that chapter in my life; he was the only person I told or talked to about how I was feeling. We eventually had children of our own, two daughters, Jenny and Jamie. I didn't realize that having Jenny would stir up so many thoughts and emotions from the past—questions about the little girl who so long ago, ten years ago, I had given away. All those firsts: sitting up, first tooth, first steps, first words . . . *how and when did my little girl do these things?* I had so many questions about her life, but I had resigned myself to never knowing the answers.

Twenty-six years had gone by, and I secretly looked at the picture in my wallet of the baby I had given up. Wondering, wondering all the time. Sometimes my husband and I would see advertisements for television programs featuring lost loves, and we would look at each other, not really sure what to say but thinking of the possibilities. I was secretly hoping, but not holding much faith, that I would have contact with my daughter. So much time had gone by; the door to that chapter of my life seemed closed, never to be opened again.

Then one evening in October 1995, my mother called to tell me that my brother had received a letter from Children's Aid and Family Services (CAFS) in New Jersey, and they were looking for a Donna Severy, and that if he had any information to please contact them. I was stunned. *What could they possibly want after all these years? Could it be that my baby was trying to find me?* Bruce and I decided that I would make the call to CAFS. Now the questions were beginning to come. *Twenty-six years. If she is looking for me, what does she want? Is she broke and in need of money? Is she a drug addict? Is she looking for something I can't give or don't have?* On my lunch hour a couple of days after I had talked to my mother, I made the call to CAFS. Upon speaking with the social worker, I was told that my daughter wanted to make contact with me. I just started crying. I thought I would be able to handle any situation that the social worker presented.

I was so overwhelmed that I had trouble asking questions. As I composed myself, I asked all the questions running through my mind. This girl was well-adjusted, and she wanted to make contact, take things slowly, but only if I agreed to the contact.

Contact with the baby I had given away? *YES! YES! YES!* I wanted to make the contact. After filling out some forms for the agency, a letter came for me. I was so excited. Inside the envelope was a handwritten note from my baby, biographical information and a picture of her. She had a name, Debbi Rachel Swanstrom (Cohen). I couldn't take my eyes off her picture, so grown up. She looked a little bit like Jenny and quite a bit like her birth father's sisters. The biographical information was good and complete, but the handwritten note was great. I could sense her excitement in the written words, which was exciting for me. She truly wanted to talk to me and even meet me in person. A very warm feeling, one that is hard to describe, came over me.

A couple of weeks went by. I was building up my courage to telephone Debbi. She beat me to it. One evening in mid-November, Debbi called. Oh my, what a night. As I reflect, it seems that I probably thanked her a million times for having the courage and curiosity to do what she did. We talked quite often. Our conversations were lengthy, hours and hours of honest talk, trying to catch up on so many years. I strongly feel that Debbi and I hit it off right from the start. As the conversations were progressing, a new fear raised its head. I had told my husband before we were married, but I had not told anyone else. I would have to tell my girls about Debbi. I agonized over this for days. Jenny was sixteen and Jamie only thirteen; how would they handle this information? They have a sister. I thought they would be okay with the sister part, but what would they think of me for keeping this secret for so many years? Bruce and I decided that I would tell each girl separately. I should have known that both girls would be accepting of me and excited about having another sister. Now that my family knew, I was really comfortable with everything. Wherever the relationship between Debbi and me goes, at least there are no more secrets; things are finally out in the open.

The Meeting

The first letter arrived from Donna, my birth mother, in late November, and after several months of letters and phone calls, on March 8, 1996, I was on my way to meet her for the first time. What a journey that turned out to be! I flew from Minnesota to Boston for a connecting flight to Vermont. The plane arrived at Logan International Airport right on time. Upon my arrival in Boston, I learned that my connecting flight, however, was cancelled.

Because of a severe snowstorm moving into the area, all flights out of Boston were being cancelled. I cried in front of three different gate agents and didn't know what I was going to do. I decided to take a shuttle bus to a Boston hotel. Upon arrival I called Donna to let her know that I was not going to make it to Vermont after all. I then called my cousin Phyllis (who lives in the area) to see if she wanted to have breakfast with me the next morning, but unfortunately she was planning to leave for New York. Donna called me back a little while later and said, "I'm driving to Boston with my friend Linda to come and pick you up." Then Phyllis called to say that the weather had been so bad that she was staying in Boston, and we could get together for breakfast.

The much anticipated meeting was set. Donna and Linda were coming to meet my cousin and I at 10:30 A.M. As 9:45 rolled around the next morning, I had never been so nervous.

My eyes darted around the restaurant, watching every person coming in and out of the room. After what seemed an interminable time, I saw a woman standing at the door with her hands covering her mouth and nose, with tears welled up in her eyes. I couldn't believe it was my birth mother standing only a few feet away. I wasn't sure what to do. *Should I walk up to her or wait for her to approach me?* Well, I took a deep breath and I walked toward her. The tears were full in my eyes, and it all seemed a little blurry. We approached each other and embraced in tears.

I had been looking forward to that hug for twenty-seven years! After a while, all we could do was hold hands and stare at each other through our tear-filled eyes. It was emotionally incomprehensible—to finally meet the person who gave birth to me!

Donna began to tell us about what had happened all those years ago. We sat and talked for two hours. Donna and Linda were trying to convince me to drive back to Vermont with them. I wasn't sure it was the right thing to do, but I finally agreed.

Scared, nervous, excited, apprehensive, happy, guilty, sad—I was overwhelmed with so many emotions all at the same time. The emotions cloud many of the memories from my trip, but I did have a really great time with the rest of my newfound family in Vermont. Meeting Jenny and Jamie (my half-sisters) and Bruce (Donna's husband) and the parade of Donna's sisters and brothers was just amazing. I think meeting Frank (Donna's brother, the one who received the letter from the agency trying to find her) was one of the most emotional experiences of my visit. He and his wife Faye were so welcoming and loving that it was almost too much for me to handle.

During this visit I learned more than I could ever have hoped for. Donna is a wonderful woman with whom I really enjoy spending time. She was so open and honest, answering anything and everything

I wanted to know, although I did have to ask many of the same questions twice because it was so hard to digest everything the first time around. Throughout this whole experience, my parents Ann and Bob were there in spirit, and I knew I had their complete support. I was so grateful for their love and understanding throughout this difficult emotional journey.

A Mother's Acceptance

October 1995. It is noon, and the phone rings. My daughter is calling from halfway across the country. She is crying, and before too long we both are. She is calling to tell us she has found her birth mother. Even though the news hit me like a bolt of lightning, I felt a sense of happiness and relief for my daughter. My husband Bob and I thought that searching was the right thing for her. She had questions about her medical history and really wanted to know about it. It had taken her about two and a half years, on and off, to get to this place in her life. We had encouraged her to search for her birth mother if she was willing. We had encouraged her to do what she thought was right. We never felt threatened by her desire to learn more about her birth family.

We saw our relationship with our daughter as strong and enduring, and nothing could diminish our closeness. A few months later, the plans for the long-awaited reunion were set. Debbi was traveling from her home in Minnesota to Boston, and from there to Vermont. Well, as fate would have it, the winter weather caused a change in her plans. The airport in Boston closed after her arrival because of a major snowstorm, and there were no flights to Vermont or anywhere else. Debbi was alone in Boston, or so she thought. She called us, not knowing what to do. I told her to call my cousin, if for nothing else than to have someone to talk to and some emotional support.

Debbi called her birth mother to tell her she was stranded. When Donna learned of the delay in Debbi's travel plans, she told Debbi that she and a friend would leave Vermont immediately by car to come to Boston and pick her up. I knew that Debbi would be okay. They would all meet in the morning, and she would have Phyllis with her for moral support. Even though I wasn't there, I feel like I was with her in spirit, there to see the hugs and tears, and Phyllis was there bearing witness to this incredibly emotional scene of the reunion of a birth mother and a child separated for almost thirty years. Although I know this journey has been Debbi's to find her biological roots, I feel like I have taken the journey with her. When Debbi called us from Vermont to relate the overwhelming emotions she felt that day, my husband and I were extremely happy for all of them, even though Debbi never was able to meet her birth father.

Debbi was not the only one who had a reunion with her past. In March 2000, Debbi and her husband organized a meeting in Boston for us to meet Donna and her family. We decided we would meet at my cousin's house and have brunch together. My husband and I were on edge all morning. We couldn't relax and found ourselves pacing back and forth with anxiety. Bob had a hard time controlling his emotions, and tears rolled down his cheeks several times that morning. The plans were for Debbi and her biological family to arrive by taking the T train and walk from the train to our house. We kept peering out the window, down the street, to see signs of their approach.

On perhaps the tenth visit to the window, a group appeared walking down the street. We recognized Debbi, and upon the sight of the others we experienced a rapid increase in our heartbeats and a dryness in our mouths. We wanted to like them and really wanted them to like us. *What if it didn't go well?* We were so nervous. *Please let this go well; it means so much to Debbi and all of our lives.* The doorbell rang, and again there were many hugs, tears and flowers. We cried, we laughed, we talked, and we spent a wonderful weekend together. It was all so perfect and all too short. Donna and I keep in touch with cards. I have thanked her for what she did for us, now some thirty-four years ago. We will always be grateful for her decision, which gave us a daughter we always wanted and whom we loved so much. We have a great daughter, and she has us. We will always be extremely grateful for the wonderful gift of a daughter. Donna is now "Donna" to Debbi. We are still "Mom and Dad."

A New Relationship with My Birth Mother

In the intervening years, Donna and I have become close friends, talking on the phone and sharing stories from years past. She shared so much of her life, and she opened up to me in such a way that was completely selfless. I can't thank her enough for all she has given me. I know at times it was difficult for her as well, but she was very patient with me and my never-ending questions.

Over the past few years, we have had the opportunity to meet a few times. Donna and Jamie came to visit me in Minneapolis. It was great to see Jamie have some new experiences while she was visiting me. Jamie is deaf, and so is a good friend and neighbor of mine. He took the opportunity to show her that in a city like Minneapolis, there is a large deaf community. I was just glad to be a part of that experience for Jamie, who is such a sweet young girl. Another time, Donna and Linda, her best friend, took a road trip from Vermont to Seattle to visit Linda's daughter. The two of them remind me of the women in *Thelma and Louise*. First stop for them was Minneapolis. Every time we see each other, it's just like a couple of old friends who haven't seen each other for a while and have to catch up on events in their lives. We really had a good time, and seeing Linda again was comforting. She's such a good friend of Donna's that she feels almost like family to me.

I will always think fondly of the reunion that occurred between my parents and Donna and her husband Bruce. Upon seeing each other for the first time, Ann and Debbi hugged in a long embrace and the tears flowed freely. The moment was quite emotional for all of us. I felt like my entire family was there: my parents Ann and Bob, Donna, Bruce, Jenny and Jamie (my "extended family"), and Randy (my husband). I had many mixed emotions before this extended family meeting, and there were lots of tears, but also great enjoyment and memorable moments. Everyone got along so well, and everyone was really happy to meet each other. We had a wonderful time, with nice dinners and relaxing afternoons and great conversations. I was so happy that Donna and Ann and Bob had the opportunity to meet and share their feelings and stories with each other. They had given me and each other the greatest of gifts—my life and a loving home. The whole situation tugged at my heart in such a sweet way that I can hardly explain it. We were all sad to leave, and so thankful to have the opportunity to all be together. As you might guess, I consider myself a really lucky gal to have my extended family and know we can all share our lives and our love together. I couldn't have asked for more!

A Birth Mother's Prayers Answered

Why did the meeting of Debbi and me work? I don't know, but maybe because Debbi and I had talked so much in the very beginning, trying to be as honest with each other as possible. Remembering how things were long ago becomes a bit cloudy over time, but some things you don't forget. I think that we gave each other the space we needed, and I am a firm believer that all you can do is talk about the past. You can't change it; it is what it is. The future is the only thing that an individual can have any effect on, and for Debbi and me, we are trying to build a relationship by going forward. I truly believe that we both feel that way.

Our first contact was seven and a half years ago. Since that time, I have traveled to Debbi's house twice and met her husband, and two years ago met her mom and dad. When both of our families met in Boston for the first time, I thought I would be able to handle this meeting without a whole lot of emotion. I was wrong. When I saw Ann, Debbi's mom, for the first time, my emotions took over again. I cried and hugged them both very tightly. I had such an overwhelming feeling of gratitude. We had a wonderful weekend, visiting and touring around Boston. I enjoyed talking with Debbi's mom. I might have been dreaming or reading more into the situation than was really there, I don't know—maybe it was nervousness—but I did sense some tension between her mom and myself. As we were saying our good-byes and thanks for the wonderful weekend, I said to Debbi's mom something to the effect that Debbi would always be her daughter and to me she is a friend. For whatever reasons, I needed to say that, so that Debbi's parents could be assured I wasn't going to try to be something I wasn't: Debbi's mother. I had what I needed: a chance to know that the little girl I gave up years ago had love in her life and a promising future. My prayers had been answered.

Since this meeting, Debbi and I continue to talk on the phone, sometimes at great length, and we are working on getting together again. I would love to see her mom and dad again. I have no secrets anymore, and it sure feels good to have peace of mind. I get goose bumps every time I tell my story. I will never be able to fully describe how I feel, but I feel good knowing that my little baby has a good life and parents who really love and care for her the way she deserves. I will forever be grateful to Debbi's parents for supporting her in her quest to find me, and I will forever be grateful to Debbi for having the courage to take the steps necessary to find me. I think all of us involved are happier. My dreams from thirty-four years ago came true.

♥

You Loved Me Enough

Alex

You loved me enough to let me go
You loved me enough and it really did show
You probably cried when I left your arms
You probably shed your tears when I left my country,
Family, and when I left you forever
You probably think about me all the time
And when you do, it must hurt inside
If you are in heaven watching down on me
You are thinking, "That's my baby!"
You loved me enough to let me go
You loved me enough, this much I know

♥

CHAPTER TWO

Facing Loss
and
Gaining Hope

Journey of Destiny

Keriann Kimball

The story of how I came to be a mother started twenty-two years ago. When my story began, it didn't seem like it would end with a nice, big "happily ever after." It didn't begin as a story about adoption and destiny. It didn't begin as a story about answered prayers. If you told me as a child that my story would be a testament to the greater plan and the secret granting of a sick girl's prayers, I probably would have laughed. Or cried.

Once upon a time I was six years old. I was laughing carelessly with my sister in our bedroom with the innocence and all-consuming joy that only children can feel. We were giggling and starting to undress for bedtime when my sister pointed at me and screamed. Her scream shattered my childhood and jarred my world into a crooked place. She cried, "What is that? Mommy, come quick! There's something very wrong with Keriann!" I followed the trail of her pointed finger, down to a large bulge on my stomach.

It was determined that the bulge was a hernia. But during a routine operation to repair it, the doctors found a large mass on my ovary, so large that it caused the hernia. A doctor told my parents that their little girl had between six weeks and six months to live. Ovarian cancer is one of the deadliest and most unstoppable forms of the disease, and it is very rare in children. They could do absolutely nothing to help me.

What they could do, the doctor said, was take me home and allow me to live the rest of my days with my family. My parents would not accept this answer. They pleaded and searched for any hope, for any chance to save their six-year-old's life. Finally, a doctor mentioned an experimental study of a chemotherapy drug regimen. Desperate, my parents opted for that lone hope. The next several years of my life were empty of childhood laughter and games with my siblings. Those treasured would-be-memories were replaced with horrific operations and recoveries and two and a half years of biweekly chemotherapy treatments. Those treatments were brutal, a hellish nightmare. The moment the needle hit my vein, I could feel the cold surge of toxins begin to course up my arm and through my little body. I instantly became nauseous and dizzy. This terrible poisoned sensation would last for a full week. Just when I had the strength to walk and hold down food again, Friday would come with a trip to the clinic. The whole sickening cycle would start anew.

I remember my mother during those times, and how she held me, stroked my hair and tried to comfort me. "It's okay to cry, darling," she told me. "I know you're strong and that you're going to beat this." She would sing, "Don't stop thinking about tomorrow, don't stop, it'll soon be here." And my dad always told me, "You are a survivor." I always thought I was being strong for them, but now I know they were being so incredibly strong for me.

The chemotherapy cycle continued for over two years. I missed school, I missed friends, I missed playing with my brother and sister, I missed eating and feeling strong and being silly. Most of all I missed that last picture of my careless childhood: laughing and changing into pajamas with my sister before bed. All that I had missed—and it was gone forever. But I was alive, and it was time to start living.

The doctors said it was uncertain whether or not I would be able to have children. I did still have one good ovary, and it might be possible for me to be a mother one day. As I developed into a young woman, the remaining ovary seemed to be functioning well, and doctors assumed fertility would not be an issue for me. But in high school I was checked for something called cardiomyopathy, a condition resulting from damage to the heart tissue. The doctors said I had it. I felt fine, but I had to take blood pressure medicine every day as a protective measure. So I carried on with my life, determined to live it my way.

I became a teacher and married, but after a couple years of teaching and running myself ragged while happily married to my husband, Brett, I began to long for children of my own—children I would teach not only to read, but to walk, talk, dance and sing, and enjoy life. I wanted a child to hold and comfort in the night when they had a bad dream.

At the same time these feelings were surfacing, I started becoming very tired, like I have never been before, and I could never seem to catch up. I felt like I was eighty years old, not twenty-three. I was in congestive heart failure, and I spent the next year making huge lifestyle changes to my diet and schedule, even cutting my teaching time in half. I still wanted a baby, but doctors warned that pregnancy would be a serious risk to both of our lives given my weak heart.

They were concerned that during pregnancy, my heart—though working sufficiently now—would not be strong enough to pump effectively for both my body and a developing fetus. In addition, the medications I took daily, which were in large part responsible for my regained health, are not recommended during pregnancy. Moreover, I was told that even if everything somehow worked out and I miraculously had cardiac reserve enough to function as a parent, who was to say that the child would be healthy, given the exposure to toxins my ovaries had undergone during chemotherapy?

I cried for hours on the kitchen floor. My body had betrayed me, first failing me as a child and now too riddled with poison to bear life. I couldn't leave the house, and I made excuses for every occasion involving parenthood or children. Eventually, it seemed I could not go anywhere without seeing a mother and child. Again, I prayed in bed for another miracle, the same prayer echoed from my childhood nights.

Then I was with my sister-in-law one day on my couch. She is adopted, and she bravely asked if I had ever considered adoption.

"I won't," I said. "I can't. I'll never consider it."

She was silent. "Why not?" she asked eventually.

"What if one day that child, who I raised and held and loved their whole life, wanted to meet their birth mother? I couldn't handle that. What a slap in the face it would be. I just don't need it. I can't take that."

My throat ached as I told her that I wanted to be able to look into my child's eyes and see my husband's handsome brown eyes gazing back, or watch my child be able to paint and draw because. . . . My voice almost closed off. "Because she got it from me," I finished.

But time passed and my longing for parenthood only grew keener and my self-imposed isolation unhealthier. I decided to go back to teaching after the coming summer. I also tried to attend more family activities. At my godson's sixth birthday party, one little girl was having a hard time. She was standing away from the other children, by a side table covered with presents.

"What's the matter?" I asked her, squatting down to her tiny size.

She glanced up with shiny black eyes, then looked away. "I miss my mommy," she said.

"Yeah," I said. "Me, too."

Her eyes flicked back to me. "Where is she?"

"Well, she's in . . . ," I started. "Hey, wait. There she is!" I pointed to a little girl in a pink dress, picking gum from the bottom of her shoe.

The girl beside me stared at the gum-picking child, and looked quizzical. "That's not your mom," she said.

"What do you mean?" I said. "Of course it . . . oh wait." I pretended to squint my eyes and scrunch my face. "I'm not wearing my glasses. Maybe it's not my mom."

The girl regarded me for a moment, then started giggling.

"Do you like pizza?" I asked. She shrugged, studied her fingers, then looked up and started nodding vigorously. "Me, too. Let's go get some."

By the end of the party I had made a new friend, and she was playing musical chairs with the other children. I was actually sad to watch her leave. For the last hour I had felt like a parent; I had bonded and watched her grow from a scared little girl to one laughing while jumping on the musical chairs during the game. And she looked nothing like me. It sounds silly, I know, but I think I had an epiphany that day, as if God took my hand and held it as we walked all the way to my daughter.

Brett and I sent our application to an adoption agency and soon found out we were on our way to becoming parents. A few months later, we met our social worker at the hospital where our soon-to-be daughter had been born the night before. As we walked toward the room to meet the birth mother and the baby, I was numb with anticipation. We entered the tiny room, and our social worker introduced us to the woman who had "chosen" us. I tried to smile with frozen lips, handing her the flowers we had brought her. That bouquet of daisies and little white buds was a sorry gift compared to the one she was giving us.

She said she was happy to meet us, and that she knew immediately upon seeing our profile that we were the parents for her daughter. I thought I would feel nervous, that I would worry I didn't measure up to what she had expected, but instead the air in the room was filled with a comfort of all that was meant to be. I could tell she felt it as well and was at peace with the moment.

The nurse brought the baby into the room. At the first glimpse of the back of her head covered with a pink knitted cap, I felt everything begin to spin. My heart leapt, my eyes teared, and my husband squeezed my hand. "You can pick her up, don't be afraid," the nurse said. And when I held our beautiful six-and-a-half-pound girl, the world that had somehow been knocked askew by my sister's almost-forgotten scream gently slipped back into place.

I look at my daughter today, every day, and I know without a doubt that this was meant to be. I am grateful for every moment of pain and horror and despair that brought me to her. I wouldn't change anything, not anything. Every day, my beautiful daughter Lillian brings me the joy of new experiences. Whether it's because she fell down and cut her lip, or because she said a new word, or simply because she gives me the long-lost feeling of childhood when we gallop like horsies together in gym class, she moves me in a way I've never been moved before and like no one else ever could. And she does it every day.

We write letters to Lillian's birth mother twice a year. I always look forward to writing and sending her pictures, and I hope our letters bring her comfort and peace to know that she brought this amazing person into our world. I will raise Lillian to be grateful to her birth mother for two very special gifts: her life and her family. I hope she wants to meet her birth mother some day, I realize now. I hope she will want to say "thank you," and I hope the voice of the little girl she gave birth to will be a far better gift than the daisies we bought her on that afternoon in May.

♥

Miracle in Miami

Jessica Varn

When my husband Craig and I decided to start a family through adoption, there was never any question of where we would find our child. The only choice for us was Colombia, as my family is from there, going back at least three generations on both sides. I am very proud of my heritage, and I wanted a child with whom I could share a language and cultural background.

While I searched the States for adoption agencies with Colombian programs, I set my relatives to work in Colombia, with my cousin researching orphanages in Bogotá, where my extended family lives. The situation came together like those wonderful coincidences in life where magic, chance, fate, divine intervention and whatever else all form tiny links in a chain that brings a child home to a family. My cousin had a friend who worked at an orphanage in Bogotá and who was also adopted from there as an infant. That same week I discovered an agency that worked exclusively with this orphanage. The combination offered the perfect, and only, choice.

Within six months of starting our home study and paperwork, we received the heart-stopping news that the child was a boy, and he was waiting for us in Colombia as soon as we could get there.

Jacob was eleven weeks old when we first held him. He was all I'd hoped for in a child: beautiful, angelic looking. But my little boy had been sick with a nasty cold. The stress of our first week of parenthood, which would have been terrifying enough, was compounded by

Jacob's illness and his trouble sleeping and eating because of congestion. Within the first ten hours of being with us, our son was examined by a pediatrician, who said Jacob had a lot of lung congestion and was to be placed on a regimen of respiratory therapies. In Colombia, pediatricians and therapists come to your house and the pharmacy delivers prescriptions to your home. A therapist visited us every other day, and at one point Jacob was filled with five different medications, for the lung infection, an eye infection and colic.

Craig had to go back home after the first week, along with my dad, sister and aunt, leaving my mom and I alone with Jacob. My memories in Colombia after they left have a faint, bittersweet tinge. We moved into my aunt's house to live with her and my uncle, cousin and grandmother for the remaining four weeks we were to be in the country. I think it was a healthy adjustment period for my son, being loved and coddled and held, fed, changed, bathed and put to sleep by all of his live-in relatives, with many others visiting on a regular basis. Spending his first month with our family in the arms of a Colombian household that spoke his language was, I hope, a soothing period for Jacob, easing the transition from his foster home to ours.

But with every sweet new thing he did, each gurgle and chubby hand wave, I smiled and cried, feeling the sweetness with a fishhook of pain in my throat. He was developing before my own eyes, but not in front of his dad. We missed Craig terribly. In Jacob's crib, we placed the T-shirt that Craig had slept in the last night he was with us, hoping his son would sense his enveloping presence that way.

But unfortunately, even though we saw the pediatrician and therapist through the entire month, Jacob never improved. He seemed to be stuck in a constant state of lung congestion. At night I would listen to the raspy wheeze of his breathing, wishing I could hold him and use my love to suck the very illness out of him. Two days before we were scheduled to go home, he was put on an inhaler to help clear his blocked airways. It seemed to help a little, and he was deemed healthy enough to travel to the United States.

We were warned, however, that his system might react badly to the air conditioning at the Miami airport, since he had never breathed air-conditioned air. As we prepared for takeoff in Bogotá, Jacob projectile-vomited all over his pristine (and carefully planned) white outfit, the airplane window and my lap. He seemed to feel much better afterwards (he was the only one, mind you), but I was sure that he would get very sick the moment we arrived in the air-conditioned Miami airport.

As soon as we arrived in Miami I noticed something different, but I could not place it at first. I'd become so accustomed to his perpetual and rhythmic breath, like a small accordion under my arm everywhere I went. Suddenly there was silence. I walked for several paces, looked at him, then walked several more. I stopped. Jacob was looking around the airport with bright interest, his mouth open slightly. His breathing was quite clear, with no rasp at all! It was entirely bizarre, beautiful and instantaneous. We had scheduled a visit with a stateside pediatrician before we even flew home, and when he was examined they found nothing wrong with his lungs. No congestion, no sickness. Poof! It had all gone away. We're not sure if the inhaler did the trick, or the humidity in Miami, or maybe both. Maybe it was feeling my sense of relief and happiness that we were finally home with Craig.

So after four weeks in Colombia we were home with our sweet son, who was more than I had ever hoped for. He has brought sunshine into the lives of everyone in our family. Our family in Colombia adores him, and he has brought us closer in touch than we've ever been in the past. Our family in the States is crazy about him, too, and we couldn't be prouder.

Jacob is two now, and he speaks Spanish and English. My parents and I speak in Spanish to him, and Craig and his family speak in English. He is a Colombian with a new heritage, and with a wonderful American heritage, too. The joy he brings us, and his instantaneous recovery to good health, are a daily reminder of God's presence in our lives.

♥

The Switcheroo

Audrey Keller

July 27, 1999. 7:30 P.M.

It's hard to write in the car, and my handwriting is shooting all over the page with every bump and turn. However, I have to briefly record this moment. We're coming, Victor, we're on our way to meet you for the first time. I know we're a little late, sweetie, but we missed our connecting flight in JFK, so I think it's incredible we managed to get here in Moscow only six hours late, and with Daddy in one piece! (I got a little tense on the flight.)

It's a little too dark to see the city outside the car windows. I can only see the vague flash of steepled silhouettes against the night sky. I don't care about seeing Moscow right now, I just want to see you. We located our driver, Michael, and interpreter, Katya, at the airport and convinced them to take us to the orphanage to meet you, despite the late hour. It was already 7 P.M. They seem like wonderful people, and I can tell Michael's even driving a little faster to get us to you as soon as possible.

Daddy's quite nervous right now, staring out the window and talking to himself like he does sometimes. This writing helps contain my nervo—Whoops! We just hit a bump and I left a long ink scratch down the page. I think I'd better cut this short, so I can be nervous together with Daddy. We'll see you so soon, my darling, I can hardly wait!

July 27, 1999. 11:45 P.M.

Oh, my little Victor! I never believed in love at first sight, but it must be true, because I love you. I held you for only twenty minutes, and already I can't stand to be away from you.

Of course, when we arrived at the orphanage, it was a little crazy. At that time of day, all the doctors and daytime personnel had gone home, leaving only the security and nighttime caretakers. Many of the lights were shut off, and everyone was giving us strange looks. Katya, thank God, took charge, locating your group and whisking us upstairs to meet you. You were so sweet, a bit sleepy, but you lay in my arms and sighed and wiggled your hands, and when Daddy held out his finger you grabbed it and wouldn't let go. You didn't struggle or cry, but just cuddled with me, like you were happy to be there. I'd been excited but so terrified of our first meeting, wondering whether you would squirm away, or cry in my arms, or if you would even be there waiting for us when we arrived.

We're back in the hotel now, and I should get some sleep for our big day tomorrow. I think we'll see much more of you then. I remember at home during the months of waiting, before sleep I used to whisper in the dark, "Goodnight, Victor," as though you were in a crib just across the room. I knew it was silly, but it made me feel happy all the same just to say it. So goodnight, sweet Victor. This is one of the last times I'll ever have to say that to you from a distance.

July 28, 1999. 11:32 P.M.

What a day! Katya and Michael picked us up and took us directly to the orphanage. We could hardly wait to see you, and then a strange and funny thing happened. We went to where your group is located, and the daytime caretaker tried to give us another little boy! It was actually pretty uncanny how much he looked like you, and she was pretty insistent that this darling was Victor. For a second I almost believed her, you two looked so alike, but I know my baby and he just felt different than you did last night. He was so sweet, but I knew the difference.

The eyes gave it away. His were hazel, like a gray sea with small green waves, and yours are definitely brown. Katya noticed this too, and she and the caretaker got into quite an argument about it.

Eventually, they removed the hazel-eyed boy from my arms and brought you in, brown eyes and all. Holding you again just felt right, probably because I dreamed of the weight of your small body all night. We stayed with you for as long as we could, watching you crawl and pick up toys, and holding you whenever you'd let us. Finally, we had to go, but with the consolation that tomorrow is our big day at court to legally adopt you! I should try to sleep, but I feel sick with anticipation.

July 29, 1999. 7:28 A.M.

It's here . . . the big day is here. In a few hours we'll all be a family! Unless something goes wrong. Could something go wrong? I can't even permit myself to think that way, or else I'll go nuts! It will all be fine.

My paranoia and anxiety aren't helped by my sleep deprivation from last night. I think I got around three hours, if I was lucky. The bed was lumpy in strange places, and I could hear water rushing through the pipes in the walls, footfalls in the hallway, and the elevator door clanging open and shut.

Daddy said he didn't sleep last night, either, that he had a lot on his mind. He must have dozed for a little while, at least, because I heard him talking in his sleep. He mumbled, and then said,

"No . . . no . . . wait. But wait . . ." Maybe he was arguing with the judge in his dreams. Let's hope there'll be none of that today.

July 30, 1999. 1:17 A.M.

This has been a very strange day. It's so late, and I'm incredibly exhausted, yet completely wired at the same time. I have to write what happened at once, if only as a keepsake of this craziness. It's strange, though, writing this, now that everything has changed.

The court hearing was actually a breeze, as Katya said it would be. The judge was very kind and asked a few questions before legally making us all a family. There's only one problem.

We went back to the orphanage to get you, Victor, and take our first pictures together. But once again, the daytime caretaker brought us the darling baby with the hazel eyes. For a moment we were so happy we hardly noticed, but then I saw his face.

"This isn't Victor," I told the woman. "You did this before. This is another little boy, not Victor." I was quite upset that they had made the same mistake twice, and was even angrier for the little hazel-eyed boy. To be put into a mother's arms twice, only to be yanked away seconds later must be horrible for a child, especially one as happy to be held as him. He even seemed to recognize me, and there was a smile on his little wet lips.

The caretakers were confused, speaking in Russian to each other. The woman shook her head and said, "This is Victor."

"This is not Victor," I said. "Victor has brown eyes. Don't you think I know my son?" Of course, I was so confused and frazzled that I could not see the obvious, that the orphanage staff clearly knew the boys better than me. I had only seen him for a few hours on a few occasions. I glanced at Bill for support, but there was a strange look on his face: a sense of dawning comprehension behind the heavy lines of exhaustion and bewilderment.

The staff began to talk quickly, words I couldn't understand, checking chartboards and lists while I stood there, quietly, still holding the hazel-eyed boy. Everything was straightened out in a matter of minutes.

I don't even know to whom I'm writing right now, it's all so strange. In my other entries, I had a baby face with deep brown eyes to think of, to whisper goodnight to in the dark. I don't know whether to erase that face, replace it with another, or to keep that face in mind for another day in the future.

Victor was not the brown-eyed boy! The daytime staff had been right all along, our son was the darling with the hazel eyes. The first child was named Nikolai, and we weren't supposed to have seen him at all.

Even before I fully understood the string of errors, I looked at the boy in my arms, with the gray sea eyes, the boy we had come to Russia to get, our Victor. Amazingly, after that initial moment of shock, that plummeting sensation with my stomach on the ceiling and ice water shot in my veins, it wasn't hard to fall immediately in love with our son. Even when I held him the first time, when we thought he wasn't ours, I felt a connection with him. He was so gentle and loving, so comfortable in my arms. This was my son, our Victor, and his eye color really didn't matter.

But we cannot forget that there is another boy, a boy with brown eyes, and that does matter. Our love is not fickle, and although we found our hearts expanding for the new Victor, we cannot forget that first moment we spent with Nikolai. Even when I look back in my journal, I see that, it was love at first sight. He has been held and loved as a son, and there is no way we can leave him behind after that. We told the staff immediately that we wanted to adopt Nikolai, too.

Tomorrow, we will try to get to the bottom of this, and see what we can do about our other son. I want to feel happy, and I do, but there is a heaviness in my stomach, like I want to heave a sigh but can't take in enough air.

July 30, 1999. 9:48 P.M.

What a mess. The orphanage director is on vacation, as is my social worker from the adoption agency. They're both being called back to deal with the crisis, but for now there is a wait.

As it turns out, there were a multitude of errors, beginning with us going to the orphanage so late that night. The nighttime caretaker was new at the orphanage and did not yet know the children's names. Instead of giving us Victor, she brought us Nikolai. In her defense, the boys look very similar, almost like twins. The second error was our not listening to the daytime caretaker's insistence that the hazel-eyed boy was Victor! Because we were so insistent that she bring out the brown-eyed child, she thought we were calling Nikolai by his new given name, "Victor." And finally, we didn't listen to our own intuition, telling us that something was amiss. I remember now Bill talking in his sleep that night, and how I thought he was arguing with the judge.

Oh Victor, Nikolai, my brown-eyed, hazel-eyed boys, we love you both. Maybe some day we can laugh about all this, and tell the story to friends, when all four of us are together at home as a family.

August 3, 2000. 5:21 P.M.

It barely seems like a lift of the pen, but a whole year has gone by. I remember the night of that last journal entry so clearly. Putting away this journal, wanting to cry and shout with joy at the same time. I had hoped that the next day I would be writing again, that Nikolai would already be ours.

It didn't work out that way. There was too much confusion, getting the director and the adoption agency on the phone, sorting out the difficulties. Of course, we couldn't just adopt Nikolai on that same trip. There were complications, there always are. And I couldn't bring myself to write anymore, it was too hard. The journal was supposed to be a happy account of the most beautiful trip of my life, not a gravestone of disappointment and sadness. There was joy, so much joy with our son Victor, but we couldn't forget another boy who so desperately wanted our love. I told myself I'd continue writing when the story turned happy again. Not that I wanted to deny or forget the sadness, but I didn't want this to drag into a marathon of misery.

It took a year to write that happy ending, a mountainous year of patience and boatloads of tears to get our Nik home. But it finally happened. Victor welcomed him into our home with hugs and kisses, and they became brothers immediately. And people today will even ask how old my twins are, which always makes me smile.

Sometimes I think about the odd confluence of events that brought us here, even back to the mysterious equipment failure that caused us to miss our connecting flight at JFK, which made us late in Moscow, which led to the mistake at the orphanage that first night. I could trace it back farther than that—an electrical shortage, a lazy technician, a baggage handler who misplaced some luggage—trying to unravel all the workings of fate that made us a four-person family instead of three, that made us happy beyond imagination. Or I could be a skeptic, and put it all down to plain dumb luck and blind chance. But why would I want to spoil all the fun?

♥

God's Plan: Bringing Home Liliana

Christie Patrick Billings

Growing up a street child with numerous scattered siblings and absent parents, I was relatively free of normal childhood expectations and constraints. True, I felt constant fear and worry over how I would get the normal childhood staples of food, shelter and clothes, even as I didn't want to lose my street status. Ironically, as a direct result of my street freedom and my pursuit of life's daily necessities, I finally found the ultimate sources for my salvation: the Catholic Church and school.

At the various Catholic churches in my New York neighborhoods, the nuns and priests were very kindhearted, offering what they could in substance, but more importantly, reminding me always that our collective Father in heaven was always watching out for me just as he watched out for his own son when he walked the earth. I believed them without question. In my eyes, these nuns and priests were something bigger and better than I, people who lived in very important buildings, churches. If they said I had a Father always watching out for me no matter where I was, then I was happy and relieved and strengthened to believe them. I'm sure there are fancier ways to plant the seeds of faith and the Christian spirit, but the priests' and nuns' approach to salvation worked for me.

School was another source of salvation for me. While most kids dreaded going to school and longed for the dismissal bell, weekends and holidays, I stood at the entryway before daylight every day, waiting for the janitor to unlock the door. I joined every activity possible, especially anything having to do with music, intramural sports and clubs. I volunteered to help with every and any project, especially the United Way fundraisers; after all, I was a personal beneficiary of the United Way's good work. At the end of the school day, I would gather my things as slowly as possible so I could enjoy every last moment of the warm and safe environment of the school and the nurturing company of the nice adults who worked there. I had so many amazing mentors, people I now realize understood my circumstances and saw me as equal to my peers who had homes and safety in their lives. They never made me feel embarrassed as they stepped into my life and subtly acted as surrogate moms or dads or best friends. The ultimate result of their efforts was that I became an outstanding student, loved school and learning, and through club participation, gained experiences I could never have imagined. I developed into an above-average athlete in almost all sports, excelled in music and went on to college at age sixteen.

I ultimately realized that God's plan for me was as unique as the nuns and priests had originally told me, and while I didn't always understand some of the nontraditional challenges I faced, my faith and Christian spirit guided me to the prolific havens of educational institutions. Through my twenties and thirties, I pursued various graduate and professional degrees as well as participated in United Way activities. I was especially drawn to programs like Big Brothers and Big Sisters and mentoring programs in disadvantaged school districts. I truly never perceived my involvement in social causes as a "nice thing to do"—this kind of work was the most important thing I could do for myself and for others. I was equally compelled to continue improving myself and my financial resources so I could continue my involvement in social causes on broader and even larger scales. I knew without a doubt that I had survived and thrived in my unusual childhood that I might share my own good fortune, my own "divine intervention," exponentially. In fact, I felt that my own successes meant nothing unless they were used to pay it forward.

As my professional and personal life took me to Eastern Europe, former Soviet republics, the United Kingdom and South America, my opportunity to touch the lives of specific children and to intervene in the difficult circumstances that afflicted their lives multiplied. Moreover, working in several non-U.S. venues made me extremely aware of how difficult it is to assure that our efforts and resources extended for specific children's causes ever reach the children and change their lives in significant ways. And there were so many children with so many needs! Overcoming occasional flash feelings of being overwhelmed, I resolved to believe in the mantra uttered by so many who walked before me: *How do we save all these children with all these needs? One child at a time!*

While working in South America, I came to the realization that adoption was one way to reach a child and change his or her life. My husband and I decided to adopt, starting with two street children from the streets of Santa Cruz, Bolivia. These two girls used to follow my husband Leonard to and from his office every day. They reminded me of my childhood self waiting at my school's front doors. Gabriella and Elsa were six and eight years old at the time. Adopting street children was not done in Bolivia; these children had no statistical existence—no birth certificates, no care from any social service agencies, nothing. Undaunted by governmental impediments, we decided to push ahead and establish an important precedent. While waiting to complete our legal adoption of the girls, I was at least able to obtain birth certificates, civil identification cards, passports and visas for the girls. We even brought them back and forth to the United States four times and visited them and their entire street community in Santa Cruz as often as possible. A year and a half and several thousand "processing" dollars later, the Bolivian government uniformly closed down any international adoptions of children over four years old. The government's reasoning was children that age and older should stay "Bolivian." Even as the government shut down any opportunity for Elsa and Gabriella to be adopted internationally, the government had neither a plan nor any intention of caring for Elsa or Gabriella or any of the other street children. Despite all our efforts and evidence of our commitment to the girls, we were not allowed to adopt them. Gabriella and Elsa are now thirteen and almost sixteen and still living on the streets of Santa Cruz.

When Leonard and I returned to life in the United States, we were sharing our Bolivian children's story and the Bolivian government saga with an older friend. His eyes immediately sparkled as he shared with us the story of his newly adopted Chinese granddaughter. He told of a wonderful agency his son and daughter-in-law had used. Leonard and I knew immediately that our friend had to be an angelic instrument of divine intervention in our lives. The next day, we began the application.

However, yet another, less optimistic divine intervention awaited us. As we were seeking an agency and social worker to conduct the home study, Leonard—age fifty-one, an Olympic long-distance runner, the first Texan to break the four-minute mile, which he did in thirty-two regulation competitions, world record holder in the distance medley, with a very successful career as an international professional engineer—was diagnosed with pancreatic cancer. He died nine months later, on July 3, 2000.

About ten months later, the kernels of faith and Christian spirit, planted by the benevolent nuns and priests in the soul of this New

York street kid, flourished again, and my determination and optimism born of those many mentors lifted my spirit to action. I decided to reapply to adopt internationally on my own—still believing that we can change the world one child at a time. My own childhood experience, my involvement with children's social agencies, Leonard's and my experience in Bolivia with Elsa and Gabriella, our original application to adopt from China, and even Leonard's death had unleashed within me a sense that my life was unique and had a larger-than-one-life richness about it. I was being guided through the adoption process on the wings of many angels. My job was to continue doing everything in my means to satisfy the process, keeping my mind and heart ever open to the contributions of so many others along the way.

I visited China several months before my scheduled assignment of a child so that I might better understand the child's culture and customs. I was more drawn to these children and people than I could have ever imagined. I had complete peace of mind and soul. Whatever happened between that visit and the assignment of any child, I had complete peace of mind that all was working out as it should in God's plan—in whatever form God takes in different people's lives. So I applied for twins, hoping maybe to intervene "two children at a time."

On February 25, 2003, I received news that the Chinese welfare agency had no more sets of twins, but that two-year-old She Liang Jun had been assigned to me, pending my acceptance. When I read the e-mail announcing the assignment, I screamed with joy; I cried (my visiting Brazilian godchild couldn't understand if something terribly great or terribly wrong had happened); and my fiancé, Ed, came racing to my home office, trying to translate the screaming into some sense. I kept saying, "She's here. Liliana is here. She's really here!" After calling a few close friends, all of whom had "Mary Liliana Tatiana" on the top of their prayer lists of their respective beliefs, I shouted

Liliana's arrival at the top of my Internet lungs. Within minutes, I began receiving joyous replies from around the world. At a time when we were all thinking about terrorist threats, economic downturn and general world uncertainty, my friends across the universe, all my cotravelers in this long and interesting journey, delighted in sharing the news of the arrival of Liliana.

As the day approached for me to travel to China to bring Liliana home, any flashes of worry I had for her welfare were comforted through my faith that the same light which had embraced and protected her for the past two years remained ever-vigilant over her now. Even when the outbreak of the Severe Acute Respiratory Syndrome (SARS) epidemic threatened to close travel to China, I steadied myself securely in the thought that God had brought us all this long way—from the streets, shelters and doorways of New York to Liliana's abandonment in the doorway of a rural southern China police station and two-year stay in a children's institute. God's plan was in full execution.

Our pairing had the earmark of divine intervention. Her Chinese name, Liang, is very similar sounding to the name I chose for her years ago, Liliana. Liang means "moon" in Chinese, and last year we decorated her room with the moon and the stars. Her orphanage report listed her favorite toys as bells and musical instruments; I started college on a music scholarship. Playing outside is her favorite activity; our own home activities focus largely on the outdoors. Yes, no doubt, God's long-term plan was in full execution.

While I waited to meet Liliana, I meditated several times a day, sending her the message in my mind: "Mama's coming; the Angels are guarding you, Liliana, and Mama's coming." On April 6, 2003, in a hotel conference room in Changsha, China, several people witnessed the opening of elevator doors and the efficient delivery of a tiny, head-shaved two-year-old girl, tightly dressed in a traditional Chinese coat, pants and frilly pink shoes, barely able to walk. As for me, I saw the skies open with glorious rays of light and felt raptures of warmth and heard sounds of angels. As our eyes fixed and our fingers gently locked, the universal river of our lives flowed through us—this plan fulfilled. I whispered: "Mama's here, Liliana . . . Mama ai, Liang Jun . . . Mama loves Liliana. . . . We're home." Through tears of joy, I thanked God for this perfect personal delivery. Amen!*

---

*Liliana's first English word!

The Weight of the Wait:
And Then There Was Josie

Ana Douglass

W e tend to see moments of loss in our lives as endings rather than beginnings. I suppose it is part of the human condition to take stock of what we have instead of valuing the spaces, gaps and openings, often created through loss in our lives, for their potential to lead us to new beginnings and new opportunities. I have always counted myself among the lucky on this planet. So many of the stories in this collection tell of hard journeys and difficult choices, moments of hardship and loss, and moments of great triumph and love. My journey is less complicated than that, and I suspect its simplicity is emblematic of what most adopting parents hope for when they set out on the path to adopt, domestically or internationally. I did not turn to adoption after experiencing loss, so much as out of a sense of hope. There was a gap in my life, no doubt, the absence of a child, but unlike so many women who have traveled the path of adoption, that space in my heart and soul was not formed out of having experienced loss; I never experienced miscarriage, experienced infertility or lost a child.

April 2003 marked the one-year anniversary since we brought home our daughter, Josie, from Wuhan, China. That month also marked the time when a mysterious disease, SARS, entered into the world's consciousness, and soon after, people stopped going to China and the Chinese placed their adoption program on hold. Of course, as anyone who has adopted internationally will tell you, SARS wasn't going to keep them from going to get their daughters and sons, but the Chinese officials made the decision for these waiting families, and suddenly the ocean that separates parents from daughters, siblings from siblings, seemed insurmountable. It was not hard for me to imagine how difficult the announcement of the postponement of Chinese adoptions was to the families who had already waited a long time and were nearing the end of their journey. I can imagine their feelings because, as relatively uncomplicated as our adoption process had been, my husband and I experienced an eleventh-hour, completely unexpected setback. What we didn't appreciate at the time, but have come to understand, is that the unexpected delay set us on a slightly different path, one that took us away from a child we knew nothing about in Hunan province to a daughter we love with every fiber of our being in Hubei province.

Our story is one that many couples are experiencing right now with China. It is also the story of those couples who were ready to adopt from Cambodia, only to find out the program was being suspended, or for those couples who patiently awaited the birth of a child only to have the birth mother change her mind once the child arrived. In other words, our story is about temporary losses that lead to new spaces in our lives and unexpected turns in our fate. I don't think anyone should proceed down the path of adoption unless he or she is ready to experience loss and is able to find hope in that loss. I write to those who are caught up in the great wait, and I do so with the message that it will end, and to trust your gut instincts that brought you to this path.

Upon reflection, the details of our journey are remarkably similar to so many other families' experiences. We were attracted to international adoption after exploring different options for building our family. Before I had even met my husband, Steve, I had dreams of adopting from China. As a graduate student on the East Coast during the 1990s, I had seen numerous Chinese adoptees with their parents at my favorite cafés in Philly, at ball games and museums, on train rides to New York. I was, of course, taken by these beautiful little girls' faces and the seeming euphoria of their parents, but as I looked into the phenomenon that brought these people together, I also found myself taken by the historical circumstances that led to so many girls being available in Chinese orphanages. I quietly made a pact with myself that if I never found the right man to marry and to build a family with, I would pursue Chinese adoption as a single parent.

Then I met the right man, Steve. Still, I continued to have dreams of a Chinese daughter. When Steve and I decided to pursue adoption, we looked at other countries, but something in my heart told me that we needed to go to China. I knew that the wait was longer for China than it would be for other countries, but I still believed that our daughter was in China. I speak Spanish, not a word of Chinese, but I still knew that we had to go to China. It is hard to put into words the kind of feelings and intuitions that drive these sorts of decisions, but somehow I just knew that no matter how much time it would take, our daughter was waiting for us in China.

Now I write these words in hindsight, more than a year after returning from China. Time has a way of mellowing the memory of what it actually felt like while we were waiting. It felt like forever, even as I knew we had chosen the right path. I want to affirm to anyone who feels the weight of the wait that you are not alone. I also want to share something that happened to us at the very end of our wait for a referral, purely by accident, but something that truly tested our resolve. I thought I couldn't stand the wait any longer when we received the news that we were expected to be in the next batch of referrals. It was our time. I started to make arrangements to take time off from work, and for the first time I allowed myself to make lists of things to bring on our trip. Then the news came that, for some inexplicable reason, we were not in the batch of referrals going to Hunan province. Our agency worked overtime trying to find out what happened, and it turned out that our dossier had accidentally been left in the wrong pile at the China Center of Adoption Affairs. We would have to wait at least another month.

The four weeks that followed were some of the longest of my life. I had moments of serious doubt. I kept wondering if, for some reason at the eleventh hour, the Chinese were going to reject us. Ruthie, our contact at our agency, tried to keep me calm, but it wasn't easy. Then the day came when the adoption agency called and announced our referral. Our daughter's name was Lin Fu Mei, and she was waiting for us in Wuhan. As I pulled up her picture on e-mail, I saw an amazing little girl with eyes that spoke of determination and survival. On the personal history statement we received for her, the orphanage listed "obstinate" as her most defining characteristic. At that moment I turned to my husband and announced that I had my answer as to why we were accidentally left out of the Hunan group the month before. Our daughter was so obstinate that she had us "karmically" kicked out of line so we would come to the right place and get her.

The wait was over. More than a year later, I can't imagine having any other little girl in our lives. If you are reading this and feel like you can't stand the wait another day, you can. If you are reading this and are having feelings of doubt or uncertainty that you will ever see the day when you finally receive that referral, those feelings are real and natural. If you are reading this and feel that the political winds of a nation or the power of a microbe have more control over your life than you do, they do for now, but not forever. The day will come when you meet your daughter or son, and thankfully, time has a way of mellowing memory; the wait will become a distant memory.

♥

Saving Helena

Maria Addison

We don't go to China to save a child. We go to save ourselves. But sometimes saving a child is what we, in fact, do. Saving a child is not easy, nor is it uncomplicated or even an unambivalent process. With apologies to a someday-adult Helena (whom you will meet in this story), here is my side of our adoption story.

Our first adoption, from China, of a healthy baby, was so easy and rewarding that I felt I owed the world a riskier adoption for giving me what I had desperately sought after years of infertility treatments. By the time we contemplated a second adoption, we were eligible only for an older, special-needs child, which seemed appropriate to me. I was ready for the challenge, little realizing how much my confidence in mothering owed to the luck of the draw. Four months after we sent in our paperwork, I traveled to China to view an orphanage charity project. Because we had recently sent our dossier for a second child to China, I was hoping to find two daughters: one for me and one for a close friend, a single woman who qualified for an older child. Wouldn't it be great if I happened to find two girls who, sharing a life in China, could continue their connection in America?

In the second-to-last orphanage we visited, there were two little girls, roommates and friends, who were eligible for adoption by older moms. One little girl sang a song, and the other little girl recited a Tang Dynasty nursery rhyme. One was named Heavenly, the other was named Luck So Pure No Evil Touches It. Both looked at me. They seemed comfortable in the arms of their caregivers. They listened to the conversation around them and spoke a word or two while we quietly asked questions about the girls and a third older girl.

Time stood still that morning and through the next day as I decided whether to request that these two girls be adopted by my friend and by my husband and me.

I was wrung out by the fifteen-hour days I had been working in China, as well as by looking after my almost-five-year-old daughter, who accompanied the group documenting the charity project. Jet lag meant I had had little sleep. Despite banquets, my weight was dropping half a pound a day. Seeing the older children in orphanages, unbuffered by the excitement of adopting, rattled me to the core. I might be able to help two get adopted, just two, out of the many older children who needed families; yet even the one would change our own family forever.

Talking to my companions and, on the phone, to my husband didn't lighten my sense of responsibility. I realized that I wasn't going to know enough, that I was scared, that this might be a dangerously romantic notion and I would do this adoption just because I could. I didn't feel noble. I felt alone.

I called my friend, "I think that maybe, perhaps, there are two girls, friends, that we might be able to adopt. Yes, they are beautiful. Yes, they talk. One sings. Yes, I took a photograph."

I said yes, and then I almost said no, because the little information I received, the combination of the birth date, head circumference and height, was alarming enough to make two doctors experienced in international adoption tell me that I could justifiably back out. The birth date seemed off relative to one child's appearance, enough to give me recurrent insomnia.

The adoption agency sent a representative to the orphanage to make sure that the child was fine. I was comforted by the thought that both girls connected with people and both talked. Finally the word came through that my friend and I could travel to China to adopt, five months after I had seen the two little girls. My friend, from a famously musical family, would be allowed the singer. I, the compulsive reader, would be allowed the nursery rhyme reciter.

The evening we arrived in Wuhan, the babies and three older children arrived at the hotel. Helena's eyes searched the room as an orphanage worker smiled, clucked and smoothed her clothes before handing her to me.

"Be good to your mother," said the orphanage worker, and she was good—for about twenty-four hours.

The first day and for much of our stay in China, Helena exhibited the behavior that I expected of an older child being adopted; she preferred other people to me, was fascinated by the clothes and few toys I had brought, ate to excess, and warily eyed the wider world to which she now belonged. Her distress, however, rapidly escalated beyond that of the other two older children from her orphanage, probably in part because she was sick with the mumps and a few other things, but also because of Helena's memories and expectations. She was loyal to her Chinese mother, a mother she remembered and longed for with an intensity that had sustained her through an eighteen-month stay at the orphanage. She anxiously scanned the room for the only person she associated with the word "Mama." Instead of that mother, the orphanage worker pointed to me and said, "Mama." A day or so passed before the disappointment erupted in a stream of grief and anger that eclipsed her desire to "Be good."

On the morning of our third day, I had the opportunity to visit Helena's orphanage again. I went with the mother of the third child, who had a video camera. I took Helena, a decision that still gives me qualms. Although we documented invaluable information about the three older girls on the video, much of it translated later in the United States, Helena cried so piteously in the bus that I can't watch that part of the video to this day. It turns out she was coming down with the mumps and was suffering from the milk I gave her because of lactose intolerance (rare, even in Chinese children, at Helena's age of four) as well as having infected tonsils and h-pylori, the infection that causes ulcers. Besides the milk, I was also giving her orange juice, which produces a stinging feeling in the cheeks of mumps victims, as I learned drinking orange juice during my turn with the mumps two weeks later. I mostly block out the hellish night when I gave Helena Benadryl, to which she had the reaction that only 1 to 2 percent of children have: hyperactivity. It's hard to believe an experienced mom could make as many mistakes as I did in that first week, piling onto the child's emotional problems of getting a new and unwelcome Mama.

Starting the third evening and reaching its height seven days after we returned home, Helena's grief storms involved screaming at a volume that could be heard from the far end of a football field, throwing her toys and, major Chinese taboo, tearing off her clothes, fortunately only in our hotel room or at home. She also dug her nails into my arms, spat at me and peed on me. The look of fury and fear in her eyes was close to demonic. She retreated when I approached her.

Instead of growing used to us, her grief storms became longer and more frequent. She would rage at me for up to an hour, sleep for a few hours and wake up to another storm. One typical night she woke up four times, screaming. Sometimes putting her in the stroller and rolling her around the kitchen island worked. Mostly nothing did. My husband helped as best he could.

When Helena slept, I read or called people whom I thought

might help. *Passage to the Heart*, edited by Amy Klatzkin—full of first-person accounts of adopting children from China—gave me the hope and courage to keep looking for assistance. My older daughter's pre-school helped put me in touch with one of our city's top child psychi-atrists, who looked at her playing with a doll house, listened to me and said that inserting another person into the mother-child relationship wouldn't be helpful at this stage. As soon as we left the psychiatrist's office, Helena got in her stroller, threw off her socks and shoes, and screamed the length of the walk back to our house. Thankfully this Chinese child felt so wicked having bare feet outdoors that she didn't progress to American standards of indecent exposure. Consulting other experts didn't offer much help. Child psychiatrists did not know what to do with a child who didn't speak English.

My older daughter's Chinese teacher came every day, explaining Helena's new universe to her. The teacher also started teaching Helena, in Chinese, colors, numbers and other concepts that are the staple of preschool life. This teacher had met Helena and me at the airport in Boston so that Helena had someone to tell her about her new life as soon as she arrived. Hearing Chinese and seeing a kind Chinese face gave Helena two hours of respite each day and a grow-ing, if begrudging, understanding of her new world. Helena started preschool with her Chinese teacher and me in tow. We knew she needed other children, but she also needed us.

About two weeks after Helena's homecoming, I came across *Holding Time* by Martha Welch, which advocated holding a child firmly across a parent's lap, looking her in the eye, and articulating the child's feelings as well as one's own feelings. It seemed extreme and risky for a child who often retreated screaming at me. I was, how-ever, growing desperate. Helena was getting worse, not better, as our adoption agency and others had predicted. Fortunately a mother in our travel group, another Families with Children from China mom, was a psychologist. Although she treated adults rather than children, several of her patients used holding time for their children during divorce. "The key," she repeated several times, "is doing it six times in a row. If you start, you must do it six times in a row, or it won't work at all, and her tantrums might get worse."

I still hoped Helena would improve with gentle love and support. She didn't. I explained holding time to my husband. I made a chart with two variables: grief storm length of time and length of time between grief storms. No one would describe my personality as confrontational, or bluntly honest; rather I prefer to make points diplomatically. To try this method with Helena, I would have to try methods that caused me great discomfort. In preparation I learned the Chinese words for fear, anger and sadness.

The first time I held Helena across my lap, she screamed for sixty minutes. I held her. My husband held me. It was hard to believe that a child, whose initial muscle tone was so poor she couldn't walk up the stairs unaided, would fight so hard that it took all my strength, reinforced by my husband, to hold her.

I looked her in the eye and used my few Chinese words. I told her in English how scared I was. When she pierced my skin with her nails, I cried. If I put a towel beneath her to keep her pee off the sofa, she screamed even harder. She arched her back. She kicked me. I gritted my teeth as I had never gritted them before.

If I hadn't been keeping a chart, I wouldn't have known that at time number five, the grief storm was only forty minutes, and the time between storms had lengthened to more than five hours. I was so sleep deprived and disoriented I wasn't able to tell the difference between sixty minutes and forty minutes.

But the most important difference—a difference that I would have noticed under any circumstances—was the emergence of Helena's true smile. All the years I fought to bear a biological child, I had a secret hope: that I would see, on the face of a daughter, my long-lost grandmother's smile. And there it was, as luminous as the last time I had seen it, twenty-five years ago. "Oh Helena," I told her, "you have Grandmommy's smile."

There were and are still hurdles ahead, but Helena's progress has been steady. Helena is bright, beautiful and joyous. Her teachers enjoy her. She loves and is loved. The darker side of her grief she trusts to me. I still hold her and try to articulate her most negative feelings when those feelings overwhelm her. Four years later, this happens about once every six weeks and lasts five to ten minutes with much-diminished intensity. Helena, photogenic and outgoing, has become virtually a poster child for Alliance's older-children adoption program and the inspiration for other older-child adoptions among several of our acquaintances.

How did the other two girls turn out? The three girls are still friends; Helena fantasizes about marrying them both, in addition to her four boy fiancés. Heavenly turned out to be a great reader, despite singing for me in the orphanage. Helena turned out to sing perfectly in tune and struggles with reading despite reciting a nursery rhyme for me. The third girl is doing well and has a new sister from Russia. Neither of the other two girls went through the emotional trauma that Helena did.

When I arrive at the pearly gates, St. Peter will present a list of my sins. The scale, heavy with a thousand failures, will pitch dangerously downwards. Then he will sigh, ushering me into heaven, saying, "You saved Helena." And I will cry, not from relief and the joy of entering heaven, but because, despite my uncertainty, Helena was saved.

♥

Demystifying the Adoption Option

Nancy Hanner

E leven years ago, I arrived at my brother-in-law's funeral as both a mourning relative and the sudden legal guardian of his two children. It was the family's second funeral in the course of a year. Nine months earlier, my sister-in-law, niece and nephew had died in a tragic accident. People approached me, pressed my hands and said, "You are so wonderful to take these children."

It was a noble view of adoption, with me the rescuer, the saver of children. Buying into it was tempting, and I did at times. But once I got down to the business of raising children, I found that nobility had little to do with the reality of creating a family.

After the funeral, my husband and I moved into my brother-in-law's house so we wouldn't further disrupt the lives of our new eighteen-month-old son and two-year-old daughter. Those first three months were so stressful I developed a case of hives that I couldn't shake. The hives eventually went away, but it took a lot longer to work through the emotional problems. Despite my best efforts at forging a relationship with her, my daughter gave me the cold shoulder for the first five years she was with us. Her favorite story was "Cinderella," and I'm fairly certain I wasn't the fairy godmother.

I have a friend who became a full-time stepmother one weekend when her husband's ex-wife decided she could no longer care for the children. My friend raised the kids, monitoring late-night asthma attacks, baking room-mother treats and sitting through Scout meetings.

"My daughter invited me to the mother's weekend at college," she told me one day. "Then she found out her real mother could make it, so she called back to uninvite me."

I was shocked at her daughter's heartless treatment of the mother who had always been there for her. My friend and I are Number Two. We will never be Number One in our kids' eyes, and that is one of the not-so-nice realities of adoption.

We are quick to point out what we consider our children's misdirected loyalties, but what of our own? My friend's preference would have been to raise a traditional family with her husband. Mine was also to have children of my own, which I attempted to do without success for seven years. However much we pretend otherwise, our adopted children were second choices for us.

So there it is. Our children want what they have lost, and so do we. They have lost their blood ties to parents. We have lost our visions of family, the dream of how our lives should look.

I recently read about a family who brought a baby girl back from China. The whole family passionately wanted to do this. The oldest son came home from college more often so he can play with her. The kids developed a schedule because they all wanted to hold her at the same time. This family adopted their daughter for the purest of reasons: They had love to give and felt compelled to offer it. That's all. So many people don't start in the right place, as this family did, but those who are willing to work through the disillusionment that follows have a chance to grow into a real family unit.

A few months ago my twelve-year-old daughter called from her grandmother's house, where she was visiting for the week. She has a special bond with this grandmother, the mother of the mother she lost. "I miss the dog," she said, then laughed, "Oh, and I miss you, too." When I hung up, I was glad for all those years that we moved slowly together, circling each other—afraid to place our vulnerability in each other's hands. She did miss me. I could hear it in her voice.

My son is now old enough to understand chromosomes and the steps beyond the mechanics of reproduction. My husband's blood runs through my son, but mine does not, and he knows it. "There is a ceremony," I told him, thinking this would appeal greatly to an eleven-year-old boy, "where we can become blood brothers. We can do it if you want." He considered it and said no, I imagine because of the part involving blood. Now I wonder if it was I who wanted the ceremony, if I was still longing for the solidity of a blood bond.

I feel ridiculous for having suggested this idea, realizing he has no need for such things—that he is, in fact, exactly where he should be. He knows where his family is, both the one that is buried and the one that sits at the hockey rink, watching him play. Because he is such a great kid, he is willing to be patient with a mother who sometimes likes to make her mission much more complicated than what it really is: the offering of family, simple, sweet and pure.

♥

Grace

Lee Ashworth

The following words probably reflect many of my husband Ken's thoughts, but losing a child is an intimate agony, so I do not attempt to speak for both of us. However, this story is ours, as well as Hannah's. But mostly the story is about Grace. Finding Grace and loving Grace.

The orphanage director handed us Grace in the hallway just outside the hotel's elevator. Gracie was small for one year. Fourteen pounds hidden under three layers of clothes. Her foster mother had painted her fingernails red for good luck, and Grace held a red, paper-wrapped candy in her small hand.

We traveled to China with fourteen other families. On the bus from Nanchang airport, we learned we would meet our daughters that night, within the hour. My husband Ken and I were fighting over our lost luggage keys when the call came to walk down the hall to receive our baby.

That night we went to bed with a baby in our room. Gracie slept in a blue crib that the hotel had set up in anticipation of our arrival. I stayed up most of the night listening to her breathing and taking in her lovely sleeping face.

For ten months we had believed in the potential of finding Grace. The belief that we would parent again sustained us. Ten months before finding Grace, we lost Hannah.

Our first daughter, Hannah—also from China—died suddenly

in her sleep on January 3, 1998. She died after a day spent happily shopping for Elmo decorations for her upcoming second birthday. When we returned home that afternoon, Hannah began to run a temperature. Ken and I made all those decisions that parents make when their child is sick, and after Motrin, Popsicles and a mandatory reading of *Goodnight Moon*, we put her in her crib. We checked on her every twenty minutes or so over the next two hours. She was sleeping very soundly. When I finally decided to rouse her, I picked her up only to discover she was already gone. She was still warm. Her beautiful face was pale, but unquestionably peaceful. Hannah left our life as mysteriously as she entered it. An extensive autopsy was not able to determine the cause of her death.

The night Hannah died, Ken and I told each other that we would adopt again. Loving Hannah had taught us that to love your child is a unique joy. In the beautiful memorial statement that Ken wrote for Hannah's funeral, he said, "The big question we must ask ourselves now is this: Can there be any sense to make of the loss of a child so loved and loving, so joyous and joyful? How can we stand losing someone so quickly whom we longed for, for so long? I wish to God I had an answer. I wish I understood. I don't. But I do know this. Hannah taught us about hope and faith and love and the possibility of miracles."

Somehow, despite the confusion and craziness of our grief, we knew one thing with great clarity: We would parent again. We knew we could either move to the dark, or move to the light that Hannah had shown was all around us. Our choosing to love another child would be Hannah's legacy.

Before boarding the late-night flight that would take us to China and to Grace, Ken and I ate dinner at an all-night diner near our home in Manhattan. As we ate, fireworks exploded a block or two away over the Hudson River at Chelsea Piers. Maybe because the old aluminum-clad diner was so well insulated, or maybe because this is just the way I remember it, I could see the fireworks, but not really hear them. To me, now, those soundless fireworks are an apt metaphor for Gracie's adoption trip. The beauty, happiness and energy of the formation of new families exploded all around me in Nanchang and Guanzhou. But it was all so surreal. I remember experiencing things without really feeling them.

Gracie favored Ken during the ten days we spent with her in China. In an effort to assuage my hurt feelings, I remember coming up with a convenient theory that Gracie—or maybe God—knew somehow that Ken needed this special treatment because he was more vulnerable than I. In truth, Gracie's lack of interest in me made me cry on more than one occasion, and it also sort of relieved me. Maybe she would never really love me, so losing her might not be as bad.

Rationally, I knew that once we returned to Manhattan, I would be Gracie's primary caretaker, and we had all the time in the world to find our way together. But I was scared and overwhelmed at times by my desire to hold on to Hannah and my fear of falling in love with Grace. Mistakenly, over the next several months, I assumed that to love Gracie was going to somehow diminish my relationship with Hannah.

When we arrived home with Gracie, all the caretaking felt wonderfully familiar. I knew how to take care of a child. For the ten months as a "childless mother," I had longed for the familiar: little wet socks stuck to the sides of the washing machine, wiping down the highchair after a meal, filling tiny plastic bowls with Goldfish crackers, and smelling and kissing a newly washed head of my child's hair. All of these incredible, yet ordinary things were once again a part of my daily routine.

This mothering I did instinctively. I needed the physicality of our relationship as much as Gracie did. We were both wounded souls. Cautiously, we eyed each other.

During our first few weeks with Hannah, just looking at her sleeping or eating or playing—just being—could fill me with love, gratitude and wonder. We flew home with Hannah on the Fourth of July 1996. As we crossed the country, a constant silent display of fireworks accompanied us. Ken told me later that it was as though each city, town and neighborhood was celebrating Hannah's arrival.

There were times in our first few weeks with Gracie that I could actually feel myself pulling back from her. Gracie was and is now an engaging, charming, bright, rascally little person. Even as a baby she smiled a lot. Each developmental step she mastered pleased her immensely. I loved being with her, and I waited to feel "filled up."

One night carrying Gracie into her room, I whispered, "I love you." I believe it was the first time I said it directly to her. Her blue-black eyes caught mine and she smiled, an enormous, silly, toothless smile. A secret exchanged—we loved each other.

Because we arrived home with Gracie on October 30, we headed almost immediately into the holiday season—our first without Hannah, our first with Gracie. That first Thanksgiving and Christmas are both blurs to me. Like all other areas of my life, the simple had become complex.

In my house as a child, the Christmas season began the day after Thanksgiving. My mother loved Christmas, and each year she would drag out boxes of familiar decorations. Our tree was never color-coordinated or decorated by a theme. It was instead a fantastic patchwork of remembrances—hand-blown glass ornaments that belonged to my father's grandmother, paper angels, clothespin butterflies and assorted ornaments that my sister and I chose each year. Souvenirs of a hundred Christmases wrapped in pine and light. As an adult I had managed to set up a Christmas tree, even in the tiniest of apartments, every year except the first Christmas without my mother.

Christmas 1998 marked the only other time I have not had the energy or the heart to put up a Christmas tree. I thought I wanted to, because I knew that Gracie would love the smell and lights of a tree. But as I began to unwrap the ornaments, I found Hannah's crystal angel and the two still-packaged ornaments she had picked out at an after-Christmas sale just days before she died only eleven months prior. I knew that I couldn't do it.

We spent Christmas Eve and morning with Ken's parents. Christmas morning we watched our delightful Gracie delight in the Christmas tree, her presents, empty boxes and wrapping paper. Later, on the way to Ken's aunt's house for Christmas brunch, Ken and I stopped at Hannah's grave. It was a bittersweet time for all of us, but Gracie's joy and goodness provided us with a comforting balm.

Gracie sneaked into my life in an almost imperceptible way. After a year of firsts, we now live in uncharted territory. Gracie's second birthday was excruciating for me, and an enormous blessing. She will be three this October, and the day-to-day comparisons that occur between siblings no longer exist. She continues to amaze us with her charm and intellect and sassiness.

Now, when Gracie runs to me or sings or tells me one of her convoluted stories, I am filled with my love for her. Her naughtiness, sense of drama and temper, as trying as they can be, are also sweet reassurances of how far we have traveled together.

Christmas 1999 was a complicated time, but a happy one. That year, we set up the tree. Ken, Gracie, our dog and I went across Ninth Avenue to Rite Aid and picked out the perfect one. This time as I unpacked the ornaments and picked through the layers of tissue paper and discovered souvenirs of so many Christmases, I managed to believe in the Christmases to come. With each ornament that I handed Gracie, she dashed across the room, hung it with great care and let out a Gracie squeal—the mystery and beauty of Christmas, of Grace. As in the past, our tree was decorated with a hundred Christmas remembrances: of my mother, our grandparents, aunts, uncles, friends and Hannah—and was full of light.

♥

CHAPTER THREE

Embracing Our Differences

The Color of Skin

Deborah Egan

M y daughter has beautiful skin. It's smooth and feels like satin to touch. She has laid her small brown arm across my pale white one and noticed the difference in color. But until her first day of camp, I don't think my daughter had felt her "brownness" before. "Brownness," not as a difference in shade, but as a divider between her and everyone else.

Some people are fortunate enough to live in a multiracial community where there is a mix of people with a variety of cultures and skin colors. Others, like us, live in a community that is pretty uniformly Caucasian. My husband and I adopted our two children from Latin America, and we have been open with them and with our community of friends and family from the beginning. We have always let others know we are proud of our choice to adopt children from backgrounds different than ours, and how proud we are to be a multicultural family.

In our family, there are no secrets kept from my daughter, but she never had cause to feel that brownness before camp. Brown is just a color, a shade, and it needs a point of comparison to emerge as "different" or apart. My daughter had always been exposed to multiracial environments, from our circle of friends to her playschool group, and never saw herself as racially distinct from anyone else.

She was six when she first went to summer day camp. When she arrived home after the first day, she excitedly recounted the highlights of the day's events to me, filled with animated tales of swimming, singing and making puppets. Then, suddenly, the enthusiasm slipped from her face when she mentioned that she was the only person with brown skin at the camp, and what did I think about that?

I tried to keep my calm, but I felt winded, like a punch in the gut. I'm sure my daughter had felt the same earlier that day. I was expecting the worst, but as we discussed the comments that were made by the other children, I discovered that no one had actually said anything nasty or derogatory to my daughter. It seemed that the other children at camp were just curious about my daughter being adopted. Apparently this was their first exposure to an internationally adopted child living in a multiracial family. We talked for a while about how it felt, and she determined that she would get used to it. My daughter even considered what it would be like to have white skin like the kids at camp, and eventually decided that she really liked her brown skin because it went well with her black hair!

Although my daughter appeared to have resolved the issue, I lay in bed that night, staring at the ceiling and wishing I could go to the camp in the morning to talk with the children, or at least tell the counselor my anxieties. I envisioned several scenarios in my head, each running to ludicrous polar extremes. In one dream fantasy a big rainbow arced over the entire camp, and everyone was holding hands and singing and eating ice cream while little cartoon hearts floated in the air. In the other I was chased out of camp by a rock-throwing hoard, and I had to dive in the water for safety. It felt too much like some after-school special, and however much I tried, I couldn't find the right, and realistic, way to handle it. I decided to sleep on the issue for a day to consider how I would proceed. I wanted so badly to address my daughter's concerns and help her feel better, but I didn't want to create a raging scene and outburst at camp that would embarrass my little girl.

Amazingly, while I was doing all the thinking and worrying, my daughter's counselor, Diane, had actually conceived a plan. Diane had noticed the attention my daughter was receiving from the other kids, and had quickly devised an activity to address it. It was so simple and yet so perfect, and when my daughter told me about it the next afternoon, I gave myself a little back pat for having chosen such a lovely camp.

"Well," my daughter told me in the kitchen, describing the game. "Diane split us up into three groups. Each group had three people in it, a first-grader, a second-grader and a third-grader. Then she gave us a paper and pencil. She had the third-graders be the list makers, 'cause third-graders are good writers.

"On one piece of paper, we all had to write down all the ways we were different. In my group, we found out that one of us was born in the United States, one in England and me in Ecuador. We all had different color hair and different color eyes, and I had different color skin. And, of course, we were all in different grades." That was the extent of the list of differences. It was very short and it appeared that the counselor tried to emphasize this to all of the kids in her group. "Then," my daughter continued, "she had us use another piece of paper to write down all of the ways that we were the same. We found out that we all like to swim, sing, dance, wear the same kinds of clothes, listen to the same kinds of music, play games, paint our nails and stuff like that."

Diane then showed the children that the list of similarities was quite long—longer by far than the list of differences. And that was that. I wouldn't say that every child instantly understood the intricacies and nuances of adoption and multiculturalism, but kids absorb more than we think. And at that age, a common ice cream flavor is enough to spark an immediate and fervent friendship.

All these kids needed was a prod in the right direction, and Diane gave that push with simple eloquence and subtlety. My daughter made many friends that summer and never again commented about her difference. As the summer wore on, the children came to appreciate each other for who they were—just kids who all loved to swim and play and laugh and make puppets in the sun.

♥

Fitting In

Michael Kilmurray

I've always felt at home anywhere I go, yet at the same time I've never really felt at home at all. This is a strange paradox, I know, and it's difficult for me to describe. I guess I'm the guy who fits in everywhere simply because there's no single place where he belongs. Does this make any sense? Probably not. I've spent my whole life trying to figure it out, so how can I explain it so briefly right now?

I'm twenty-five, and I was born in Bucaramanga, a city outside of Bogotá, Colombia, over toward the mountains near Venezuela. I stayed in a church orphanage and was adopted at eleven months by my parents, who were living in Colombia at the time. I have no record of who my birth parents were, what they did, where they lived. A bad case of pneumonia expedited the adoption process, and I was living in Boston by the time I was one.

I've always thought of Jamaica Plain—our area of Boston—as divided into three sections, starting the farthest away from downtown and working their way in. The first is the upper-middle-class neighborhood, near Brookline. Moving on, there's the main business drag—our neighborhood—where the middle class lives, mostly Irish descendants. The last section makes up the biggest chunk of Jamaica Plain, and that's the Hispanic neighborhood, mostly composed of Puerto Ricans and Dominicans, with some Cubans as well.

I remember an experience that first made me notice my appearance, especially compared to my parents. When I was a child, I was shopping with my mom in a grocery store my parents frequented, in the Hispanic section of Jamaica Plain. Two ladies were speaking in Spanish in the other aisle, and from the way my mom stiffened, I could tell they were talking about us. My mother's face grew tight and dark in the eyes, and she dropped her can of beans and marched into the other aisle.

She spoke loudly and angrily in Spanish to the women, and everyone in the store stopped, their attention drifting to the scene. Not only were these women getting chewed out, which is always amusing, but a white woman was chewing them out in Spanish. Everyone almost looked guilty, as though a spy had been discovered in their midst who knew all the secrets they thought she hadn't heard. I'm probably overdramatizing the scene greatly, but in retrospect it's how I felt at the time.

Later, my mother told me what the women had said. It was wrong for a Hispanic boy to be brought up by white people, they said, and were wondering what business my mother had with me. My mom told them that she was my mother, and probably some other nastier things that she didn't reveal to me at the time. She didn't have time to explain the whole situation to the women, my mother said, but I should be aware that we were not quite like other families. That didn't make us wrong, of course—just different.

I began to learn then that how others perceived me was strongly related to how I was presented to them. Walking by myself, I never felt part of my neighborhood, even though my parents were involved in the community. But being alone in the Hispanic neighborhoods felt more natural, as though my skin color was an access pass to those streets. And yet being with my parents in the Hispanic communities, I suddenly felt out of place again.

I was to feel that strange shuffle even more when school began. I went to an excellent elementary school in a terrible neighborhood.

Sometimes recess was cancelled because there were gunfights roaring near the area. I could come home to clean, quiet suburban-like streets, and my head would reel with the contrast. The bombed-out buildings with busted brick ramparts and black, burned lots clashed harshly with my after-school life, and reconciling the two was difficult.

In elementary school, I was never the minority. There were maybe one or two white children in the classes, and I was never treated like I didn't belong. But even though my skin wasn't distinctive from the rest, I still felt out of place. When I stood up for roll call, there was always a hesitant moment for the other children as they tried to place my Colombian face with the Scottish name that was often mistaken for Irish. And I never spoke Spanish, partly because I didn't remember, but mainly because I fought against relearning it as a child. This, too, made me an outsider in the Hispanic school culture, and I sometimes felt shunned from conversations.

It was like a stake sharpened at both ends. Anywhere along the middle I could move freely, and only at the bitter ends did I feel the sharp sting of prejudice or rejection. This frustrating dichotomy would arise again when I, much older, would drive my parents' expensive car around town. In my own neighborhood I would get pulled over by cops, who most likely thought, *Here's this Hispanic kid probably stole someone's car from around here.* And in the poorer neighborhoods I'd still get pulled over by some cop who thought, *Where'd a kid from around here get a nice car like that?*

I don't want to cast myself as a victim, because I never really had that complex. But I do feel the workings of my little world were illustrative of a greater trend in Boston and the world. I learned more about the real world in elementary school than I did about addition and the fifty states. Rather than make me bitter or discouraged, my circumstances forced me to be that much more outgoing and accepting.

My bus route to school passed through many neighborhoods, picking up a very diverse range of kids. I liked one kid in particular, and we quickly became friends. I was impressed by his ability to rap and freestyle, his sharp memory, his clever lyrics. He was in fourth grade, like me, and he was incredibly friendly, outgoing, bright and talented. He also had a policeman stepfather who used to beat the hell out of him and his mom, and he'd come into school with iron burns, whip marks and cigarette blisters on his arms and neck.

We were great friends, but sometimes he would fight me, as a show in front of the others. No one in the school picked on me because of his friendship, except him. Once he even pulled a knife on me. I always knew that he'd never really hurt me in front of the others, but I was sometimes terrified of what he'd do if he lost it when we were alone.

My parents were wonderful in helping me work through my anger and hurt, and trying to understand him. They told me that you can never really tell where someone is coming from, you can never understand the horror that some people have to face. I never knew why he would fight me some days; maybe he'd been beaten especially hard that morning.

But I think even more than my supportive parents, my adoption gave me the perspective to view my world. I knew what my life could have been like in Colombia, for all I remembered of that country was a life of pneumonia and bad health. I knew what my life could have been like here, if I didn't have such incredible parents to raise me. I think having that knowledge of a harder, more brutal life that never was, but could have been, made me more appreciative of what I had. It made me try harder in school when I wasn't always interested, and it made me open to finding friends wherever I went, regardless of their background or where they wound up. I met some amazing people that way, unlikely friends I never would have made without that openness and that perspective.

When I was nine, my parents took me back to Colombia. I wandered around my old orphanage, with no memory of the church or the grounds. We walked into the hills on dirt roads, where the towns became smaller and less developed, more broken down, and little children started running to us, begging. They weren't begging for food or money, as I was used to, they were begging for fireworks. My father explained to me that it was two days before the New Year, and they were trying to get enough fireworks to stuff the traditional scarecrow to blow to bits to welcome in the year. "For a few days," he said, "they don't beg for money or food, they just beg for fireworks and a new chance, a new beginning."

The idea of these children forgoing food in order to prepare for their cultural event stuck with me. I looked at them and realized that I could have easily been one of them. Not that I pitied them, but it again produced that strange mirrored schism through which I could view my two possible lives unfolding at once. The difference was that mine had afforded me many opportunities, and it was my responsibility to make the best possible use of the chances I was given.

Even now, in my midtwenties, I'm not always sure where I belong. Sometimes I feel like a chameleon, like I can feel comfortable and blend in any neighborhood in Boston, or in any city. But the thing about chameleons is, I wonder if they eventually forget their natural color. It's considered nice to master the art of fitting in. I also think chameleons must be lonely.

I've experienced anger, sadness and confusion in my life, as many have, but now I have a medium to express it. I finished high school and graduated from Williams College in western Massachusetts. I studied sociology and pursued studio art. I now work as a production assistant at the local PBS affiliate, working on educational productions. Being involved in educational programming combines my desire to reach people with my love of the creative arts, and I think I'm finally closing in on what I want to do, where I want to be. I hope to reach anyone who wants to learn but sees walls everywhere. I was blessed with many opportunities, and I just want to show others where their chances lie, that there always are chances, even if you haven't been as lucky as me.

For the same reasons I became and stayed friends with my elementary school friend, I hold no resentment or anger toward him or the way he treated me. I was upset at the time, but I never lost sight of the fact that if all the people in his life cared about his interests and noted his talent as much as people did with me, he may have been a happy kid and had a different life. I valued his artistic talents, how he could express his happiness, his pain and his indifference. He simply valued my acceptance of him. The experience that was our friendship has reinforced my open perspective and taught me the value of artistic expression—most importantly when no one will listen to you. As I learned in fourth grade, you can live a lifetime by the time you are nine years old. No one is too old to learn or too young to teach.

♥

Navel Gazing

Lindsay Davies

At fifteen months, Gemma Leigh found her tummy button. Her fingers poked and tugged at the uneven folds of skin tucked low in her taut belly and circling inward: neither an "innie" or an "outie," hers is a neat, pretty "inbetweenie." "My baboo," she solemnly dubbed it. This discovery accompanied others: her silken lashes, for instance, and, inevitably, her nostrils! Yet while we were caught up in the general amusement of her bodily fascinations, her navel-gazing also stirred me in the profundity of its innocence.

One of the meanings *Chambers Dictionary* provides for a "navel" is a "central point" (related to "nave," the hub of a wheel). The human navel is a central point in that it marks the complete connection of mother and child in utero. Thus for Gemma, a child adopted from China, her navel is the sign on her flesh of her deep loss. It marks an actual physical connection to the woman who gave her life; the woman whom, later, no doubt, she will try to imagine, try to grasp in her mind and heart; the woman for whom she will cry and yet never be able to know. This fleshy knot attaches her to a past she can never access and to people who will remain as elusive as shadows.

For her, somewhere, in a place we don't know, on a day we can't be certain of, under conditions we can't imagine, the severing of this cord meant the severing of herself from her biological origins—from the folks who gave her that tremendous will and fire, that wise look of hers, that brown wispy hair that surprised us by its lightness, those gymnast's legs, that gorgeous grin. Often I have wondered about the scene of her birth: Who cut the cord? Who tied the knot?

On contemplating this knotty depression in her sweet tummy, I have been struck by the fact that all lives begin with this wound to the flesh. This necessary cutting apart is the first act of individuation for the infant—an act not willed but imposed. The navel marks a separation, a cutting off. It is the first mark of experience: life's first scar. Since Homer's *Odyssey* at least, and perhaps before, a scar on the flesh has signified two things automatically: the experience of pain and the individuality of the scarred person. This is true, for example, of the new children's hero Harry Potter. The lightning-bolt scar on his brow is a continual reminder both of the death of his parents at the hands of evil and his remarkable ability, even as a baby, to resist and combat the darkest of powers.

The scar marks the individual, marks the flesh, displaying a rupture of perfection, of wholeness. But it also marks, in the sense of "points to," the unique specificity of the bearer. The scar marks the flesh like a brand, and the experience of pain marks the consciousness. So Odysseus's scar is the means by which his identity is affirmed by those who had long awaited his return. But Homer's digression into how the scar was received during Odysseus's first hunt, a story that so oddly cuts into the drama of homecoming and recognition, is a reminder that identity is formed through experience and pain. Odysseus's scar signifies the moment when he became a man.

I consider the navel to be an identity-marking scar that we all bear, though we do not consider it as such. That odd whorl of knotted tissue at our center we so sweetly call the belly button marks the end of absolute intimacy and the beginnings of selfhood. The expression "navel-gazing" means colloquially an obsession with the self. Young children are blessedly free from such introspection. Yet there comes a time when the child will, and must, discover her origins. I waited for four and a half years for the moment when Gemma would seriously ponder hers. What would she make of the balance of losses and gains, separations and unions, scars and healing that already made up her brief life? For those who adopt infants especially, this waiting period is spotted with anxiety. Should we just wait? Should we nudge her? And what do we say when the moment comes—when she is ready to ask how she came to be with us? How indeed? The mysterious and magical matching of adoption never ceases to astound.

Gemma Leigh, born in China, an American citizen, a New York resident, with a British mummy and an Italian American dad, now (temporarily) lives in Florence, Italy. "Citizen of the World," we call her, emphasizing her entitlement. But she has grown slowly to realize origins are more specific than that. She has reached the moment when she needs to know how she fits, exactly, into the complicated network of life. Her navel-gazing has begun.

For quite suddenly, not so long ago (June 26, 2000, to be precise), Gemma reached down into the deep pocket of her memory and pulled out a detail I had given her several months before about her preadoption history. We were sitting in a café near our apartment in Florence, having just ordered a celebratory lunch. That morning, my five-year-old took off on her two-wheeler for the first time without the training wheels. Yet she rode round and around the fountain in Piazza D'Azeglio, the sun glinting off the chrome, as if she'd been doing it all her life. I had watched in delight and amazement. Another milestone reached, with such ease and confidence. *I hope she will meet all life's challenges this way,* I thought. And then, in the café, as if the step forward into life she'd taken that morning required a reflective counterpart, a glance over the shoulder at what was past and gone, she suddenly and quietly asked, "But how did I get to that house where they looked after me in China when I was a baby? Why did I go there?"

My thoughts mustered themselves into some kind of alignment as I realized this was it, the moment when I had to explain to her clearly and honestly the existence of the shadow people, her birth parents, and their importance in her history. So, in simple but truthful language, I talked to her about the rule in China that decides how many children can be in a family, and about the man and woman who gave her life and then felt they had to let her go. "They were very, very sad they could not keep you," I said. Her faced creased with pain. She hid her head in the folds of my shirt and wept, big heaving sobs. Plates of spaghetti were put in front of us, the waitress smiling at the capricious moods of children. And just as suddenly, the crying stopped. Gemma sat up and wiped her eyes, then we both noisily blew our noses and began twirling the pink strands of pasta on our forks.

Over the past year I have seized any opportunity to feed Gemma tidbits about her origins. She has known she is Chinese from a very young age, but she has been without curiosity about this fact. It had been normalized by the wonderful network of adoptive families we were part of in New York. Many of her best friends there are also adopted from China. But this lack of curiosity grew perplexing to me, in particular given the presence of her little brother, born when she was almost three as a result of the joy she had brought—the sense of striving for a family having ceased. She watched me breast-feed Julius, but never inquired whether I'd fed her this way as well. Nor did she ask whether she had grown in my tummy.

One doesn't want to rush these things though. So I waited, dropped nuggets of information, and continued to wait and hope that she'd ask me before someone else clumsily filled her in. Once I told her she'd lived in a house called an orphanage for a little while, until

Mummy and Daddy could come and get her. Another time, after watching some images of pregnancy on TV, I told her gently, "You grew in someone's tummy, too, you know." "Whose?" Wide eyes turned on me. "Yours?" "No." But she was off, skipping onto the balcony to play with a tea set or something.

Despite this effort, I often wondered if I'd somehow encouraged her lack of curiosity. For as much as I wanted her to know about her beginnings and about the people who had made her but who can never be identified, located, pinned down, I feared the changes this knowledge would bring. I feared, and still do, the sadness, the awareness of profound loss, and the difference from her brother she might feel and be hurt by.

But I don't fear the shadow people themselves anymore. I confess I used to worry that they would haunt me more than her, as competitors for her attention, her thoughts, her imagination. How much would their elusive presence affect my place in her life? Yes, I did worry about these things. Then Gemma herself, without even knowing, enabled me to embrace these shadows, who are people, of course, not shadows. People who contributed the nature part to the nature/nurture equation of identity. People who are present in her in ways we can never exactly know but who constantly provoke my imagination. People who gave her life and ensured she would survive by keeping her for six weeks before giving her up. People whose agony over her I cannot begin to comprehend. People whose deep loss produced perhaps my greatest joy—the moment when my exquisitely beautiful six-month-old daughter was placed in my arms five years ago.

As we ate our spaghetti, the conversation continued. Her curiosity was piqued now. She especially wanted to know about the other mummy, the one who had her in her tummy and fed her milk. I told her what I knew, which wasn't much. I told her that she was born in the countryside, that her birth parents were poor, that they were probably farmers of some kind. I told her that her other mummy had probably been very afraid and sad, but that she had gone into the big city to leave the baby Gemma in a place with lots of people so she would be found quickly. As I struggled to find the right words to tell her this traumatic part of the story, I saw Gemma smile. She focused on the positive and was clearly comforted by the fact that someone had gone to so much trouble to keep her safe until her "real" mummy and daddy could come and get her. Hearing me tell of the joy we had felt at seeing her for the first time, she concluded with devastating accuracy, "It's a happy story, Mummy. But the sad bits are quite sad."

Indeed it is a happy story, though born of agony. Knots, after all, don't only tie things off. They also tie things together. The finality of the knot in her belly, which severs so absolutely her connection with her origins, also signifies the beginning of her self—her story, which magically wrote her daddy, her brother and me into its contours.

♥

Success Story

Anonymous

I was adopted at three years old as the youngest of three siblings. I have a brother one year older and a sister three years older; both are the biological children of my parents. It's hard for me to say if I believe my adoption was a success. On one hand, growing up I remember feeling like my parents treated me differently. On the other hand, I know that I was brought up to be a successful and contributing member of society and a wonderful mother. Today, my husband Michael and I have five beautiful children. Four of our children are adopted. I am thrilled with the choice that I made for my family. They have given me far more joy than I'll ever be able to repay.

Yet when I was younger it seemed like everything was unfair. When my siblings and I sat in the backseat of the car I always had to sit in the middle. At dinner I always sat in the odd chair next to the table leg while everyone else had his or her own special seat. When I would ask for ketchup for my dry meat, my mother would refuse and get insulted. One time, I recall having a tablespoon of ketchup forced into my mouth. My brother got strawberry Quik with milk, but this was refused to me. When my brother went to overnight camp I can vividly recall the care packages that were sent to him. When I went to camp the next year, I didn't get any. When I was little, my sister went to dancing school and then decided that she did not like it. I begged to go and was told that I was too clumsy.

These examples were minor infractions, but they contributed to my sense that I was an outsider. They are just some of the negative experiences I recall that contributed to my feeling as if I did not measure up. Today, my parents and I do not speak. This, of course, makes our story a tragedy. I ask myself, *What has caused the rift between us? Is the fact that I was adopted a contributing factor?*

Many of my experiences growing up caused me to believe that it was. Am I sorry that I was adopted? Absolutely not! I am grateful for countless things: trips to places like Washington, D.C., Canada and New York, summer camp, Hebrew school, people to care for me when I was sick, and people to take an interest in my schoolwork. My parents instilled in me many moral values. I just wish they had tried harder to show more love and affection. I wish they had tried harder to treat us children more evenhandedly. But, mostly, I am grateful that I had a home and a family of my own!

The reasons that we don't speak now are complicated, but part of it is that I do believe that I was never truly regarded in the same way as my siblings. This point, of course, draws back to the question: Can you love adopted children the same as biological children? Although in my personal experience growing up I didn't feel like I was loved in the same way, in my own experience as a parent, I know that I do!

I can honestly say without hesitation that I love all five of my children the same. The true test would be to ask them what they think. Because some of them are shy and won't write, you'll have to take my word for what they feel. At different times they have each complained that I don't love them all the same. This includes my biological child. Like in most families, I hear, "You like her better than me!" Sound familiar? Each one for different reasons has said this about the other, and at times I stand back just baffled. *How could they* not *know how much I love them? Where have I gone wrong?*

Not one day goes by that I don't tell each one individually that I love him or her. I hug and kiss them constantly, and I go out of my way to treat them fairly. The fact is that not one of us is perfect, and no matter how hard we try, there will still be plenty of room for criticism. I'm sure every mother worries about this. It is probably natural for kids to wonder if their parents love all the siblings the same, which is the source of sibling rivalry. It's a story as old as Cain and Abel. In this sense, I wonder if it is unfair to criticize my parents.

Perhaps, but in my mind the difference is due to the fact that I am constantly trying to do better. I am always aware and sensitive to this because I suffered myself. I would never allow the same fate for my family. I would never let it degenerate to the point where we're not even speaking. If I feel that I have made a mistake, then I apologize. My mother has never apologized. My children and I talk openly, and I think that they *must* each know that they are incredibly loved.

We are a large, happy family with the same problems and trials of any normal, loving family. Certain sensitivities spring up because the children know they are adopted. I know how they feel. We talk about their concerns, and my husband and I do our best every day to show them how much we love them as individuals and for the special children they all are. We do this by taking a tremendous interest in their schoolwork and their friends, by going to their sporting events and recitals, and by spending quality time with them.

My husband and I expose our children to many different activities where they can explore their own talents and affinities. This effort can be a challenge to schedule, as we often have to be in two or more places at once, but we always find a way, even if it does make us crazy at times. I couldn't imagine putting any of my children down. Even if they can't be successful at everything, at least they should have the opportunity to try.

In my case growing up, it wasn't about my mother worrying about my failure at dancing. Instead I think she worried that I would succeed and show my sister up! We can't protect one child from another in that way. It is harmful and unfair. If I had succeeded in dance, I am sure that my sister would have succeeded in other things, such as sports, which I hated.

If you're reading this and wondering whether or not to adopt a child, think instead about whether or not you wish to be a parent. Adoption is not much different from biological parenthood. However, unlike accidental pregnancies, adoption is always a choice! For this reason, extra thought may go into the decision as a family embarks on the adoption journey. An adopted child may not look like you, and you can't guess what traits he or she may possess, but you can explore these together. It's the same as with biological children. My children are all unique. The challenge comes in bringing out the best in them, helping them to feel secure not only within the family but also with themselves.

A Father's Calling

Linda Matchan, The Boston Globe

Psychiatrist Aaron Lazare is on the luncheon circuit, addressing the Westborough Rotary Club over creamed chicken with potatoes.

The topic is not his academic work, although certainly it could be. Lazare, sixty-four, is chancellor of the University of Massachusetts at Worcester and dean of its medical school. Nor does he talk about his research interests, which include the healing process of apology and forgiveness. Instead, he talks about something much more personal: the fact that he is father to eight children of three different races whom he and his wife, Louise, adopted between 1966 and 1977. Now his interest has gone beyond the personal and has led him to take action on behalf of all children in need of adoption.

"If I stop and can't go on for a few seconds, don't worry about me. I recover quickly," he says to the group, his voice breaking. "There is something powerfully moving about seeing your children's lives flash so quickly before your eyes."

Now there are seven of them; their first child, Jacqueline, died five years ago, from breast cancer. All are grown, ranging in age from twenty-three to thirty-four, and it is clear from his hour-long slide show that the Lazares' three-decade adventure in parenting was not always Brady Bunch–delightful. There were times—like when seven of them were teenagers at once—that the kids "pushed us to the wall," Lazare confesses. "We have gone through stormy times with most of our children. Some situations, at times, seemed overwhelming."

But now the toughest work of fathering is done, and he can look back, this Father's Day, and reflect on some of the lessons his children taught him that he "never could have learned from any psychiatry textbook"—lessons that inform his stewardship of the adoption research center the medical school opened three years ago.

He learned that the power of family life surmounts differences in racial backgrounds. He learned that the joys and suffering of adoptive families "equals or exceeds those of biologic families."

Above all, he learned that children adopted at various ages are more resilient than is often imagined. It's an important lesson for these times, when the adoption of children from other cultures and races is becoming more mainstream, when adoption is heavily promoted as an antidote to the problems of the tens of thousands of children in foster care nationwide.

Although they adopted their children decades ago, the Lazares, who were unable to have biological children, serve as a model for what social workers and reformers are preaching: adopting difficult-to-place children at vulnerable points in their lives can have a satisfying and joyous outcome.

"Experts like to say you take a great risk by adopting, especially older children, and that their character is already formed," Lazare says in an interview at the Newton home where he and Louise raised their children.

"We decided to take the risk, and maybe we were lucky, but we didn't want anyone to tell us to be cautious. We made an ethical and moral decision, not a scientific one. And yes, they were all resilient."

His children are living productive lives, doing work that ranges from music and acting to computer troubleshooting and carpentry. Two daughters start law school in the fall. Four, including the daughter who died, married, and another will marry next month.

The Lazares have five grandchildren, and another is on the way.

For years, Lazare declined to speak publicly about his children. But now that they are adults he does, often. "I feel I have a calling to enhance the idea that every child who needs to be should be successfully adopted," Lazare says.

And this includes interracially. "People often ask me if our children get along, and you know what they are really saying is, 'Do the different races get along?' Yeah, people can get along. We didn't think about race when we were raising them. We just thought about: How do you raise eight children?"

Roll Call

The Lazares never meant to adopt so many children. Nor did they plan a multiracial family. They started conservatively enough, with two traditional adoptions of Caucasian babies.

The first child was Jacqueline, a three-week-old baby from an Episcopalian family, who arrived in 1966. Then came Sam, who came at two weeks of age in 1968, and "became Jackie's soul mate." He is now a gifted pianist, enrolled at the Berklee College of Music.

In 1968, months before the assassination of Martin Luther King Jr., the Lazares learned that many children of color were going homeless and decided they wanted an African American child. "The agency social worker thought we were crazy and tried to discourage us," he recalls. Lazare's father sent relatives to his home to talk him out of it.

It didn't work. Sarah—whose mother was Caucasian and father was African American—arrived at the age of three months. The extended family relented and welcomed the girl, now a Smith College graduate who starts law school in September at City University of New York.

By 1970, they were ready for one more. It was Thomas, a ten-month-old African American boy, who had already lived in two other homes. "He cried so much for the first week I thought he'd die of dehydration," Lazare says. "He was shy and anxious for two years and rocked himself to sleep each night." Now twenty-nine, Thomas is an actor in Los Angeles. He's starring in *The Promise,* a film that the Museum of Fine Arts screened last week.

Hien came next, in 1973. The Lazares decided that the children who seemed most in need at that time were Vietnamese American children fathered by American soldiers, and they applied to an adoption agency in Saigon. Hien, whose father was African American, was four and a half when she arrived, and "looked like a sad, sad little girl," says Lazare. All her teeth were decayed. She hoarded food in her bedroom and would not speak for several weeks. But the four Lazare children helped her learn English and taught her games. "In six months, she appeared to be a normal child," Lazare says. Hien is now married and begins law school next year at Northeastern University.

Then came Robert and David from Vietnam, half-brothers with different Caucasian GI fathers. The boys, who were eight and nine at the time, "were more than a handful," Lazare concedes. "Having been abandoned by their fathers, they were not sure how to relate to me." Eventually, they joined the military and "their respect for me increased," Lazare says. Today Robert and David, both married, live nearby with their children. Robert, his dad says, is a "computer whiz," and David's a master carpenter.

Finally, in 1977, Naomi arrived, a six-month-old African American baby. The Lazares were finally done. "We were too tired, too old, and too much in debt," Lazare says.

Trying Times

There were days, of course, when Lazare questioned what he and his wife had undertaken, even though the bulk of the child care fell to Louise, whom he calls "a saint."

Louise, for her part, says her husband "is the person who read stories to the kids, because he thought reading was very important, and encouraged any kind of education. He was very in tune with the kids."

Sometimes, Lazare felt his career suffered because of the conferences he missed and the business trips he declined in order to be home with the children. "I used to say, 'God, if I could travel I could really be a contender. I could be famous,'" he acknowledges.

He did not bank on the rebelliousness of his adolescents, of the runaway episodes and shoplifting escapades and court appearances that taught him firsthand about humiliation and shame. "We needed to get outside help," Lazare admits. "There were times when we had what we came to think of as our live-in psychologist."

He didn't count on the academic difficulties some faced, or the subtle racism the African American children would confront in public school—like the time Sarah was told she had the highest SAT scores of any black child in her high school. He didn't expect his youngest daughter to become a single parent.

And surely, he was not prepared for the death of his beloved Jackie, just a year after her wedding, at the age of twenty-nine. But if anything convinced him that the effort of raising these children had been worth it, it was the response of her seven siblings to her illness.

They surrounded her with love and kindness, he says. Hien and Tom, who had been planning to move out of the house, stayed to be close to Jackie. Naomi gave constant nursing care. David, the carpenter with whom she had frequently quarreled, completely redecorated a bedroom for her. Sam quit his job and moved home to help provide twenty-four-hour nursing care.

"This experience of suffering transformed me and my entire family," Lazare says in his speech to the Rotary Club. "The adoption of children is an important social structure that makes such interconnectedness possible."

Now all the hard work is yielding benefits, one of which is his joy over the upcoming marriage of his African American son Thomas to an African American woman. Her parents invited the Lazares to their twenty-fifth wedding anniversary celebration in Roxbury, and although he felt initially awkward being the only white man present, he was so moved by their warmth that he made a speech about how wonderful it felt to be part of this interracial family. He and Louise adopted Thomas twenty-seven years ago, he told the group, "and now I am asking all of you to adopt us."

Coming Home

He segues to his second favorite subject these days, the Center for Adoption Research at the University of Massachusetts, of which he is executive director. It is the first university-based adoption center in the country with academic resources dedicated to providing practical solutions to adoption issues.

"Everyone talks about how wonderful adoption is, but no one studies it to figure out how to make it work right," Lazare says. "The adoption center is the missing link."

But to Lazare's seven children, the home in Newton is the ultimate adoption center. They come back often. "They move in, they move out," Lazare laughs.

In separate interviews, the children say Lazare managed to accomplish something exceptional in his parenting: He was able to cultivate a special bond with each one of them. "Instead of a generic sweep of love, my dad (was like) a large feather who would graze everyone individually," Sam Lazare says.

For Thomas, the bond was around a mutual love of sports: "He'd take me to Celtics games." Sam shares his father's interest in music.

"I was into athletics, and played softball and soccer," says Hien. "He'd always want to do the carpool." Sarah remembers "a relationship that was special to me." When she was small, he took her to medical conferences at which he lectured "and I was the one who would give out the index cards for people to write down their questions, and then collect them all. I remember feeling very, very special because I was the daughter of the man at the front of the room."

To this day, Lazare says, when any of his kids phones him at work, his secretary knows to interrupt immediately. Sarah, who coordinates tutorial services at Smith College, says her father comes to Northampton to tell her students about his work.

"When the students see us together, they often say we look alike," she says. "It's not because we look alike. It's because we listen alike. We communicate the same way."

On Sunday, Father's Day, the Lazare children will acknowledge their dad "in our usual endearing way," Sam says. "We'll probably have a barbecue. It will be very casual. It will be very chaotic."

♥

CHAPTER FOUR

Adopting the Older Child

Elya and Elena

Gaynor Ellis

I t's a dream, Mom," declared Elya. "It's a dream," she repeated again and again as we drove away from Elena's new home in Miami. "I just can't believe it!"

A year and a half earlier, in St. Petersburg, Russia, Elya had become my daughter. Even at our first meeting in July 2001 in the Children's Home in Slantsy, Russia, Elya had begged me—first through a translator, and then in ever-improving English—to find a family for her friend, Elena. Maybe she even hoped that I would adopt her friend so she could have a familiar playmate for a sister.

The two girls had lived in the Children's Home for six years. They had played together, gone to school together, fought together, sometimes cried together. At the Children's Home, older children had to request to be adopted. Some chose not to be adopted, but both Elya and Elena asked to be adopted, though it was especially difficult finding a family for the older children. Elya was almost twelve when she became my daughter. Elena is a year older than Elya.

On the day Elya and I first met in Slantsy, I also met Elena. I took photos of her to share with people back home in the hope that someone wanted a bright, lovely daughter. That day, Elya was so excited. Elena was sad, but trying to be happy and brave for her friend. Elya was hugging Elena, holding her hands and saying, "Don't worry, I'm going to find someone for you. Don't worry."

The two girls are quite different. Elya is bouncy, blonde and out-going. Elena is shy, brunette and quietly funny. Elya is a ball of fire; Elena is a thinker and a scholar—the smartest student in her school, I was told.

When we came home to New York, Elya continued to talk to her friend in Russia by telephone. She was quiet when she got off the phone, and didn't say much when I asked about Elena. Often, she was homesick for her friends and her birth country. Elya finds life in New York City loud and crazed with a frenetic energy. It is not quiet like Slantsy, a small city on Russia's border near Estonia. Elya jokes about "all the drug dealers" in New York. She misses her friends in Russia.

I sent the photos and description of Elena to Ruthie, the wonder-worker at our adoption agency who had made Elya's adoption go smoothly. I told Ruthie how passionately Elya wanted to find a family for Elena. During those early months after Elya arrived, we were very busy as Elya started school, learned English and adapted to her new life. Her language skills improved enormously, and after a year she spoke English quite well.

Meanwhile, Ruthie had included an article about Elena in the adoption agency newsletter, an article that caught the eye of Shirley Silva in Miami. Shirley and Alfonso had already adopted two-year-old Lani from China. Shirley had not planned to have another daughter, but she read Elena's story and showed it to her husband. "I didn't know I had a Russian daughter," he joked.

Shirley and Alfonso discussed the idea with their children, Alfy (sixteen), Nick (fourteen), Daniel (twelve), Yvonne (ten) and Lani (now five). How did they feel about Elena joining the family? Adoption costs would be a strain, Shirley told them. Alfy offered to contribute his car fund, savings he had hoped to use to buy his first car. The other children promised to help in any way they could.

In early 2002, Elya and I heard that the Silvas were completing the paperwork for Elena's adoption. Elya "let the cat out of the bag" in a phone call to Elena, and despite Elena's excitement, she was hesitant to fully let herself go. The girls had lived so long with the dream of having a family, of having a sense of permanence and belonging. In the Russian Children's Home, once the children reach the age of sixteen, they are given an internal passport and move out on their own. Teens look forward to this freedom, to emerging from the strict rules of the home and school. But there is loneliness and apprehension as well, as though a timer is slowly counting down, marking time until that step from the Children's Home, completely free and completely alone. The children live with hope for so long, but that hope perhaps becomes numb with constancy. Elena, suddenly faced with having her hopes fulfilled, was at first scared to believe it.

Elya said that Elena was frightened of the plane ride, but there was something else. She was also afraid that something might happen to deprive her of a family now that it was so close. Elena waited, unsure whether or not her dream would come true. It did. By early June, Elena was home with the Silvas in Miami. Elya was on the phone at once, so happy after that first call, jumping up and down.

In the months that followed, both girls pursued their new lives and friendships—Elya in New York City, Elena in Miami. Elena learned English fast, spent a summer becoming accustomed to sun like she had never seen, and learned to be part of a lively, large and loving family. Elena and Elya did not talk often, but each knew the other was there for her.

Christmas vacation gave us a chance to visit, and we booked a flight to Miami. As our departure day neared, Elya grew more and more excited. Not only would she see Florida, a new state to add to her list of places visited, but also she would be seeing Elena.

I was a bit nervous about the reunion. After all, the girls had not seen each other for more than eighteen months. They had both changed at lot, I was sure. Would their friendship survive the dramatic change in their lives? Would seeing each other bring painful memories of the past? In the end, I need not have worried. The Silvas are a lovely family, warm and generous. I watched Elya and Elena walk along Miami Beach, testing the ocean waters in a cool December breeze. They might have been playing back at the Children's Home in Slantsy. They spoke in Russian, although their English was excellent. They giggled and teased and laughed like they always had, but this time with a difference. Each had their forever family waiting at home.

♥

Jadra's Story: Miracles Do Happen!

Meredith Browning Bishop

I had four children at home, but I had always wanted to adopt. Finally, through a mutual friend, I met a social worker for an agency in my area that did international adoptions. At the end of October 1994, my husband and I went to an information meeting, after which we submitted our application to the agency. Little did I know the long and winding road that awaited.

Our first choice was Guatemala because the travel time was short and children were available. A couple months later, we were informed by the agency that we were not eligible for Guatemala because my husband was previously divorced. During the time we were considering Guatemala, I had been looking at pictures of little girls from China and falling in love. With a sigh of half relief, half frustration, we gave up on Guatemala and decided to pursue an adoption in China.

Gathering the papers was not difficult, only time consuming, and in March 1996, we received our referral. Her name was Chen Yueying. She was three and a half years old, and lived in Xiamen, an island in the Taiwan Straits. The referral photo was very small, but the child was adorable and became mine in my heart almost immediately. Travel was arranged, and on May 15, 1996, my forty-fourth birthday, I left with my friend Jeanne for China.

After a very long flight, we arrived in Beijing. We met up with the agency representative and our national guide, along with the other eleven families that would also be traveling and adopting from Xiamen. For three days, we were escorted to various historical sites and temples in and around Beijing. To find ourselves actually standing on the Great Wall of China was quite awe-inspiring! Though touring the Forbidden City and the Summer Palace was very interesting, I was growing impatient to see Jadra, the name my family had voted on for Chen Yueying. We left Beijing and headed for Xiamen.

In Xiamen, we met up with our local guide and were taken to our hotel. Xiamen is a special economic district with government funds dedicated to promoting tourism, so we stayed in a lovely, modern and convenient hotel. The next morning, we were to go to the orphanage to meet our children. We felt quite lucky to be allowed to see where our children had lived.

The orphanage was impressive; it was a welfare center housing both children and elderly people. There was a grassy area with a fountain in the back, and the room we were escorted to was surrounded by windows and pink velvet curtains. Our group was invited to sit, and we were served tea. Of course, we were all impatient and may not have been as polite as we should have been during our tea party.

Finally the caretakers began to bring in the babies. I spotted Jadra but waited for them to call my name just to make sure it was really her. She cried at first, but I held her and played with a little felt doll I had brought, and pretty soon she settled down. She had been taught a little dance and performed it with the other three-year-old in our group. It was the first time I saw her smile. Soon, I discovered a large, bumpy black spot on her head. *Okay,* I thought, *a birthmark of some kind, I can handle that.* We went back to the hotel, and I began to change her clothes. I was shocked to see over fifty smaller black spots on her body. Luckily, I was traveling with two experienced pediatricians, so I called them in. They were worried, but needed more information. A call to the orphanage confirmed their worst fears. The staff insisted that the lesions were all new. If this was indeed the case, they were most likely malignant.

What followed was an intense couple of hours of thinking about what to do. I had come expecting a child who I could take home and watch grow and flourish, not a child who I would most likely have to watch die. I considered how difficult this kind of illness would be for my other children to watch and how much of my time would be taken from them. I decided that I would leave Yueying there and take a child who had a better chance for a normal life.

Jadra had spent one day and night with me, and in that time, while never speaking a word, had learned to kiss me gently on the cheek. Dressed in a new light blue outfit I had brought for her, I watched her turn her back and be led away from me. It was one of the most profoundly emotional moments of my life.

The little girl they gave me was Liu Li Juan, age seventeen months. I was very aware that I was not taking home a three-year-old anymore, but a baby. She had been at the orphanage for only four months, and in that time, had been in a crib in the baby room, and so could not stand or walk. Her front teeth were broken off at the gumline, making it very difficult for her to eat properly. I think that the orphanage, being fairly small, had a difficult time finding an available child. Little did they know that they found the perfect child for me. Though my first instinct was to hug her, I held back, thinking maybe she would be taken from me, but within a few minutes, she was mine. Calls were put in to get out the crib, exchange the clothing, and prepare for diapers one more time. After completing the paperwork, we were on our way home with one angry baby. We named her Emma, and within a few weeks, I was—and I remain—completely in love with her, and I could not imagine her being with anyone else.

Though I wondered what had happened to Jadra, I was too scared to inquire. I figured I could picture her living there in good health, though I knew it was probably not true. As time went by, I convinced myself that she was dead.

In early 1999, one of the families in the group I had traveled with was preparing to return to Xiamen for a visit. I halfheartedly asked them to please inquire as to what happened to Yueying. When they returned, I heard the astonishing news that she was still there, apparently fine, very outgoing and sweet. I immediately decided that I would do everything I could to go back and get her. People were a little confused and astonished at the decision, but I didn't have to think twice. She had been my daughter from the moment I received that little photo over three years before, but never did I think I would be so fortunate as to have the chance to finally bring her home.

My initial inquiries through a couple of local agencies were not promising. China was no longer doing identified adoptions, I was told, and furthermore, Xiamen was no longer doing any international adoptions. Then I met a man who believed in the impossible. He carefully informed me that while "in general," no identified adoptions are allowed, perhaps he could do something for my case "specifically." He was Weihang Chen, the China program coordinator for Alliance for Children in Massachusetts. So I had an agency. This man kept me up-to-date on everything, helped me write a letter appealing to the Chinese sensibility and talked to people for me. At last, in January 2000, my papers left for China. Within two weeks, I had my answer. A connection in Beijing had hand-delivered my papers to the CCAA and then waited while the director approved my application. I couldn't believe it! Now it was just a matter of waiting for the process to grind along until I could pick up my daughter at last.

And grind it did. The first approximate date I had was toward the end of May. No way. The papers proceeded at their own pace from desk to desk. Perhaps June? No way. The provincial officials had to make sure Jadra's parents were not going to claim her, and to that end they had to advertise for two months. Finally, the departure date was set for August 4, 2000. I decided that my thirteen-year-old daughter, Carisa, would travel with me, and we applied for visas and made sure our passports were up-to-date. We packed a few clothes and a ream of papers, and we were ready to go! I had been divorced two years earlier, and the other children were able to stay with their father. I found myself on my way to China for a second time.

We flew into Beijing once again, and after spending a night there, we headed for Fuzhou, the capital of Fujian province, where the orphanage representatives would bring Jadra to us at last. We were not allowed this time to go to Xiamen as they no longer had the facilities to process international adoptions. We arrived in Fuzhou on Sunday morning, August 6. We were met by the local representative who was to process our paperwork. Fuzhou was hot, sticky and dirty, but the hotel was lovely—right on a lake, and right near a McDonald's! This later proved very useful, as the plastic toys in the Happy Meals were some of Jadra's favorite things. At 5:00 P.M. on Sunday, August 6, Jadra arrived at our hotel with her orphanage director and two caregivers, and we were called to their room. Anticipating separation problems, I figured we would be spending a long time with the orphanage representatives before we took Jadra, perhaps reluctantly, to our room. Didn't happen. She screamed "Mommy," flung herself into my arms, and never left. After a few minutes of asking questions and being polite, I asked Jadra if she wanted to give them a hug, her response was "No, bye-bye." My family was suddenly complete.

We have been home for two years now. She is a remarkable little girl, affectionate, resilient and apparently happy with everything. Yes, she still loves to perform. It has not been an easy two years, but it has been tremendously rewarding. Jadra was seven years and eleven months old when she finally arrived home. We had been waiting a long time for her and she for us.

❤ ❤ ❤

The spots have been diagnosed as dysplastic nevus syndrome, at present benign, and there is a good chance they will stay that way. The large spot on her head was removed in China, and she has a large skin graft on her head, making it necessary for her to wear bangs. She knows that we don't consider her scar important, and when she feels comfortable enough, maybe someday she will pull her hair back and show it to the world. She had no mirror in China, and she was not aware that she had a black spot, nor was she aware of the scar, except that she remembered it hurting at first.

The challenges of bringing home an older child are unquestionably great. A child who has been in an orphanage from birth has huge gaps in their understanding of relationships, rules, general knowledge and thinking. Everything was always done for Jadra; she had no choices in her life. When she arrived, she could not put on her own underwear. She had no concept of ownership, no idea how to behave in a home or in school, and no concept of friendship or even right and wrong. But she is learning. After two years in second grade, and multiple calls from the school concerning her misbehavior, she has moved on to regular third grade with only in-class extra help from her ESL teacher. She is reading almost up to grade level, spells pretty well, shows a spark of understanding of how numbers work and is working very hard on how to be a friend. She will be having her first-ever birthday party next month when she turns ten. She is fascinated still by her longer hair, and she is beginning to take care of her clothing. There is so much she has had to learn from scratch. Her brother and sisters have been as patient as they can be, and I am very proud of the whole family. Jadra has brought us closer together and taught us what is really important.

I look at her sometimes, and I still can't believe she is here—that we really pulled this off. Jadra Yueying Bishop is home.

♥

A Gift of Life

Lynda Fielstein

When our six-year-old daughter, Jodie Bea, came home with us from China, we were a little worried about her at first. It was as though she couldn't control herself, such was her wild excitement and joy. She ran around the house, almost hugging herself, laughing constantly and holding us so tightly that her little arms trembled.

Elliot and I were thrilled by her sweetness and exhilaration, but for a few days we actually wondered whether she had ADHD. Her wildness and hyperactive elation never died down, but rather seemed to increase with every passing day in our home. Of course, when I realized the simple cause of her happiness, I felt almost ashamed to have attributed it to some disorder. It was just the pure joy of a child who never wanted anything but her own family.

When my husband and I were contemplating the age of the child we wanted to adopt, we recalled the words of a wise Chinese friend and advisor, Dr. Weihang Chen, the director of the Chinese adoption program at our agency. He said, "If you adopt older children, they know what they have left behind, and they will always be appreciative of what you have done." Appreciation is a rare and endearing quality, which unfortunately I think we do not see often in American children. Many children have known comfort and pleasure all their lives, so they don't even recognize what a gift it is to be warm and loved. As my husband and I approach our fifties, we have observed many of our friend's children come of age, and rarely have we witnessed any signs of appreciation for their good fortune.

Of course, parenting is a selfless act (or it should be). It is not about receiving gratitude for your work. Having an appreciative child might be nice, but it is certainly not expected and is never a reason to parent in the first place. What moved us to adopt an older child was probably Weihang's second comment, which was that "Older children hardly ever get a chance for a new life, because adoptive parents seem to want the younger children."

Elliot and I had spent most of our life together thinking about ourselves. We are not necessarily self-centered or selfish people, but we were in love with each other and that was enough for us. A life can move so quickly, and sometimes when you grow older, like my husband and me, you look around and are pleased with what you have, but something is still missing. I think that Elliot and I wanted to do one thing in life that wasn't about us, one thing that was entirely for someone else.

Jodie's excitement eventually lowered to a milder, quivering pitch, but her gratitude has not lessened over the three years she has been home. Not a day passes during which she does not tell me how happy she is, or how we are the most wonderful parents in the world. It is wonderful to see such appreciation, but rather than an ego massage (as it might sound), sometimes it fills me with deep sadness. I think of my little girl, abandoned by her father at age three at night outside an orphanage in China, crying herself to sleep. This story is the horrible circumstance of many, many children around the world. I think of her in a place she feared and hated, praying every night in her bed as she grew older and older that one day she would have a family, any family. Any family that would take her away from that place.

Jodie still suffers from post-traumatic stress disorder from her experience in the orphanage. She cries if she's left in a room alone.

Frequently she'll ask me to stand outside the door while she brushes her teeth upstairs.

But she loves to hear the story of her adoption, of how Mommy and Daddy saw her sweet picture, and Mommy said to Daddy, "You go to China right now and bring my daughter home to me." (I am a terrible traveler, and decided it would be wise for Elliot to go alone, rather than have to care for two babies instead of one. This little story makes Jodie smile, and makes it easier for her to understand why I did not go to China for her.)

Jodie will inquire, "But how did you find me way over there? And how did you know that I was the one?" We respond, "God found you. He knew you were the one for us." I'll never forget the day someone asked me how we got Jodie, and I launched into this long-winded explanation regarding the adoption process. Finally, Jodie blurted out, "No, Mommy, God gave me to you!" That adults have taken the miracle of adoption and turned it into a convoluted and laborious paper trail is truly unfortunate.

Nor will I forget the day that Jodie ran out of toilet paper in her bathroom, and she looked so disheartened. Since she could not yet speak English, I took her by the hand and led her into the kitchen; I pointed to the top shelf in the pantry. She caught a glimpse of an economy-size package of toilet paper. Her face lit up like a Christmas tree, and she twirled around our kitchen, squealing with laughter at the mere sight of twelve rolls of toilet paper! Who would have thought paper products such as tissue paper, Kleenex and napkins (which we tend to take for granted) could create such a state of bliss in a child?

About six months ago Elliot was talking to Jodie as he tucked her into bed, and she asked him to retell the adoption story. After he finished, she exclaimed, "Then we must thank God right now! Let's pray, Dad, for what God has done for our family."

Jodie is appreciative, but I feel that we are the truly grateful and thankful ones. She has opened our eyes to a pure and honest perspective. We are grateful to Jodie for transporting us beyond ourselves and the daily grind to a world we never knew existed. Or if we did, it must have faded from our memories with the passage of time. Everything we once had and cared about, all of our priorities, pales in comparison to simply loving Jodie. In retrospect, we had overindulged ourselves, and in the process failed to recognize simple pleasures, or even to find satisfaction from those scholarly and material accomplishments.

While Jodie languished in an orphanage uninspired because of deprivation, we languished in America uninspired by comforts and indifferent to security and safety. We lay in bed at night, both praying for something to complete our lives, to make us whole. I had sensed the empty space, and all the while a little girl in China was waiting to fill it. She articulates every day what took me half a lifetime to discover: Family is truly the greatest achievement of all.

♥

Living the Fantasy

Cathy Rogerson

There are many strange twists and dips in the road of life, and sometimes you can control it and sometimes you can't. Often the events you can't control turn into the biggest blessings, and that's how I now look at my infertility. What started as a blow from which I felt I'd never recover turned into an eighteen-year-long process of growth, pain, anguish, and ultimately, joy and fulfillment.

If I could go back and change the circumstances such that my body functioned properly and my offspring would have my genes, I wouldn't. I would never trade this amazing blessing of receiving my children through adoption. Our oldest son came home to us at five days old, our second son came home at seven months old, and our daughter Sarah came home to us when she was three. Sarah's story is the one I want to share with you.

We did not set out to adopt an older child or even a Russian child, but rather an infant American girl. Because we wanted a daughter, we were discouraged from pursuing a domestic adoption because of the many couples waiting for a child regardless of the gender. We already had two boys, however, and we were set on a daughter, so adopting internationally seemed to be our best option. My husband and I were particularly interested in Russia, so that became the country of our focus.

Two years passed while we tried to find the right agency. At that point, we changed our age range from an infant to a girl under two.

Finally, in October 1996, we were ready to begin what was starting to seem like a journey without end. We left the adoption agency that day with a familiar and dreaded stack of forms, countless questions, and the added concern of U.S. immigration issues.

Vigilantly, we filled out each form and had the necessary interviews, and roughly a year later we got the call telling us about our precious little girl. Sarah was two and a half, but by the time we were to bring her home, she would be three. As soon as we found out her age, my eyes began to pick out every three-year-old girl they could find, analyzing their size and their development, trying to envision what my child would be like. I bought clothes and dolls and pictured endless hours rocking and reading and cuddling and playing games. I projected far into the future the chats we would have over tea, the walks on the beach sharing our hearts. The day when I would be able to hold this little girl in my arms seemed as if it would never come.

When I first saw her in the orphanage in Russia, she didn't look like the picture I'd seen. There was no disappointment, but rather a strange jolt, the instant readjustment of a mind-set that had been six months in the making. It was not about physical beauty, for she was neither prettier nor less attractive than I expected. But I had already fallen in love—with a picture no less, but I was in love—and it took a moment to transpose the living face before me over the one that existed in my heart. For although Sarah was full of joy and wonder for each day, she was also strong-willed and high-energy, and she wore her emotions on her sleeve. She was different from the fantasy daughter I had concocted in my head.

I wanted to say and share so much with my daughter from the start, but I could not speak a word of Russian. All of this was built up inside me like swollen river behind a dam. All of my communication with her had to be physical or through mime, and my reaction was to pick her up, sing songs, rock her and hold her. But Sarah did not want to be held. She didn't like to be picked up, and if I tried she would push me away. She would hold my hand at times, but that small contact was only a droplet compared to the flood of affection I wanted to shower on her.

She was not interested in cuddling, petrified of dolls, and unable to play games because she had no understanding of what a game was all about, and she would literally pass out from fear if she couldn't find me.

This period was a strange and confusing time for me, and so different than my experience with my sons. Infants have a chance to build a relationship, to be cuddled and hugged, to trust and love you as you learn how to love them. But Sarah had spent three years in another place. She was suddenly lifted up and plopped down in another country with people she'd never met and who didn't speak her language, and with a woman who expected such love and affection instantly.

I had to learn to be patient and realize that this time was about Sarah's process of growing, not about my feelings of rejection and disappointment. Restraining myself felt so unnatural, so unfamiliar. Our bonding was a slow, gradual process, and over a year passed before Sarah made it to a place where she trusted me, where the full bonding could grow in both our hearts.

Additionally, even though she was healthy, she was very speech-delayed, and her learning process was slow. I needed help, and as far as I could see there were no wise old sages in my midst, nor were there any books that I could find duplicating my scenario, to give me the road map that I so desperately needed. Patience was hard to muster. Faith in our future was a challenge.

Now that Sarah is six and we know each other so well and love each other so much, it feels wonderful to be able to write this story. I am so grateful that we are glued together for life, and I've learned that the bonding process grows on its own time. I know I probably did a million things wrong. My list of wishes is long. I wish I could go back in time with the confidence I have now. I wish I could have been sure that, even though my daughter was beginning her life with me at age three, she would indeed go through all the physical and emotional steps my boys did. I wish I had known that we would ultimately bond and that we would love each other. I wish that I had had the confidence that our love for each other would happen, that it was not a question of "if" but "when."

Ultimately, my lack of confidence in the bonding process and the fear that Sarah and I would never be close caused many moments of impatience and many shed tears. Now I see that Sarah is her own unique child of God, and that God created her just the way she is. Her temperament is not that of my "fantasy child," but whose child is ever their fantasy child? A birth mother cannot choose the makeup of her child anymore than I could mold Sarah to fit my dreams. I have learned to see her for the person she is and to love her both for her strengths and her weaknesses, as one would with any child.

We have had many challenges, mostly stemming from Sarah's lack of a family during her three years in an orphanage, but my daughter is a fighter and has more strength of character than I ever will. I admire Sarah so much, and it is a testament to God, not my parenthood, that her zest for life is such an inspiration to so many people. Sarah is a gift, and my husband and I feel blessed and privileged to have her in our lives.

In the next few months, we are going back to Russia to bring home our second daughter, who will be four years old soon. I hope I can relax and enjoy this ride, and instead of trying to force love, to just give it. We know now that a relationship is a process that never ends, and that love, patience, prayer and, most of all, faith are the key ingredients in grafting a child onto our family tree.

♥

Of Signs and Wonders

Elizabeth B. McGowin

I adopted my spectacular daughter, Tatum, in early 1999 in Hubei province, central China. She was about three and one-half years old, and a most beautiful child. Even the other adopting mothers said so. The true blessing was discovered in the following weeks. Tatum's heart and soul outshone even her outward beauty. I might have questioned the chance that such a child was really meant for me, except for the signs. I had had signs. Not mere coincidences, but irrefutable signs that let me know this was my daughter. They just kept coming for months after her arrival home, off-the-wall stuff that stopped me in my tracks. "He will send you signs and wonders," it says in the Bible. I realized with awe that's what was happening. Suffice it to say, I knew the decision to adopt Tatum was the right one.

On May 8, 2002, Tatum's seventh birthday, I contacted the adoption agency that I had used back in 1999. I told Ruthie, the coordinator, that I was ready to begin the process of adopting a younger sister for Tatum from China. Ruthie accepted her mission, and quickly told me the probable timeline for this second adoption. We would need to begin work on my dossier in July, and she asked that I call her then to get started.

Two weeks later there was a message on my voice mail. "Hi, Beth. It's Ruthie Rich calling. I'll bet you're surprised to be hearing from me." She was right. "I'm calling you because I have a beautiful ten-year-old girl in Russia that they are looking to place quickly." *So?* I thought. Her message continued, "I'm calling you because I know that you know a lot of people, and maybe you could find a family for her. She's fabulous. I have pictures and information. Give me a call and we can talk." "Why is she calling me?" I asked aloud. "She knows zillions of people! Who do I know, for heaven's sake?"

A minute later, a thought occurred to me. I did know someone, actually. I recently had a phone conversation with a woman from my church. We'd never spoken before, but she had called me to discuss some church business. She had brought up the subject of adoption, saying, "You're the one with the little Asian daughter, right?" We had ended up talking for forty-five minutes about international adoption of older children. She and her husband were middle-aged and had never had kids. I could tell that her interest was piqued, and I felt that I'd shown her an option. I hadn't given the conversation another thought until this out-of-the-blue call from Ruthie.

Two days later, I had the photos and information on little Karina Nurutdinova by e-mail, and thus started a week of the old "Reply/Send" back and forth as Ruthie and I wrote and responded to each other in our joint effort to place this child. With confidence, I called my church acquaintance, only to find that, after some discussion with her husband, they didn't think it was right for them just now. Gosh, to me it had seemed such an obvious match. Then another memory surfaced. Another church friend had talked to me on several occasions about adopting an older Russian child to join her one daughter. I was sure this was it! This family was the reason Ruthie had called! Sure enough, my friend was excited and hopeful. I was honestly shocked when she called me back two days later to tell me with a sad voice that her daughter and husband did not feel ready to add to their family. She had to say no. I was nonplussed. Why else would Ruthie have called me, out of the hundreds of people she knew around the country, to help find a home for Karina if she weren't meant for one of these couples that I knew?

Soon after these disappointing phone calls, I took the information and pictures of Karina to my friend Trish's house. We had both admired the pretty little girl looking for a new mother. Another neighbor, Lynda, joined us. Lynda is the mother of a little girl from China (Tatum's beloved companion), and then, just seven months before, Lynda and her husband had adopted a ten-year-old girl from Russia. Lynda works for an adoption agency here in our city. I wanted her to see Karina in case she knew of anyone who might be looking for just such a daughter. But Lynda immediately looked at me and said, "This is a special child, Beth. What about you? Then our daughters would be a matched set!" My reply was quick and sure. "Oh, no. No, not me. I'm getting a younger Chinese child. That's what I'm doing. That's been my plan all along."

As we had perused the printed information on Karina, I had noticed something and casually pointed it out to Trish. Karina's birthday was listed as 2/3/92. *The third of February? Hmm, same as my grandmother's. Not only that, but also the very date on which I had adopted Tatum three years earlier.* (Yes, that had been one of the Tatum signs.) *Well,* I had thought, *What a coincidence!*

Because we had been holding Karina's info for too long already, I wanted to contact Ruthie to let her know as soon as possible that we could not find a place for her in Nashville. I sat down, pulled up Ruthie's latest e-mail, pushed Reply and typed out the sad news: no takers. I asked Ruthie to keep me posted on her progress. I pushed Send. A minute later, still sitting at my computer, I saw a new e-mail had come in: MAILER DAEMON, the moniker for returned e-mails: my message to Ruthie. It had come back. "What? That's impossible!" I said to the screen. "I pushed Reply! It can't be the wrong address! We've been back-and-forthing like this all week!" I tried again. Wham! MAILER DAEMON reappeared. To make matters worse, it was Memorial Day weekend. I had absolutely no other way of delivering this message to Ruthie. Suddenly, I was desperate for her to know now, at the beginning of the weekend when she no doubt would be seeing and talking to lots of people. By the time I could call her on Tuesday at the agency, several valuable days would be lost. I remembered that Ruthie had another e-mail address, one with a different Internet company, and I typed that in. Incredibly, five seconds later that one also came back undeliverable. At that point, I was ranting and raving at cyberspace while stamping around my study. "I'm telling you, this is impossible!" I kept shouting. Furious, I finally gave up and walked away.

This frustrating e-mail fiasco was the culmination of my grand efforts to place this child, and I felt that my hands were tied. I tried to put it out of my mind and joined Trish at yet another neighbor's home for dinner. Trish shared the story of Karina with them, and they, too, asked why I didn't take her. What was it with all of these people? I already had my plan underway, and going to Russia for a big sister for Tatum wasn't it! Trish insisted on telling them about the birthdate "coincidence." At that point my hostess, Jane, said, "Well, heck, Beth, just what does he have to do to convince you?" I knew who she meant when she said "he": the purveyor of signs himself. In that instant, I felt myself break a sweat.

"Please," I protested. "She's not for me!" They all shrugged, and I went muttering to the powder room, replaying their words in my head. Suddenly, I froze, more sweat breaking out all over me. The MAILER DAEMON problem came crashing back to me, only now with some sort of eerie sense to it. There was just no logical explanation for that message not going through. I thought about what my friends in the other room would have to say if they knew about the cybersign.

My mind was off and running. *Had I been being bombarded with signs without even noticing? Was my own plan so firmly fixed in my mind that I couldn't recognize a different one taking shape?* The amazing signs that had unfolded during Tatum's adoption had all come after the decision to adopt her had been made. They were comforting reassurance that the decision had been the right one, the inevitable one. I hadn't even thought about the possibility of signs coming out of the blue regarding something not yet in my life.

Back at home, Tatum in bed, I sat down at my computer and pulled up the copies of the returned e-mails. I looked at Karina's picture on my desk, and this time stared hard at her face and eyes. I whispered to her, asking if she could be my child. Inside my chest, and in Karina's photo, I felt a shift. Small, but real. *Oh my gosh, could this child be mine?* Then I spoke directly to God. I felt very timid and awkward. "Excuse me, God? I hate to bother you with techno stuff, but this MAILER DAEMON thing is just nuts." My voice got even smaller. "Could this be you trying to tell me something? I honestly don't know what to think. I hope that this isn't too presumptuous, God, but I need to know. I am going to push Reply to Ruthie's e-mail address one more time, only I'm going to change the message. I'm going to tell her that I would be interested in adopting Karina myself. I don't mean to play games with you, God, so please don't take offense, but if this e-mail goes through, I'm going to assume that is your answer."

I suppose anyone having read up to this point can guess what happened. Yep, that e-mail went straight through. I stared at my inbox for an hour, waiting for MAILER DAEMON to show back up. It never did. Instead, a reply from Ruthie came shooting back to my screen. Stunned, I was shaking and felt afraid to move. Finally, I opened it and read her message, part of which is burned into my brain. "You are right," Ruthie had written. "This must be meant to be. Karina will be yours. I think that this will be a wonderful placement for everyone."

The next day I told Tatum that something crazy had happened. God had decided to send her a sister, but that instead of being younger, she was older, and from Russia. I braced for a disappointed little face. *Bam!* Tatum leapt into my arms and said, "Mama! It's what I've always wanted!" Huh? Then as she literally danced all over the room, she turned her face up and said, "I feel like I'm in heaven! And you know something funny, Mama? I had a dream last night that God told me I had a sister in Russia, but he didn't tell me how old she was. I put my pillow over my head, because I didn't want to hear him say that she was younger." I've found that once the signs start, they cascade. The first people we called were neighbor Lynda's family. We wanted to tell them that now our girls would be a matched set.

Six months later, in November 2002, I traveled to Kazan, Tatarstan, Russia, with my grown niece accompanying me. There we met my new daughter and lots of her friends in her little village orphanage. We spent four days visiting and cried when we had to leave the other children because it was time to take Karina and go. A few weeks later, my heart broke when we heard that at the orphanage's New Year celebration, Karina had been unanimously voted "Luckiest Child of 2002."

We arrived back in Nashville late one night, with Karina rousing herself after the thirty-hour trip, and asking, in Russian, "Are we home? Is this our house?" As we stepped out of the car, Tatum came tearing up the street from a neighbor's house, eyes looking past me, searching for her new sister. They fell into each other's arms and have been truly in love ever since. One night, soon after Karina's arrival, Tatum was upset about something at bedtime. In a flash, Karina climbed into her sister's bed to comfort her. She stroked Tatum's hair, saying, "My baby, my princess." Each girl was born in a different country, worlds away, only recent acquaintances, miraculously sisters. Sometimes I think how foolish I was trying to deny fate, refusing to see the signs. Sometimes I shudder to think that I almost missed my daughter. Signs and wonders, doubtless peace. As an adoptive mother, what more could I ever have asked?

♥

Mya Papu

Denise Brown

W hen we walked into the large playroom of Moscow's Orphanage #17, we were surprised to see our family photo posted on the bulletin board for all the children to see. From across the room, I immediately spotted the young blond boy I had only seen in a Polaroid photo and on videotape. As I approached him, he seemed to know who I was, but he was shy and backed away. After all, he had only known the women in the orphanage—a woman director, women doctors, and women nurses and caregivers. But suddenly, the little boy looked up, and with a flash of recognition and a broad smile, he ran to the doorway where my husband, Tom, was standing. *"Mya Papu! Mya Papu!!"* he said.

That greeting from our new four-and-a-half-year-old son melted our hearts and began our family with him. Unlike other couples who adopt infants, we could not whisk our new son away to another room for privacy to get to know him. He was old enough to indicate he wanted to stay in *this* room, with his friends. And so we sat, with our little Yurichka practically Velcroed to his dad's lap, which is how he remains to this day.

While we were getting acquainted with Yuri in the main play-room, we sat on the floor, and the other children came and hugged us and clutched us and sat with and on us. One little six-year-old girl gripped me around the waist as she looked up at me sobbing, "Mama, Mama . . ."

Most older children give back affection and acknowledgment almost immediately. An infant usually grows to relate and respond to new parents over time, but with Yuri his affection and attention were instantaneous. Although we only spoke limited Russian "baby talk" we were able to communicate with some key Russian words we learned—like *machina* for car, or *samolut* for airplane, or *sabacka* for dog. More important were the Russian words we learned dealing with daily life—food, drink, eat, sleep and potty, and "my son," and that pretty much covered all we needed to know initially.

On one visit to the orphanage before we had completed Yuri's visa paperwork, we brought apples we had bought from a street vendor. The children in the orphanage were so hungry, and some seemed malnourished. They ran to us and grabbed the apple wedges as quickly as we offered them. When we held out cups of milk as well, our little Yurichka held pieces of apples in both hands while also trying to raise the cup to drink. It would have been a comical sight, except that Yuri knew that if he set the apple pieces down, even for an instant, they would vanish, taken by the other children.

Our first trip out of the orphanage with Yuri was to the American clinic for his exam. He was terrified of the car, and he clutched an apple in one hand and a small shovel in the other. (It was October in Moscow, and Yuri had been playing in the snow.) The only way we could undress him for his examination was by shifting the apple and shovel from hand to hand, as he would relinquish neither.

On the day we were able to take Yuri to our home from the orphanage, we dressed him in the clothes we had brought from home and took photographs of him in his first baseball cap. In a toy store, we encouraged Yuri to pick out a toy or stuffed animal he would like to keep. Yuri would look at things, hold them for a while, then set them back on the shelves neatly. He didn't understand the concept that he could actually have something to keep. (That would soon change, mind you.) From the orphanage, the only thing Yuri brought with him was a small yellow hard-plastic *sabacka*, his dog.

The airplane flight with Yuri was full of surprises. He was our littlest politician, running up and down the aisle of the plane, pointing to us and shouting "Mya Mama, Mya Papu!" He endeared himself to everyone. Being constantly fed on the airplane meant many trips to the restroom too. On one of these trips, Yuri would not put down either the dinner roll in one hand or the sausage in the other. After the roll hit the floor, Yuri tried to dive into the trashcan to retrieve it. He knew too well what it was like to be hungry. What he didn't yet know was that he would not have to go to bed hungry ever again.

With an older child, you have to be aware of the impact of your surroundings on his emotions. We arrived home on Halloween evening, October 31, but we stalled at the airport and had dinner to delay going home right away. How could we explain all those witches and goblins and scary faces and the constant doorbell ring to someone who didn't understand? We did not want our son's first impression to be one of monsters and ghouls ringing our doorbell all evening.

At home, one of the biggest differences with an older child was Yuri's sense of freedom, space and high energy. My new exercise regimen was nothing more than chasing Yuri. Friends commented on how exhausted we must be trying to keep up with our little lightning-fast waterbug! Yuri's exploits sent him through our old house slamming doors and flushing toilets, since he had never before run free in such expanded space. Everything was novel. It was exhilarating, trying and rewarding for everyone. But when he was quiet, and I sweating and panting, he was so sweet and affectionate, seeming so happy that we are his mama and papa.

There were, of course, challenges in communication. I was lucky that a Russian friend told me of a Russian-English childcare center nearby. It allowed Yuri to immediately become part of a group of young children, much like what he was accustomed to. He could communicate with the Russian and American caregivers, and very quickly Yuri learned to speak English. As a mom, I was able to return to work without feeling guilty. It was the best of all worlds.

There was an adjustment period at home, too, for Lauren, Yuri's new sister. Lauren had been an only child for five years. She wanted a sister, but was happy to have a new brother. There is only a one-year difference in their ages. Once Lauren realized she shared the pedestal now and had to make room for Yuri, some resentments began to crop up. But this situation was not so different from a two- or three-year-old's jealousy at having a new infant around the house. Soon Lauren was reading stories to her new brother, playing games with him and helping him learn the alphabet once he started school. They are true siblings; they play, they battle and they do love each other! It's so gratifying, now that Yuri is ten and Lauren eleven, watching them play soccer in the yard or horse on the basketball court!

One big difference in adopting an older child, especially one who has been confined to an orphanage, is the lack of life experience. We take for granted all that an American child learns and assimilates day to day: unending food, cars, trucks, toys, TV, video, vacations, the beach and the ocean and boats, skiing, airplanes, taxis, even tools and various rooms around the house. When Yuri arrived, he had very limited language skills and limited life experience, so he was constantly playing catch-up. While most dads might say to their toddler, "Where's the hammer?" we first had to show Yuri what a hammer or screwdriver was, because he never had occasion to see one before. Similarly, "Dad is in the living room" would be perplexing when Yuri was in the empty family room looking for Dad. He needed to learn what the rooms of the house were, as well as the various utensils around the house. Everything was foreign: watering can? spatula? ladle? whipped cream? We began with baby steps, teaching him everything, assuming he had not had exposure to each new thing. Yuri got the concept of Christmas quickly, though: "more presents!"

Yuri started school a grade later than other kids his age, allowing him to develop more language skills and maturity. The extra year has paid off, and Yuri is thriving. With the help of a tutor each week, Yuri is able to keep up with his peers, with so much new to learn! Of course, some things he has learned on his own. He loves basketball, and now is an ace at shooting foul shots after hours of practicing on his own. His reading is improving, and he goes through the sports page of the newspaper every morning to keep up with the teams and players. And he is a computer whiz. It's amazing how much kids can learn about computers on their own! Yuri loves computer games, such as Math Blaster and Midnight Rescue, and he is even learning to type with Slam Dunk Typing software.

Adopting an older child presents different issues than adopting an infant. A younger child requires more physical assistance, between feeding and diapering and carrying, while older children need more emotional nurturing and support. I do not mean to suggest, of course, that babies don't need emotional care, but infants aren't quite cognizant enough to recognize the dramatic change they are experiencing.

Infants cannot, as Yuri did, look at photographs of their mother and father and recognize them when they step foot in the room. We fell in love instantly with our child when he went running to his new dad with open arms for the first time, and we feel Yuri was able to instantly reciprocate his love for us.

♥

Welcome Home, My Daughter

Rosemary Zibart

As we tour the streets of Minsk, Belarus, searching for the orphanage where my daughter grew up, I ask Tanya if she has butterflies in her stomach. Like a flip American teen, she replies, "Of course not!" But a moment later, she says, "It feels like bugs."

I'm tense too, perhaps more tense than I felt this week nine years ago, when I arrived in this former Soviet bloc nation to claim Tanya. At the time, I knew almost nothing about the eight-year-old child beyond a flimsy snapshot that had been pinned to my refrigerator door for the previous six months.

In 1992, countries like Belarus had just opened the doors of their numerous orphanages, allowing international adoption. From the beginning, most prospective parents sought infants or toddlers, but I was beguiled by the pictures of older children. Unlike the horror pictures of Romanian orphans, these kids seemed bright and well-cared for. They looked like an easy fit for life in the United States. Plus, they were immediately available! After years of longing for children, my husband and I were impatient.

I traveled to Minsk in June for Tanya, and my husband went to Tula, Russia, for seven-year-old Sergei six months later. We quickly learned how wrong we were about expecting an easy transition. Faced with problems ranging from mental deficits to emotional turmoil, my husband and I found that we'd embarked on a roller coaster of excruciating highs and lows with no chance to climb off.

Quick-witted and charming, Sergei made friends and succeeded in school. Any painful feelings remained tucked behind a big smile. Tanya also had wonderful qualities, but because of a history of abuse, her problems were greater. Though clearly craving affection, she was as prickly as a porcupine—so difficult to touch, we often quit trying. She resisted joining our family, retreating into a fantasy of happiness before her adoption. Through therapy, we learned that Tanya's behavior was typical for older adopted children. Such boys and girls never stop asking, "Will you abandon me just as I've been abandoned before?" Often, they don't wait to find out and instead push away the adoption parents first.

Years of rejection had bruised my husband and me. We questioned whether we'd done the right thing in pulling Tanya away from her native culture and bringing her to the United States.

Last year, while these questions were painfully brewing, I learned of an international conference to be held that summer in Minsk by the Belarus Ministry of Education and National Adoption Center. Families from countries such as Denmark, Canada, Sweden and the United States had been invited to share their experiences with each other and Belarus officials.

The timing seemed perfect for Tanya to revisit her homeland. She'd kept open the door to the past. Now she needed to make choices. We even decided that if Tanya wanted to stay in Belarus, we'd try to find a way.

Before making the final decision, however, I consulted Donna Clauss, director of Rainbow House International, an agency that has placed more than sixteen hundred children with American families. "Lots of people seek their child's roots," she said. "For most, it's a positive experience. But for a few, it's traumatic." Despite concerns, I bought the airline tickets, believing the trip was the key to Tanya's and our family's future.

We all flew to Germany and took an overnight train to Belarus. We were met at the Minsk train station by Linda Baldwin, an adoptive mother from Denver who was helping with the conference. Linda had started her own adoption process as a single parent in 1993. When she arrived at the Belarus orphanage for her four-year-old daughter, Tatiana, she decided to adopt Tatiana's best friend, Julia, as well. Two days after arriving back in the United States, Linda married her fiancé, Brad Baldwin. "I told him it was a package deal," she told me. "The three of us or nothing."

Linda eventually founded Guardian Angels, a nonprofit organization that ships thousands of dollars' worth of medical supplies and clothes to Belarus each year, transported without charge by United and Lufthansa Airlines.

Thirty-five children and their parents were at the hotel for the conference. We soon met Julia and Tatiana, both twelve and both wearing dresses matching their mom's. We also met Alexandra, a captivating four-year-old from St. Louis. "Her IQ is higher than the rest of ours put together," said her mother, Elizabeth Engel. Since she and her husband, Tom Otto, are orthopedic surgeons, adopting Alexandra, who lacks one hand from a birth defect, was "no big deal," she said.

"We came here," Dr. Engel explained, "to show how happy and loved adopted children can be in the United States."

Seeing these bright, lively youngsters made me a little sad. While Sergei made friends, Tanya didn't interact and instead withdrew alone to our hotel room. I realized that our family's agenda lay outside the conference. We located an interpreter and set off with our daughter in search of her past.

As the taxi neared the orphanage, Tanya peered tensely out the windows. Passing dingy tenements and weed-choked yards, she finally spied a low building surrounded by playground equipment. "That's it!" she called out. We entered a long, gloomy corridor and found an office where a heavyset woman with henna-dyed hair sat at a desk. Seeing us, the woman—who turned out to be the orphanage director, Gallina Petrovna—broke into a big smile.

"Tanya, Tanya!" she cried out and rose to embrace my daughter. This hug was the high point of Tanya's trip. The low point occurred moments later, when we requested information about Tanya's biological mom. *"Nichevo"* (nothing) was the reply.

Next Tanya asked for what she wanted most in the world: a baby picture. But the answer was the same: *nichevo.* Tanya sank as she heard these words. Before the trip, we'd seen a cute photo of an infant with its lip defiantly sticking out. Tanya loved the picture, and I bought it for her. Now it would have to substitute for the real thing.

The director led us into the living quarters of the orphanage. Several girls looked wistful as our daughter was introduced as a child who had once dwelled there but now had a family. Tanya handed out stuffed animals, which the children squeezed tightly. I was reminded of what Antoine de Saint-Exupery wrote in *The Little Prince,* that one's devotion to a particular rose bush is what makes it unique. How much more true for children: It's our "favoritism," the attention we dedicate to our own, that enables them to thrive.

The orphanage visit had a great impact on all of us. My husband and I were chastened by a glimpse of the "dreadful alternative"—what Tanya's life might have been like had she not been adopted. Without saying a word, Tanya also seemed to have turned a corner. Back at the hotel, she played with others for the first time. Like *Eloise at the Plaza,* kids ran up and down the halls.

That night, as she slept in the hotel bed beside me, Tanya uttered the word "Mommy" and threw her arm over me. I wondered what was going on inside her head. The next day, at a talent show given by the adopted kids, Tanya confidently crossed the stage and pounded out the American classic "Stand by Me" on the piano. Recalling the scared little kid she once was, I clapped loudly, my eyes damp with tears.

"Don't ever think you don't make a difference," Linda Baldwin said to the conference audience. "Everyone involved in adoption has changed the world for at least one child."

When it was time to go, Tanya's bag was the first one packed. At the airport, we saw couples carrying infants. "Are you adopting?" I asked nosily, and the new parents nodded. Smiling proudly, I pointed to Tanya and Sergei. Nine years ago, my husband and I had embarked on the same adventure, and just look what we had to show for it— gray hairs and stretch marks on our heart muscles, but neither of us would have skipped the ride.

Unlike the first time, when I dragged Tanya screaming and kicking onto the airplane, she now knew where she was heading. And no one was happier to get home. She raced in the front door.

I realize now that what we carried to Minsk but did not bring back with us were dreams: dreams of a more perfect daughter, dreams of perfect parents. The experience helped us all commit to the family that we are. While the path remains bumpy, Tanya's feet seem more firmly planted here. When explosions occur, she makes amends more quickly.

A week after our return, Tanya surprised me by asking, "Mom, can you please help me wash my hair?" Moments later, gently sudsing her head over the bathroom sink, I relished a joy of motherhood I was finally privileged to experience.

♥

CHAPTER FIVE

Embarking on the Lone Journey

To Lay Open One's Heart

Rita Cheresnowsky

I t's late—9:30—and the girls have been asleep for nearly an hour. The house looks like it's been vandalized, at least once, maybe twice, by a frustrated burglar who appears to have been a Barney fan. Crayons, Play-Doh, Duplos and chalk litter the front room and spill out into the hall. My only goal: lights out before Ted Koppel says "Hello."

Up since 4:30, showered, dressed, fed the cats, scooped the poop—then fed, undressed and redressed, diapered and/or pottied two very strong-willed little girls, ages four and two. Packed them and their lunches (made the night before), sleeping mats, coats, hats, gloves, boots and at least four "can't-leave-home-without" toys into a car, which also bears that just-been-vandalized look. In the car seats—once, twice—then out for pee-pee time . . . dash into the house. Back in the car seats to try again. Drove thirty minutes to the day care that collects one-third of my take-home pay, then unpacked, hauled in, hugged, kissed—waved good-bye. Subwayed in, walked, worked (nine hours, ten-minute lunch). Subwayed back, picked up, packed up, drove forty-five minutes home. Unloaded, unpacked, fed, bathed, brushed and combed. Storied them, blessed them, explained why dead bugs don't fly and again why the sky is pink just before dark. And now, the mess— the cleanup, tomorrow's lunch, the dirty floor. My bones hurt, my eyes burn, I am sleeping beside angels. Koppel never had a chance.

What was I thinking? Good Lord, what could I have been think- ing? Once? Then twice? At my age? And single? A "perimenopausal moment" perhaps? Answer: I wasn't (thinking, that is) and certainly not in the "list-making" way. Adoption, for me, isn't really about thinking. We sometimes try to make it about thinking. Thinking is so much safer and so much neater, and doesn't require nearly as much guts. It makes us feel like we are in control, as if the outcome should logically be predictable and fair. *I can adopt because this list I just made shows that I can. I can adopt because I have it worked out. I have a plan.* Or, in some cases, *I can't adopt, I'll never make ends meet.*

I tried the thinking route. With each of my two adoptions, I tried thinking the responsible, worst-case-scenario thoughts. *Am I strong enough, am I woman enough, am I healthy and smart and selfless enough to mother a young child—to mother two young children—at my age, in my home without a mate? Do I make enough money? What if I die? How will I ever afford college? What will people say when they see we don't look alike?* Answers to my thinking varied with the day. The "Don't Do It" list could be very long at times. It almost always outnumbered the "Go Ahead" list, at least two to one. Just to be clear, there is a place for thinking in the adoption journey. Adoption is obviously not something to be done thoughtlessly, or without at least some planning and common sense. But in the end, bottom line, with all my planning and list-making, I'm lucky if six of the twenty-three things in my "Reasons That I Can" list actually turned out the way I'd planned.

So why did I do it? And how did I do it? Why and how did I, a single white woman in her forties with a human services salary, take on the stress and expense of an international adoption, to enter the Mommy Club when most of my friends had just repainted their empty nest? I did it because my heart could not *not* do it. I did it because deep inside, when all was said and done, it felt more right than not. I did it, not certain that adoption was definitely going to happen, but knowing, beyond a doubt, that I needed to take each step as it came, and that at each step, I would know if and when to take the next. I did it, telling myself that if it ever stopped feeling "right," then I would wait or not ever make another move. My journey into adoption was one of trust—of saying "yes" over and over again. It was not, in the end, a decision based on thought.

Was I scared? I would have been crazy not to have had fear. But the "rightness" I knew deep in my heart propelled me through that fear, into a place of courage and resolve. I did vow, from the start, that no matter how little I had, I would not let money alone be the reason not to take the risk. Money—so fluid, so unpredictable—was not worthy of becoming the deciding force. And miraculously, the money did come, each time as a gift—an unexpected, unpredictable, unimagined gift. It came, I believe, because it was always meant to come.

The money came because, as I realized early on, the journey into adoption is so much bigger than me. It is so much more mysterious and sacred than we can ever know. We think we know. Agencies, seasoned social workers, adoptive parents . . . we all think we know what to do, how to think, how to make it happen. But we don't. We are part of something that is all about risk—all about the unknown, the uncertain, the unpredictable, the unsure. We can fill it with paperwork. We can find all kinds of reasons that it might or might not make sense, but we cannot know the magnitude of the plan. We can only step into the mystery and wait, then step in some more.

To pledge one's heart as "home" to a child, to lay open one's heart to the possibility of receiving that most sacred of trust, is not about lists and day care costs. It is about transformation, about opening one's life to the possibility of things never ever being the same. It is about reaching deep into the fear and the anxiety and the unknown, with a blind certainty that you are part of something right and holy and beautiful and rare. Adoption is about risking the possibility of pain, rejection and loss—your child's, her birth parents', your family's, your own.

Adoption is messy. Nothing about it—not the applying, not the waiting, not the receiving nor even the living of adoption for that matter—is neat or predictable or emotionally safe. Parenting is messy, backbreaking, heartbreaking, soul-stretching work. Loving and transforming, becoming a family, is sloppy and shaky and packed with unbelievably wondrous joy.

So why did I do it? I've come now to believe, as so many adoptive parents have affirmed, that "I did not choose adoption; rather, adoption chose me." I laid open my heart, I listened, and I said yes—over and over again at each step, yes. *Yes, I will open myself to the possibility of this chance. Yes, I will jump, blindfolded, my heart on a platter, over this cliff without a net.*

And so I did. I opened my heart and my life to receiving my first child. She was birthed in Guatemala in November, and at seven months she was home with me. This little miracle turned my life (and my heart) inside out. Chaos, unpredictability, worry, intense joy . . . such a circus. I had never laughed so much, or cried so much, or felt so full. And I did not lose myself as I had feared, but rather found myself in ways that continue to unfold. I was transformed, not the same. I was me, but more me than me before. My age, rather than a drawback, was in fact a gift. I might not have been the fastest with a diaper change, or the most awake at 3 A.M., but I was seasoned in living and adapting. My years had taught me what really mattered in life. I was able to give over to the experience of giving over, with an abandon that only the wisdom of age, and the wildest of risks, calls forth. *What did I have to lose but the rest of my life? And what better way to spend it than caught up in the fray?* I was more patient and loving. I was stronger and more alive. And more frustrated and more exhausted and more surrendering—over and over again surrendering into the experience of surrendering itself.

Two years later, adoption again chose me. Again I knew, in that deep knowing place, that there was room at our table, room in my arms, for at least one more. I knew, again, not with lists and logical thoughts. Good Lord, this time the "Don't Do It" list was three pages long. But as before, I knew that if I opened my heart, what was meant to be, would be, and if not, then not. Again the financial gift— another unexpected source. My second child came home just after 9/11, following three major terrorist alerts and during the middle of the anthrax scare. At a time when loss and fear and unpredictability were everywhere in my world, this little blessing came home, and my life was further transformed.

The journey into adoption can be so complicated and fraught with worry and waiting and disappointment and loss. But for me, it was and continues to be a sacred journey into the stuff of life, into the mystery that leaves words far behind. It is not easy. Do not adopt if "easy" is at the top of your "Can Do" list. The paperwork can be intimidating, the invasion of privacy an annoyance, at best. The scrutiny can feel demoralizing and the wait without end. But the journey into adoption is so like the journey into parenting. When all is said and done, it makes so much sense that it would be so. All it takes is one high fever, or one toddler with a tantrum in the middle of the mall, to know that parenting is no more in our control than was our referral wait, or how long before our 1600 was approved. For me, it is all part of the same movement, the same journey, the daily laying open of one's heart, the daily surrender into love.

My children and I are witness to the miracle. We are living the miracle, so blessed in the muck and the snot and the tears with more delicious joy and wonder than I could ever hold. What was I thinking?

God, I actually can't remember. These days, if it didn't happen yesterday, it's long gone from my head—to be replaced with the toilet overflowing or the next case of strep, or that waterfall of giggles when the three of us get caught in the rain.

♥

Sadie and Me

Myra Alperson

We're sitting at the breakfast table, seven-year-old Sadie chewing away at her pasta (she eats spaghetti for breakfast, with sprinkle cheese), when she says, suddenly, "Mommy, do you know Britney Spears?"

I almost moan. "No," I lie. "Who's that?"

"Mom-my," she says. "You just don't know fashion!"

"I guess I don't," I concede. "I'm not a fashionable person. So what do you know about Britney Spears?"

"Well . . . it's about fashion!" Her voice tapers off. Silence. I get a funny feeling.

"Sadie," I say, "is Britney Spears a man or woman?"

Her eyes veer away. One phrase that Sadie refuses to learn is "I don't know." She usually responds to this type of question with: "Well, do you know?" And that's what she says now.

I say, "Well, I think I do know," but won't tell her.

And we leave it at that.

It's a fragment of our life together that I record in the journal I started on Valentine's Day in 1997, when Sadie had been with me for just four months. (Adoption Day was October 14, 1996, when she was ten months old.) That day I wrote extensively about her accomplishments to date.

Here's one of the journal entries:

You're saying words. As of today, these include hot, up, cah (for cat), appa (apple), pah (pear), bah (bear). When I picked you up in China, you could make the sounds ba-ba-ba and pa-pa-pa in a soft, whispering voice. Your voice is very firm now. I love the sound of it. There was a time when your only word was baba—a catchall for everything. Now your sounds vary. For a while—in November and December—you were saying Mommm. You have stopped saying that, and you don't say Mama, either, but I'm not worried. You're babbling a lot and words are coming out, even if I don't understand them. I do think you say Enta for Yenta (our cat)—who scratched you on the face yesterday. I hate to say it, but I think you deserved it!

Now I write in the journal every few days—or weeks—and it's over three hundred single-spaced pages long. I keep telling myself that I need to start printing it out, and I have bought a ream of three-holed paper so I can put it in a binder. The compulsion to record our lives together is very strong, and I want to do more than take pictures because images don't capture its essence; I vividly recall the warning of another mom while I was still waiting for the referral: "Spend as much time with your child as you can. You'll never get those days back." Writing about our lives helps me hold onto those days.

That mother was so right: Sadie is now in second grade, for goodness' sake! Where did the time go? The day you took your first steps? (In our local Barnes & Noble, January 21, 1997.) The mikveh (ritual bath for Jewish conversion)? Your first performance at Chinese Culture Day? Your first haircut? The first day of kindergarten? Your first time on ice skates? Your first lost tooth? The day you mastered the bicycle (on your sixth-and-a-half birthday!)? And so on!

The desire to be a parent is very abstract when you're still waiting.

And when your child is with you, it's as though you've made a leap to some "other side." I sometimes refer to my pre-Sadie days as "When I was single . . ." But I'm still single: I'm a single mom. But becoming a parent has brought me into an entirely different existence—the "other side"—and has affected every aspect of my being.

Let's start with work. I was never a workaholic, but I was able to attend all sorts of work-related extracurriculars before I adopted Sadie, and I could also pursue many hobbies and go to all the movies I wanted to, and did. I'm an avid bicyclist and used to bicycle everywhere I needed to go in New York City, any time of day or night and in all sorts of crazy weather. At one point I had developed a bicycle touring business and spent most of my nonworking time doing that.

My priorities changed dramatically once I became a parent. Well, everything changed: my frame of reference, my friends, my schedule, the rhythm of my life, my ambitions. Forget movies. I certainly went out much less. I downgraded my professional aspirations and ultimately created a new professional template, which has involved working at home, working on projects that give me more flexibility, putting more emphasis on having time to myself—for us—and not working late. All of this also means much less income. It's not easy to achieve a balance, but at present I'm working from home, producing a newsletter for a nonprofit, doing regular editing jobs, and running a small business that includes walking tours and my own newsletter. I've written three books since bringing Sadie home.

Choices I've made to keep our lives going smoothly and economically include doing as many activities as close to home as possible. We're lucky to live in a Manhattan neighborhood that has lots of advantages: a wonderful park one block away from home, a terrific public school a five-minute walk away, great shopping, very good public transportation and lots of friends nearby. I economize: I do much more cooking now (which I love), and we see lots of videos. I bless the public library (a ten-minute walk) for its great video library.

As a single parent, I'm lucky to live in a so-called full-service apartment building, which means when electricity or plumbing problems arise, the staff helps me. I like to joke that I always have a man around the house but don't have to deal with the hassles!

Sadie would like to have those hassles: She has become fairly vocal in the last year about wanting a dad. She used to not discuss it, but now she does so freely, I think, because three of her best friends have fathers, although several others are in families like ours. She has imposed a deadline of September, and I have to remind her that it doesn't work like that. (She also likes to refer to my pre-Sadie boyfriend as "dad potential," even though she has never met him!)

She wants to have a dad because she very badly wants a sibling, and thinks a dad would automatically mean a baby brother or sister. (Dream on, dear daughter!) I know quite a few single moms who are raising more than one child, but I don't see myself among them. I lack the emotional or financial wherewithal to raise more than one, but this realization has been wrenching, because when I was younger I envisioned having at least two children, and because I know how badly Sadie wants a sister or brother. She has always loved babies (something I never particularly did when I was little), and she is remarkably patient and affectionate with them.

Watching Sadie grow up has been fascinating and precious. She is very aware of her Chinese-ness, although we don't make a fetish of it. Sadie took Chinese dance and language classes from the time she was a toddler until she started full-day kindergarten, when she didn't want to continue. Life in "big girl" school changed her, and she didn't want me to schlep her to these classes anymore. (The first two weeks of kindergarten were so exhausting that she took a nap every day upon arriving home.) Also, she is in a program where half of her instruction is in Spanish. Now in the third year, she is becoming quite fluent. Top that off with Hebrew school, and she is receiving a lot of language stimulation.

We do a fair amount of Chinese-related activities with and without Families with Children from China. Our proximity to Chinatown makes this easier. Her two key interests—chess and origami—have brought us in contact with more Chinese and Chinese American families. Tomorrow, I will be taking her to a chess tournament at a public school in Chinatown that has a huge team.

It's six and a half years since I journeyed to China to meet my daughter. Sometimes I think about those first ten months she spent in China without me. Ten months of empty pages in a journal I hadn't yet begun. At times I'm sad that those journal entries are lost to me forever. But then I remember that Sadie and I have the rest of our lives to spend filling our pages together.

♥

My Choice

Anne Unterkoefler

I've always had an idea of the family I wanted to have. I think many people do. Some people go so far as to picture the house and backyard, the pool, the car—but I never cared about all that. I just wanted it to be me, my husband, and a son and daughter. Of course I'm missing one from that picture now, but when you're twenty years old, you never think you'll have to sacrifice anything at all.

Luckily for me, I learned about sacrifice very early. I married in my twenties and quickly learned that I couldn't have children. A divorce soon followed. My husband wanted biological children and was unwilling to consider any other option. I'd always been comfortable and open to the idea of adoption. My brother Kurt was adopted, and as a clinical social worker, I'd spoken to many families who came together through adoption.

I knew what I had to do, and I began preparing myself to take this step, even if I had to do it alone. I moved back to Pennsylvania and into my parents' house for a year in order to save money. And when I was just about to begin the adoption process, I met a man, fell in love and decided to take another chance with marriage. He was nine years older than me, but he said he was willing to adopt. Yet all through the information sessions, I could see him shying away, becoming alternately anxious and distant. Then one day he said he didn't want to go through with it, that he couldn't do it. He was just too old for it all, he said.

All I'd ever wanted was a family, and children most of all. I'd been with other parents' children for so long, helping them, smiling and playing with them, and in the beginning I was content with that appetizer, happily anticipating the main meal to come. Later, those small tastes of family life, only enough to whet the palate and sharpen my hunger, were just a horrible teaser. The thought that it might be the only taste I would ever have was almost too much to bear. I didn't want to live in regret, growing old with a husband who'd denied me the single joy I'd wanted most, hating him and hating myself most of all for accepting a life that I didn't have to live.

We were divorced on October 18, and my adoption papers were submitted the next day. I had already chosen an adoption agency and didn't want to waste any time getting started. But I was clear about one thing from the beginning: I wanted to adopt two children at once. I'd always wanted two children, but I was getting too old to suffer twice through the process, the wait and the traveling. And there was something else. My adopted brother, Kurt, always had a wonderful relationship with his brother and me, but I always sensed he might have felt more comfortable in our family with another adopted sibling, a sibling with a similar background or history. I wanted my children to have that advantage. I hoped that maybe having each other would make it easier for them to have me as well.

A referral and video of a Russian boy, who I named Dylan, came in February, and I immediately agreed to adopt him, hoping that his sister would follow soon after. She did. I called her Emily, and her video came in April. From the information provided me, they seemed to be smart, beautiful children, inquisitive as well, and only five months in age apart. I said yes the next day.

I flew to Moscow in June and had to wait in the airport for my flight to Perm, a city to the west on the Kama River. The flight was delayed because of mechanical trouble, and I sat staring out the airport window at the gray sky, trying to reconcile my fear of never arriving at the orphanage with my quiet terror of the frail old plane that sputtered on the runway in the distance. I sat and prayed it wasn't mine.

It wasn't. We were finally led outside on the tarmac and walked around a jet and some baggage handlers to find our plane. Suddenly I found myself wishing for the other one. It looked like a low-slung steel crop duster, and as we waited to walk upstairs to board I noticed the left tire seemed flat. The crew noticed this also, and with a nonchalant sense of concern they approached the tire and kicked it, like I do with my Taurus at home. It was clearly deemed acceptable and we were board-ing, up the stairs into an old train compartment with brown vinyl seats that folded back and forth, and no overhead bins. This fear was mild compared to what was to follow. At least I could sleep through the flight. I had a strange dream of little Dylan and Emily dancing together on my living room floor. When I awoke we'd touched down in Perm.

My first official act was going to the Department of Education for permission to visit the orphanage, and after the meeting I felt like cry-ing. *They can't do this to me,* I thought over and over. *They can't do this to me.* But through my pain and anger, there was a sense of unreality, as if I were in a movie. It all seemed too horrible, and yet so contrived and familiar, to be real life. On the drive to the orphanage, the movie camera would show my face pressed to the glass, with a blank stare in my eyes, perhaps the look of defeat. In actuality I wasn't defeated yet, or if I was, I was too furious to realize it. But beneath the fury there was a deep, heart-wrenching sadness, for already all the fantasies I'd devised had been shattered.

At the orphanage they brought out Dylan and Emily, and I held them one at a time. When I put them down, they crawled together on the floor, already at home with each other. I had no idea how to choose between them, nor how to leave one of them behind.

That's what they had told me at the Department of Education. They said that I wasn't allowed to take both home, that they'd only received my paperwork for Dylan. However, I was allowed to choose one to adopt, whichever I wanted.

I'd already fallen in love with both of them, with the idea of them, before they were ever put in my arms. I'd rearranged my home, my life, to fit two small but growing bodies that I'd only seen for minutes on a scratchy videotape. When I held them, I wanted to give myself over, to allow myself that moment that so many adopting parents feel. I'd read many stories describing that moment: the moment when a parent first holds his or her child in the orphanage and feels the bonding in a sudden burst of light, in the sudden realization of one's being a parent. It sounded so clichéd, but I wanted that. I wanted that moment with Dylan and Emily, and it had been robbed from me.

I couldn't allow myself to feel anything at all. It was as though they weren't even mine. I felt myself holding them from a great distance, as though I didn't want to become attached because it would kill me to give one away.

That night I barely slept. It was the summer solstice in Perm, when the sunlight lasts all through the day and into the night, only fading into a bright twilight for a few hours before dawn. I was reminded of being a child, having to go to bed in the summer when it was still light, lying awake and hearing the neighborhood children playing all down the street. I tried to lie still in the hotel bed, a towel over my eyes, but the light still found its way in, through the cracks in the blinds, through the pores of the towel, through the tight press of my lids. And when I finally did sleep, there were nightmares. In my dreams I spent hours trying to force two large bundles into a suitcase, but no matter how I tried, there was always one that didn't fit.

In the morning the situation seemed to have more hope. I called my contact in the adoption agency in Massachusetts as early as possible to tell her the situation. She assured me not to worry, that there was no rule stating that I couldn't adopt both, and it would be sorted out. I started to have some confidence, too. I told myself that I had come so far, and I was absolutely not going to leave a child behind.

Of course, for the time being I had to leave both behind at the end of my first visit. This was the normal procedure. I returned home to chew my nails to shreds and wait. This was much worse than the referral wait, much worse than my time in Russia. At home all I had was time and my doubts, which returned like ghosts with a wicked vengeance.

After eight weeks had passed I returned to Russia to lay myself at the mercy of the courts, which would make the ultimate decision. I overprepared the night before my court hearing, memorizing all of Dylan and Emily's information, their charts, medical history, everything. It was something to keep my mind busy.

In court the next day the social worker from the orphanage was on my side, which was comforting. As the proceedings began, I felt a strange lightness, as though a heavy cloak had been taken from me. In a way, I was glad to be rid of the responsibility, free for the moment to relax while someone else handled my fate. Yet at the same time there was a panic. This was the most important moment of my life, and I had no control whatsoever. Someone who had no idea what I'd been through, who didn't know me at all, was going to design my salvation or doom.

We were ordered from the courtroom while the judge deliberated, and I settled myself in the stiff wooden benches for the hours ahead. I couldn't help feeling as though I'd done something wrong, like a murderer or thief waiting in the wings before going to prison, trying to enjoy her last moments of freedom. Fifteen minutes later they called us back. *Fifteen minutes!* I thought to myself. *Is that good or bad? Is my case so preposterous that they don't even need time to consider it?*

Many times now, when my house is quiet, I think about that day in the courtroom, and I wonder how my life would be if the judge's decision were different. It's like torture to think about. But all the same, I think about staring up at the judge like she was God and I a sinner awaiting judgment. I think about the silence in the court, the only sound my heart thumping in my throat, just like the kitchen clock on the wall in my home.

And then Dylan and Emily will wake up from their nap and start laughing and banging around upstairs, wanting their lunch or their mommy, and I don't have time to consider the past. There's no time to remember how the judge finally smiled and said to me, "You are a brave woman."

Why would I want to imagine life without my two children? I know they wouldn't be able to do so, themselves. They are quite different: Emily, so smart and quick to learn, and Dylan, with his natural charisma. But they are as close as brother and sister could be, Dylan always looking out for his sister. When someone gives him a piece of candy, he'll ask for another for his sister. They hold hands when we're in public, and sometimes they play Cinderella and Prince Charming after watching the movie. They dance together with tiny, clumsy and loving steps, and it always gives me a strange, beautiful chill.

At times they speak with such adorable sweetness and innocence that I can barely respond. The other day Dylan was telling me the story of Snow White after he watched the Disney movie. He said that "the bad queen turned into an evil witch, and made Snow White sleep with an apple, and then the Hi-Ho's came to rescue her." It makes me smile just to write it.

I am open with them about their adoption, although I think they are too young to truly understand. I was explaining to Dylan about how babies grow in a mommy's stomach. Dylan, knowing he did not come from my stomach, considered this for a while before saying, "We were never born, Mom." When I told him that he was grown inside someone else's stomach, he thought about this, too, for a while. "Did we grow in Grandma's stomach?" he asked.

Other times they speak with such wisdom that I'm filled with both pride and sadness. "What was the lady's name?" Dylan once asked me, meaning the name of his mother. I had to think for a while before I could remember.

I also think about what it might be like for my children to have a father. They consider this, too, and sometimes go so far as to make up imaginary daddies. Just the other day Dylan told me he was playing with Daddy in the tree fort they made, and Daddy fell out. I didn't quite know whether to laugh or not.

Emily and Dylan see my brothers often, and my uncle too. But they know it's not the same. One day Emily approached me as I was reading. "I'm sad that I don't have a daddy," she said. I picked her up and held her. "Me, too, sweetie. But I think we have a nice family, though. Don't you?" She nodded her little head in my arms.

I believe that, too. This is the family I've always wanted. All I need to convince me of this is the feel of my children's arms around me and their cries of joy when I wake them in the morning. All I need is to see Dylan wrap his arm around Emily, spontaneously, like he did today, and whisper into her ear, "You're my best friend."

♥

READER/CUSTOMER CARE SURVEY

BB1

We care about your opinions. Please take a moment to fill out this Reader Survey card and mail it back to us.
As a special **"thank you"** we'll send you exciting news about interesting books and a valuable **Gift Certificate.**

Please PRINT using ALL CAPS

First Name | MI. | Last Name

Address

City | ST | Zip

Phone # (___) ___ — ___   Fax # (___) ___ — ___

Email

(1) Gender:
___ Female   ___ Male

(2) Age:
___ 12 or under   ___ 40-59
___ 13-19   ___ 60+
___ 20-39

(3) Marital Status
___ Married
___ Single
___ Divorced/Widowed

(4) Did you receive this book as a gift?
___ Yes   ___ No

(5) How many Health Communications books have you bought or read?
___ 1   ___ 2-4   ___ 5+

(6) How did you find out about this book?
Please fill in ONE.
1) ___ Recommendation
2) ___ Store Display
3) ___ Bestseller List
4) ___ Online
5) ___ Advertisement
6) ___ Catalog/Mailing
7) ___ Interview/Review (TV, Radio, Print)

(7) Where do you usually buy books?
Please fill in your top TWO choices.
1) ___ Bookstore
2) ___ Religious Bookstore
3) ___ Online
4) ___ Book Club/Mail Order
5) ___ Price Club (Costco, Sam's Club, etc.)
6) ___ Retail Store (Target, Wal-Mart, etc.)

(9) What subjects do you enjoy reading about most? Rank only **FIVE.** Use 1 for your favorite, 2 for second favorite, etc.

	1	2	3	4	5
1) Parenting/Family	○	○	○	○	○
2) Relationships	○	○	○	○	○
3) Recovery/Addictions	○	○	○	○	○
4) Health/Nutrition	○	○	○	○	○
5) Christianity	○	○	○	○	○
6) Spirituality/Inspiration	○	○	○	○	○
7) Business Self-Help	○	○	○	○	○
8) Teen Issues	○	○	○	○	○
9) Sports	○	○	○	○	○

(14) What attracts you most to a book?
(Please rank 1-4 in order of preference.)

	1	2	3	4
1) Title	○	○	○	○
2) Cover Design	○	○	○	○
3) Author	○	○	○	○
4) Content	○	○	○	○

TAPE IN MIDDLE; DO NOT STAPLE

BUSINESS REPLY MAIL

FIRST-CLASS MAIL PERMIT NO 45 DEERFIELD BEACH, FL

POSTAGE WILL BE PAID BY ADDRESSEE

HEALTH COMMUNICATIONS, INC.
3201 SW 15TH STREET
DEERFIELD BEACH FL 33442-9875

FOLD HERE

Comments:

Practically Perfect

Barbara Schrier

I watch as my six-year-old daughter, Lily, stands before the mirror assessing her outfit for the day. She has spent considerable time rummaging through drawers and closets this morning to look "fancy" for school, despite my increasingly urgent warnings that we'll be late if she doesn't move *now*. So here she is, adjusting the hem of a too-small purple plaid skirt. Completing the ensemble is her beloved pink Barbie University T-shirt and two pairs of socks (red Santa ankle socks layered over pale blue knee socks) because "My toes want to be cozy today." Determining that an essential ingredient is missing, Miss Lil arranges her hair into three ponytails secured with glittery pipe cleaners. Finally, finally her work is done. As she looks at her reflection, she exclaims, "Oh Mama, I'm practically perfect!" Indeed she is.

Moments like this are now a regular part of my life, but I can still conjure up the uncertainty and anxiety that I felt six years ago as I waited to hear my adoption social worker say the magic words, "You're going to China to meet your daughter." My thoughts then were focused on the many challenges of caring for an infant. When I occasionally daydreamed about Lily in the future, she was older. In my mind's eye, she was up on a dais delivering the valedictory speech at some impressive college, thanking me for creating the perfect environment for learning. Or coming home after a date and sharing whispered secrets about a boy, followed by the words, "I am so lucky you are my mom." Or accepting a music award for prodigies—well, you get the idea. I was able to practice a highly selective form of fantasizing that took me from infant to adult without any of the messiness of those in-between years. But you also need to understand that to this day, I have my perfect Oscar acceptance speech at the ready—just in case.

My image of raising a Chinese daughter was equally naïve and uninformed. I would learn to serve a proper Chinese New Year's feast. Lily would to grow up bilingual, and, of course, her multicultural background couldn't hurt when she applied to that impressive college. My brother, Tom, came at it from a marketing perspective. He traveled with me to China, where he perfected his fantasy. This was just when Tiger Woods exploded onto the scene, and Tom became convinced this would be Lily's future, as well. "Just think, Barbara, of the up-close and personal stories that Jim McKay will do." Forget the fact that Lily at ten months couldn't sit up without assistance and was holding her bottle with her feet. Tom now approached the video recorder as a man on a mission. "I know they will want to include shots of her hometown in the documentary," he assured me.

After watching home movies of Tiger, at age three, working his way through buckets of golf balls with focus and great determination, Tom decided that three was the logical age to introduce Lily to the game. Starting slowly, he took her to a miniature golf course. After struggling at the first hole, Lily threw down the club and began kicking the ball into the cup. Dodging windmills, hurdling bridges and forcing the clown to keep his mouth open permanently, she navigated the entire course in two minutes and thirty-eight seconds. As she raised her arms in triumph, Tom was still struggling to get the lens cap off of the camera. Later when I asked her if she had had a good time, she said with all seriousness, "I like golf. You know, it's a lot like soccer."

I must also confess that at age six, Lily has yet to master, or for that matter even start to learn, Mandarin. She does, however, profess to speak Chinese to her dollies. To be fair the sounds coming from my daughter's mouth definitely have a distinct cadence and inflection, but to my untrained ears, it sounds more like an Italian Mr. Rogers speaking with a heavy Swedish accent. Despite my fervent feminist pleas, a bride costume handily beat out Mulan for this year's Halloween costume; no amount of historical explanations about negative cultural stereotypes can stop her from belting out the score from the *Flower Drum Song;* and chopsticks in our house are rarely used as eating utensils, but are just "perfect" as microphones, a conductor's baton or skis for Barbie when she hits the slopes.

For Lily, being Chinese is part of who she is, but not the first adjective she uses when describing herself. When her first-grade teacher posed the question, "What makes you special?" Lily wrote, "I am sweet, I make my mama laugh, I am a good paintist (an artist who paints, obviously), and of course, I'm Chinese." Final trump card—case closed. Happily, we live in a very diverse community that embraces the notion of being different. Recently when I went to pick Lily up from her after-school art program, two of her pals were lamenting the fact that they weren't Lily. "I just wish I was Lily," one sighed with a dramatic flourish. "I know," the other girl said. "She's got such a great life." When I asked why they felt this way, the response was "Because she's Chinese."

When we talk about the fact that she and I were born in different countries, Lily adopts the mannerisms of a solicitous social worker delivering bad news. "It's going to be okay," she comforts. "Just try and remember that not everyone can be Chinese." And she draws on our difference to make sense of the ultimate conundrum—why she doesn't have a dad. As she said to me recently, "I don't understand it,

Mama. People say you have a nice personality" (note: heavy emphasis on "say"). We frequent a local Starbucks, and everyone there knows Lily. Assuming the role of matchmaker, she sidles up to the male du jour and whispers the alarming fact of my single status along with an abbreviated list of my charms. It's as if I am being shadowed by a forty-two-pound madam, who is desperately trying to direct any male eye my way.

Moments such as these surface again and again, piercing the frenetic static of everyday life. Because my imagination failed to sketch out the vitality of Lily's presence in my life, each day is filled with surprises. Yet I have come to cherish that lack of clarity and now realize that there was a reason that the details of Lily's growing up refused to come into focus: One of the leading ladies was missing. The dreams that I conjured up while waiting to travel to China were monologues; the richness of a dialogue had yet to be written. Almost six years later, Lil and I are traveling companions in this adventure, finding our way together and composing our own narrative. This intertwining of two lives—outstretched limbs supporting, nourishing and sometimes competing for that patch of open sky—marks the compass of my heart.

♥

A Life Interrupted

Sarah Stangle

The images we create for ourselves of early parenthood usually include a spouse and a tiny, smiling baby. Most people can't help but have this image; they've seen it thousands of times in commercials, and it seems the most natural. I never saw this picture in my mind, though. Whenever I pictured myself with a husband, we were always holding an adopted child—and not an infant or a toddler, but an older child. A child who had grown in an orphanage, who had only a vague idea of what love was and was waiting patiently to experience it.

After many years, the right husband has yet to come along, or if he did, my nose was pressed too close to the career grindstone to notice. But the desire to adopt was with me in my twenties and thirties, and by the time my late forties rolled around, I was ready to make it a reality.

I decided to adopt a little girl from China, and initially my age range was five to seven years. I wanted an older child, knowing that being adopted might elude such children forever. I did not need a baby to mold to my preconceived image, but a child whose personality was already formed, who needed some support along the way. With an older child, I wouldn't have to wait to take her to playgrounds and museums, to give her bubble baths and have tea parties, to teach her ABCs and how to ride a bicycle. I thought of all the artwork that would soon grace my refrigerator door. I started to rehearse all the answers to the "why" questions that might arise: Why is water blue? Why is this toe longer than that one? But the best thing I could imagine was not having to wait too long to be called "Mommy."

But then I remembered that I would be alone on this job, a single working parent. It might not be easy for a child of seven to make the transition culturally, linguistically and educationally under my care alone. Without a spouse, would I be able to give my child all the time she needed?

After some serious thinking, I changed my request to a three- to five-year-old girl. I thought that since I was willing to take a child as old as five, that was what the Chinese government would give me. So I waited for my daughter through the months ahead, and I spent Sundays buying her clothes, especially little dresses, anything from a 3T to a 6X. I figured I'd cover all possible sizes; I would donate anything that was too small to the orphanage, and my daughter would grow into anything that was too big.

Time passed, and my referral from China finally came. Imagine my surprise and shock when I was told my little girl had not yet passed her third birthday. I was almost immobilized. Three! As I raced home from my office where I had received the news, I mentally rechild-proofed my apartment as other realities came into place: two years of childcare before kindergarten, possible need for potty training, stroller, car seat, choking hazards. Was I up to this? I had to regroup. Then her picture came, and there was nothing more to think about. I fell in love. She would soon be mine. I couldn't get to China fast enough.

She was, of course, the most beautiful child I had ever seen, probably the most beautiful ever born. Her name was QiaoQiao (pronounced "ChowChow," meaning "handy little person" or "cute cute," depending upon who translated for you). With her adoption, her new name would be Helen Lark Qiao Lin Stangle. I decided to continue calling her ChowChow until she felt comfortable with her new name. She just turned three several days before my arrival; she was the oldest of the nine children in our group to be adopted, and she wanted no part of me.

Like all adopting parents, I had my fantasies about what our first meeting would be like. Some fantasies can survive the actual reaction of a small child confronted with the newness of this kind of situation, and some simply shatter, like mine did. To this child I had fallen in love with even from her picture, I was the enemy. The moment she laid eyes on me, she was prepared for battle. I had learned before I went to China that she had been in a foster home for some time. I didn't know, however, that she had been with the same family for more than two years of her young life. Being with her, I could immediately see how loving the foster home had been and how much she loved her foster family. She was a happy child—healthy and crazy about her foster dad. She cried inconsolably for him. A hardy child, she went to everyone except me. I felt rejected. I guess I almost thought that I would be her savior, a positive force in saving a child from certain doom. I hadn't even considered that she might be happy where she was, and may not want to be with me at all.

I had sent her a little album before I left for China, with pictures of me, my family and her new home, along with a teddy bear that she was clutching the first time I saw her. I imagine that when the pictures were first shown to her she was told, "This is your new mommy and soon you will go to live with her." When she saw me in person, all she recognized was a woman who was going to remove her from the only family and the only life she'd ever known. I was the one who was interrupting her happy life.

During my first night alone with her at the hotel in Nanning, sleep eluded me. I simply stared at her all night as she lay asleep in the bed next to mine. I monitored her breathing, counting every breath. I memorized her face and jumped when her eyelid flickered. I recalled old tunes from the sixties that I could use to sing her back to sleep if she awoke, songs like "Scarborough Fair," "Let It Be," and some old Peter, Paul and Mary tunes. Lullabies were not my forte, but I remembered enough of "Hush Little Baby" to get by. The rest I would make up along the way. I just lay there waiting for the moment when my hopefully soothing, yet not too terrific, voice would be called into action. I thought of the awesome responsibility, the gift that had been given to me. No sleep, all nerves, trying to take her in with every pore of my body. I was a bit of a wreck. *Could this little girl—would this little girl—eventually accept me?* In the dark, waiting for dawn, I worried whether this beautiful girl would ever love me. I hoped dawn would bring new hope for our future together.

However, the next morning provided no relief. The instant ChowChow got out of bed, she ran to put on her little sandals that she had neatly lined up next to mine the night before. It was as if she wanted to be ready for anything, perhaps a quick escape, or to run into her papa's arms the moment he came to take her back home. For the first four days, she insisted on wearing the same sundress she wore the first day I met her, and she'd strap on the backpack that was the only link to her past. Each night, she would put the dress under her pillow, sometimes burying her head into the folds of the skirt. Some nights in the hotel she did fall asleep to my singing, as I carried her back and forth across the room trying to soothe her broken heart. Over and over, it would be the same few fragments of songs that I knew, but somehow they worked.

On our last day in Nanning, before traveling to Guangzhou, the adoption agency facilitator took us on a group tour of a park on one of the highest hills outside the city. On this hill stood a fifteen-story pagoda, which was incredibly high for someone with acrophobia, such as myself. As I stood on the second floor trying to appear completely satisfied with the view from two stories up, I learned that my daughter was leading the troop to the top. After hearing of her whereabouts from someone who had already made the return trip, I started the long climb. Hyperventilating and with weakened knees, I finally reached the top, only to find her perfectly fine, laughing and enjoying the sights with all the others.

One Sunday when I was alone with her in Guangzhou, I took ChowChow to a small amusement park. After getting off one of the kiddie rides, she started to follow a Chinese family out the gate. As I went to pick her up, she screamed for her foster father. She continued crying the entire way back to the hotel. Her cries were so distressing that at least three Chinese people came up to me and asked me what was wrong. I couldn't explain anything that they seemed to understand. I wondered if they thought I was abducting the child. This situation made such an impact on me that for the first two weeks back in the States, I would not venture outside with her without taking someone else along.

That same evening, exhausted and deflated, I could not envision an evening in the hotel dining room without incident. So I called room service, ordered several things I thought she would like and hoped for the best. She wanted no part of the milk I ordered to accompany dinner, and she headed for the small refrigerator in our room to extract a beverage. (Since her discovery of that appliance, its contents had cost me a small fortune.) All that remained was a cola and a Tseng Tao, a wonderful Chinese beer. Even though I had vowed years ago never to give a child a cola drink, and beer was not a usual libation for me, our choices were limited as to who would drink what. As we sat at the table trying to keep our eyes open, chopsticks in hand, I felt a nudge to my glass and a little voice saying something that sounded like *"dom bay."* I was too preoccupied to notice until ChowChow lifted her glass to mine three more times. It was then I realized *dom bay* was a toast and something she must have learned from her foster dad. *"Dom bay,"* I whispered back as I raised my glass to hers.

After processing the final papers in Guangzhou, the time came for us to return home. The return trip lasted thirty hours, including a night in Hong Kong, a flight to Tokyo and then on to New York. At last, ChowChow and I were home, alone, together. Thus we started our new life as a family, she in her corner and I in mine, waiting for any sign of acceptance.

The first challenge was overcoming the time difference and jet lag. I am not exaggerating when I say it took us three and a half weeks to get on a routine. Because I was on my own, I slept when she slept and was awake when she was awake. I realized I would get back to normal when she had finally adjusted. In the meantime it was a challenge to keep my daughter busy, yet somewhat quiet, from 3:30 A.M. until 7:00 A.M. when my neighbors would be rising to get ready for work.

Our middle-of-the-night games included dropping coins into an empty plastic milk jug (eyes closed for more intrigue) or washing dishes. I soon found that ChowChow loved playing with water and especially washing dishes. In fact, she loved it so much and it kept her attention for so long that some 3 A.M. mornings found us washing the same dishes over and over again, five and six times, lost in the hypnotic rhythm.

I took three months off from work to be with my new daughter. We soon settled into a pattern of watching *Barney* and *Sesame Street,* reading word books and playing. Lunch was followed by naptime (I couldn't wait for this; I took one too). After that it was off to the playground on her tricycle, a stop at the ice cream shop (her sense of direction was immediate and acute), a video tape while I prepared dinner, a bath, story-time and then lights out.

During the first two weeks, she never stopped repeating the names of her foster family. She followed the neighbors to their front doors and cried when I tried to bring her home. I came to realize that the road to bonding was going to take a long, long time. But now I was mentally and emotionally prepared for it. This child was so precious, so bright and so personable, with a sense of humor beyond compare and a smile that would light a ballroom. I was ready to keep trying if it took a lifetime.

Then very early one morning as I lay half asleep in my bed next to hers, I heard a little voice say "Mommy." Into my bed she crawled, and she snuggled to get close. I felt my own tears running down my face as I realized the bonding, however slight, had begun. I never remember being so happy. She must have seen my wet face from the glow of the nightlight, for she cocked her little head to the side and murmured a questioning "Hmm?" I shook my head and said, "It's okay, these are happy tears." Within a minute, she was fast asleep. I savored the moment and held her in my arms until she woke again in the morning light.

February 24, 2000, marked the sixth-month anniversary of our family. The bonding continues in so many ways. It is a beautiful process, especially with a child who remembers her past. I can see now that acceptance is not something meant to happen overnight, or in a day or month, but that it takes a lifetime. I believe one's bonding should never be thought of as completed. I want ours always to be growing, not necessarily in giant steps, but in the small, steady patter of feet, building and building all the time.

Every day is a joy. Helen, as she is called by her teachers and new friends, has been enrolled in preschool since December and attends

Mandarin classes once a week. She seems to be thriving. Every night when we're together, I marvel at what she has learned that day. There is artwork on my refrigerator, tea parties on Saturdays and Sundays (you're all invited), and every day, over and over, I hear "Mommy, Mommy." Who could ever tire of that?

♥

CHAPTER SIX

Experiencing Fatherhood

E-Mails from Ekaterinburg

Walter Anderson

August 27 Re: I'm home

Friends, well-wishers and bewildered onlookers,

Just a quick e-mail to let you know I've returned from Russia, where on Tuesday I filed the legal papers asking to be installed as Papa to the world's most angelic human being, tiny Oleg, who if a Russian court approves will become Theodore Oleg Anderson later this year. By coincidence, Tuesday was also his third birthday.

Oleg loves his toy cars and playing on the swing, and he can sing his little heart out in a manner that irresistibly steals away the heart of even a roughened cynic like his prospective papa. He is also good-hearted enough not to laugh at my attempts to speak to him in Russian.

Now begins the long wait, perhaps six to eight weeks or even longer, before I make a second trip to Russia for the court proceedings and copious paperwork that will (I hope) result in my bringing this admirable little person back on the plane to begin a new life as an American boy.

October 24 Re: Court Date

I'm happy to report that after worse-than-usual delays, I've been given my court date to come back to Russia to complete the adoption of little Theodore Oleg. Most likely I'll leave around November 12 and return, accompanied by America's newest citizen, around December 4, but everything might change. Cross your fingers. . . .

October 31 Re: Delays for Dad

My agency said I ran into some paperwork delays because of the single-dad business. But another family I talked to said that they heard a judge in Ekat was sick or indisposed and that many families' paperwork had therefore been delayed. I was told to show up a week in advance because the judge wants to be sure I really, really know what I'm getting into—the single-dad skepticism again. I don't mind the added time exactly, because seeing Oleg again is what I want to do most in the world.

I've been nervous at times, like everyone, being a single dad aged forty-eight, a first-time parent, having to deal with mysterious bureaucratic requirements. But for me, all doubt vanished once I had a chance to see and get to know Oleg, the most wonderful child I could imagine. And it's been inspiring to visit with several families hereabouts in New York who've adopted from Ekaterinburg, and see how their children are thriving.

November 18 Re: Oleg's wild side

Sorry I haven't written in a while. I'm in Russia now, but Net access has been really dreadful. It looks as if the main chance is going to be in the early morning. This morning, however, the streets were a sheet of newly frozen ice, and I didn't dare venture out. I am stealing an hour at lunch.

Well, it didn't take removing him from the orphanage to bring out Oleg's wild side. Saturday afternoon he began to seriously test limits, as they say, and then Sunday morning was just a constant effort to keep him under control as he threw balls around randomly, kicked wildly, threw his books on the floor, hit me once or twice laughingly, tried to grab my glasses and generally saw what he could get away with. It was exhausting. Sunday afternoon he went back to being just the sweetest, most affectionate little guy and spent forty-five minutes wrapped up in a little pegboard game I bought him. He hugged me and looked adorable. As for this morning: first half pretty good, second half pretty bad. Welcome to parenthood, I guess.

He seems to really enjoy roughhousing and likes to draw me into it, and I often respond to his naughty initiatives with some vigorous activity to distract him. The intervention of a caretaker typically leads him to resume passive good-boy behavior. He continues to get more verbal and to name animals, etc., with less hesitation.

The clothes I brought him fit very well. The caretaker said, *"Conechno doch illi tyetye"* (assuredly a daughter or aunt [helped me]). I have concluded there is a widespread suspicion that I am fronting for a woman who is the one who "really" wants to adopt but for some reason cannot.

Heavy snow Sunday, and translator Slava and I built a little snowman. Oleg really wanted to destroy it with his snow shovel and was disappointed that I only let him tear off a little of the arm. A curious thing: I made snowballs and called for Oleg to watch as I three times threw a snowball at a brick wall and left a white mark. Each time he ran up to me and buried his face in my lap, little-boy style. I think he must have seen it as an assertion of power—Daddy can do strong things so I'll go to him for protection, something like that.

The streets are a sheet of ice, and it is still dark as night at 8 A.M. Winter has set in in earnest, and they say it will last until the end of April.

They tell me I am in good shape for court Thursday at 9 A.M. The orphanage director quizzed me on Oleg's diagnoses and what I planned to do about them, and they said I gave very good answers.

It's curious that he sometimes now seems to understand the sense of what I say in English, especially the commands. Is he getting the words yet, or is it my body language, or what? I gave him the little silver bell from Carrie and Chip's wedding and repeated the word "bell" several times. He said, unmistakably, "bell." Of course he still ignores a high percentage of the commands, understood or not.

November 21   Re: Proudest New Papa in Ekaterinburg

Just a note from one of the Internet cafés in Ekaterinburg to say that the city has its newest and proudest papa. This morning, after a court hearing that I believe was unusually long and searching—I still think a single mother would meet with far less skepticism—the judge pronounced me the new father of Theodore Oleg Anderson, aged three and a quarter. I will spend the ten-day wait delightedly helping him prepare for the transition to his new life in America.

When we get home, it'll be time to adopt another cat. We are going to need one with a play-fiend type of personality to keep up with Theodore Oleg's incredible appetite for play.

What a merry spirit he was yesterday afternoon. (I hadn't seen him in the morning, because of court.) He didn't seem consciously aware of the change—I told him several times *"Sutka skazal ya tvoi papa"* (The judge said I'm your daddy) to no visible effect—but he sang his little heart out on the swing, facing the painted images of a cat and dog on the playground walls, with alternating verses about *"keeka" (kiska)* and *"babaka" (sabaka)* and what sounded like Russian versions of meow and woof effects. When we came inside he smiled a whole lot, proposed games, made better eye contact and had the energy only of one wild horse, rather than a whole pack.

November 22 Re: Saturday morning Oleg observations

Oleg and I are both stopped and congratulated in the halls of the orphanage by a steady stream of different caretakers. I have been repeatedly told that my adoption is considered special, that the orphanage was "pulling for" Oleg to find a family before he had to leave. Lara, the orphanage director, graciously accepted my gift bag, modeled the Nordstrom scarf and said the question she couldn't get over was: Why was I single?

Oleg really loves the talking photo album. Yesterday in the music room he stopped at the picture of our living room and pointed to the picture of the piano. Then he pointed across the room at the physical piano. He didn't have words for it, but his excitement at making the identification shone out. I asked *"Kto ana?"* (Who's she?) of the picture of Karin and he said *"tyotya"* rather distinctly. So we've got him identifying *baba* and *tyotya* (grandma and aunt).

Almost everyone has said something about how he appears to be a "different child" than he was before my arrival—far more animated, smiling, energetic, laughing, more verbal, etc. Slava said, "It makes a difference when a child is taken off the shelf." The caretakers say he now sprinkles his talk back in the gruppa with non-Russian words that they assume are English. He is getting better at imitating English words when I ask him to repeat them. Yesterday we began venturing into "let's pretend" and "silly" territory. I "hid" (making sure he could see part of me) and he erupted in howls of laughter, and then ran past me to provoke a chase. When I saw him doing a silly walk, I immediately imitated it with a similar silly walk. More gales of laughter from him. I can see that silly/pretend is going to be a fertile field for us to work.

I learn to use more Russian every day, too. *"Spakoina"* (calm down) and *"podozhdi"* (wait) are real lifesavers.

November 24   Re: Crime, disobedience, hunger, winter

We (including Oleg) suffered a crime yesterday. I had paid my morning visit and we stopped at the local shopping area near his orphanage to buy some medicines, books and candies. When we got back Volodya's (our driver) white Zhiguli car had been broken into and ransacked. His radio was gone, apparently his only loss but a dire one financially to him ($150, I am told). So was my toy bag, with all of Oleg's favorite toys. This at high noon while parked on the main street of a busy shopping district.

The toys are replaceable; what I really miss is the talking photo album that Oleg loved most to play with, pushing the buttons to get my voice. Now I have no picture of the house, Fanny [cat], Mom, etc., to review with him over the two weeks ahead.

I will probably offer to replace Volodya's radio instead of giving him less useful gifts such as a tie. Don't know if he'll accept it, though. They feel bad.

Oleg is no longer the perfectly obedient little boy of yore. I think one reason is that, lacking in-depth Russian to reason with him, my main way of correcting disobedience is to walk over and pick him up and take him to where he is supposed to be.

However, being chased, wrestled and roughhoused with also happens to be his favorite activity, so disobeying is the ideal way to get more of it. So now when I ask him to come here or sit down I not infrequently get noncompliance coupled with eye contact and this huge anticipatory smile of delight as he dares me to come over and wrestle him.

I am now bringing a few cookies for him each visit, having been told that the orphanage staff has less leverage to boss me around on this. (On my second day an orphanage doctor had emerged on the playground to instruct me not to bring Oleg food.) He is just so hungry and devours the food so greedily. The poor little guy. I can't wait to get him safely home.

This morning was the first really chilly, piercing wind, and the first time I actually was glad to be wearing the thermal underwear. I am now officially sick of the Russian winter. Dima said he likes his city best in the summer, when it is green, and winter, when it is white, and worst in the spring and fall, when it is awash in dirty slush. It is true that with a new snowfall the city looks immensely improved.

November 26 Re: Oleg's first tantrum

"Time out" is said to be especially effective with active kids like Oleg who feel keenly that sitting quietly with no toy is a deprivation in itself. The rule of thumb is that a time out lasts one minute for each year of the child's chronological age. With Oleg, I find that for most purposes I come up with the right toys and parenting methods, as well as the right clothes, by assuming that he is two instead of three. So I don't plan to make him be quiet in time out for more than two minutes. It does take willpower, on my part rather than his—I felt that I was being accused of the cruelties of Bluebeard for having insisted that he *sedeesh spakoina* (sit quietly).

November 30 Re: Companeros

A couple from Madrid is adopting one of Oleg's mates from Gruppa #8, little Seryozha, who is just learning to walk. There is kind of a bond between us because of that. The husband calls Oleg and Seryozha *"companeros."*

One of Oleg's attendants stopped me yesterday and had me summon my translator. She was taking the next couple of days off, and this was going to be the evening she would have to take her leave of

Oleg. She said she had cared for him greatly and asked that I take the best care of him. *"Conechno,"* I said. It was touching.

November 30   Re: Circus

Oleg was pretty good at the circus Friday, considering its duration. The animal acts were his favorite, but his attention wandered during some acts that depend on our knowledge of how tough the feat is (gymnast sitting on his hand on a pole, etc.). But no crying or fussing. He did relentlessly kick the seat in front of him, which I could cure only by putting him on my lap so he kicked my leg instead. He was puzzled by popcorn at first but soon was devouring it greedily, but he never did develop an interest in their white (untinted) cotton candy.

During intermission, Oleg refused to use the unfamiliar toilet facilities at the circus. Second half of show, he sat in my lap throughout. The show ended. *Mocri* (wet) Oleg, and *mocri* Daddy's entire lap too. *C'est la vie.* I don't really care about being made *mocri*, but I do worry that this is going to continue at airports etc. in the coming week. Maybe I buy a potty and lug it with me in my carry-on at all times? Is this what real parents do? What will I do when Tuesday comes and there's no escaping that I am a real parent?

Many people are remarking on Oleg's skill in imitating English words. I pointed to the picture of skyscrapers yesterday and said "New York." "Neoo Yawk," he said convincingly. Yesterday came his first unmistakable two-word English phrase not the result of direct imitation: "Daddy cookie," as he pointed to my supply. No more tantrums since the pair of them a few days ago, just laughing, smiling and play. He has begun running ahead of me in the corridors rather than side-by-side, shouting and laughing.

Yesterday morning, when I proposed "Horsey ride?" he promptly assumed the correct position in front of me with his back turned so that I could lift him.

December 1   Re: Reading

I guess I was wrong in thinking that watching Seryozha's new family might pain Oleg. He observed them yesterday and was happy. He even was content while I read Seryozha a little of *Repka*. I think he's secure with me now and realizes I'm not going to pick some other boy to be daddy to. Incidentally, it is more or less impossible to read Oleg a story since he wants to be in control of the book and turn/examine the pages at his own pace, which may be backward and upside down (he still recognizes the pictures). Little Seryozha, far more passive, was happy to let me hold the book.

Will be really glad to get home. The ten days have run out, so presumably we are legally secure now. Countdown: six more days. Home soon!

♥

From Kolomna, with Love

John O'Neill

As our first summer together comes to a close, it seems like so long ago that we were just dreaming of being a family of three, and yet it's also hard to believe our son has only been with us since the end of March. There's a sweet irony in the fact that the whole process took exactly nine months. The fear, anxiety and reams of paperwork seem to have belonged to some other couple, not to us. The process brought out our individual strengths while at the same time we really had to work as a team. Cathy's organizational skills and my patience definitely helped things run smoother.

Once the paperwork was done, we spent a good deal of our time trying to learn as much as we could about Russia: its culture, its history and a smidgen of its language. We felt like two eighteen-wheelers on the information highway. We bought, were given and borrowed books, and then we waited.

Our families and friends were with us every step of the way, offering support and lending their ears day or night. We wondered why we were so lucky. Did everyone get so much from his or her loved ones? Were they in awe of what we were trying to do? Was it the fact that we were traveling halfway around the world to find our child that made those around us root for us? Was it that everyone wanted to get in on doing some good? I think it's all of the above.

By the time we received the call that our son was waiting for us in Kolomna, about seventy-five miles southeast of Moscow, the Russian government had made it mandatory for foreign adopting parents to make two trips instead of only one. Going across town for us is a big trip, but we had a child to bring home, so we forged ahead. Our translator, Irene, and Juri, our driver, met us at the airport. Shortly thereafter we met Tatyana, who would be our guide through the various government agencies and ministries. We quickly learned to place our utmost trust in these people.

Our first order of business was to go to the Ministry of Education to officially receive permission to visit Kolomna. Once that was accomplished, we set out on the two-hour drive to meet Matthew Aleksei for the very first time. The anticipation we felt was indescribable. All we could do was hold hands tightly, try to take in some of the Russian landscape and remember to breathe. Kolomna is a small city founded in the early 1100s. The Children's Home is off the main road leading into Kolomna, and although it houses 105 children, it is unnervingly quiet. In the daytime most of the lights are off, but the colorful murals that line the walls are soothing and warm.

We were brought to an office with a view of a monastery across a barren field. Just as we started to hang up our coats, the door opened, and there he was in the arms of a smiling grandmotherly looking doctor: a boy with beautiful green eyes, and, as they say, the look of an old soul. We were in love.

For the next four days we drove to Kolomna from Moscow and spent the four hours between his morning nap and his afternoon nap feeding him, reading to him and just holding him. Although he was a bit weak, he was happy to show us what he could do. He could turn over in his crib. He could crawl and was inquisitive about almost everything, from the designs on our sweaters to my dive watch. He shared a nursery with nine other babies. It broke our hearts knowing that we couldn't bring them all home, but maybe, by taking just

Matthew home, the other children would receive a bit more care and attention.

Our last day in Kolomna was heart-wrenching. Matthew was running a low-grade fever, probably caused by teething. He was pale and somewhat listless. As he slept in Cathy's arms, we knew he was already home. When the moment came to leave without him, it was all we could do to keep from outwardly breaking down. Our emotions did not go unnoticed by the director of the Children's Home. She complimented us by telling us that we behaved admirably and that Matthew would be well-cared for. We knew that Matthew would indeed be well taken care of, and we realized that we were in a country where life, for most, was an everyday struggle and that hardship must be faced with one's head held high.

The next month at home without Matthew lasted a lifetime. We kept one clock on New York time and one on Moscow time. We spent countless hours looking at the pictures and video we took. We finished preparing his nursery—and we waited once more. Then Cathy and I received the call from Ruthie, a social worker at the Alliance for Children, that we had been given a court date that was even earlier than we had anticipated. Somehow we managed to get ourselves together and book a direct flight to Moscow in only two days. It seemed like more than enough time.

We had a lot more to do this time around. Having a pretty good idea of what kind of emotional and physical whirlwind we were about to embark upon, Cathy and I followed our gut feeling and chose to stay in our translator's apartment, which was a wise choice. We spent the first three days traveling to Kolomna to fulfill the required amount of time the Russian government mandated for prospective parents.

On our last trip, we had left Matthew with a rattle cube with our pictures on each side in the hopes that our smiles would remain with him in our absence. As we made our way back to Kolomna, we wondered if he would remember us. Once again, we had barely settled in when Matthew and the same gentle doctor entered the room. It took no more than a moment or two before he was comfortably nestled in Cathy's lap. When it was my turn to hold him, he reached out and rolled up my sleeve to see if I was still wearing my watch. Although we would have rather just been able to bring him home the moment we first laid eyes upon him, perhaps spending a few days at a time with him in the only home that he knew was not such a bad way for our bonds to be formed.

Now it was crunch time. Our small team went from one government building to another in preparation for our court hearing. We seemed to be moving at warp speed with an occasional stop to do a tourist thing or two. We knew that our future as a family would be in someone else's hands, and we knew that we had to be prepared to present ourselves as a couple who could and would give Matthew the kind of home every child deserves.

The court was in Moscow. Tatyana (who acted as our translator), the social worker whom we first met in Kolomna, a prosecutor, the court stenographer and the judge filled the courtroom. The judge was stern, and yet, like all the rest of us in the room, she really cared for the welfare of our Matthew. After half an hour of questions, she granted us custody and our prayers were answered. We were officially a family.

We returned to Kolomna for the last time before finishing up all the work we needed to do to enable Matthew to leave Russia. We found it to be an almost impossible task to express our gratitude to those who look after and give their love to the children. They, along with our guides and the staff at the Alliance, truly do the work of angels.

Our joy in having Matthew as our son is shared by so many, especially those who know of the journey we have taken to create our family. We are not the adoptive parents of years gone by who were often beatified and pitied at the same time. When Matthew is ready, it will be his story to tell—and hey, who doesn't like a good love story?

♥

The Miracle

Joel Barrera

For my wife Mari, adoption seemed natural and right. It just took me three years longer than Mari to figure this out.

When Mari's biological clock started ticking, I was unsure if I was ready for children. When she began frequenting the doctor's office to find out why we were having difficulty conceiving a child, I wasn't thrilled with having a doctor poking and prodding me, and Mari was adamantly opposed to fertility drugs. Mari longed to adopt a child, but I fretted about the costs involved in adoption.

Men are like that—slow to engage in emotionally wrenching decisions. Eventually, however, I grew accustomed to the idea of adoption, after talking to friends and family members who had adopted, reading articles and books, and attending adoption seminars.

Soon Mari and I will celebrate our first "Gotcha Day" with our beautiful daughter, Milagros Otalia Margarita Barrera. Her name is a mouthful, but every name has meaning. Milagros is Spanish for "miracles," which she has been in our lives. Milagros is the first of more than twenty grandchildren to carry the name Otalia—my mother's name. Margarita is the name given her at the Ecuadorean orphanage, after the wonderful woman who supervises it. And Barrera, because she is now part of our family forever.

At last year's Adoptive Parent Open Door Society conference, we were trying to make a final decision about adoption and had already begun exploring agencies. That day we met a couple who had just begun a home study with an agency in Massachusetts, and our new acquaintances Mark and Jana gave high praise to the agency's social workers. They especially shared their excitement about the Ecuador program. Within weeks, we were invited to a reunion of Ecuadoran families with a director from a private nursery in Ecuador.

I remember the shock of seeing more than fifty families who came on short notice to hear from the director, Maria Jose. Kids were everywhere, and the director remembered them all. I speak Spanish, so I struck up a conversation with Maria Jose, who asked us whether we were interested in a boy or a girl. I told her that Mari, who had longed for a child for so many years, would like to start with a girl. Immediately, Maria Jose told us about a pretty and healthy girl, Margarita, who had just come to the orphanage in Quito a few days before.

The decision itself had been years in the making, but in the end our minds were made up on the spot, right there at that reception. Our home study was completed in record time, and shortly thereafter we had Milagros's picture. For a week, Mari took it with her from room to room in the house. Five days before we were scheduled to travel to Quito, the volcano Pichincha erupted a few miles from the orphanage and stopped all international flights into the city. We flew to the Ecuadoran coast and then caught the last domestic flight into Quito.

In a unique arrangement, we were able to spend two weeks in Quito living in the nursery and getting to know the caretakers. We ate authentic Ecuadoran food, cooked elaborate meals with the staff and learned a few recipes from Milagros. We learned Milagros's daily routine and diet. We played soccer, sang and read books with the children of the nursery. But most of all, we spent quiet hours and days with Milagros, falling in love.

The caretakers clearly loved the children. Milagros's primary caretaker was Amparo, whose name means "shelter." Amparo was a kind woman, but she was also guarded and jealous of us because we had come to take Milagros to her new home in another country. Amparo began to see how much we loved her little girl, and that Milagros would be safe and happy with us. One night, in the stairwell of the orphanage, Amparo gave us her blessing to be Milagros's parents. Mari and Amparo broke down and cried and held each other on the stairs, a bond brought through our mutual love for our little miracle. The scene will always be with me.

The miracles keep on coming every day, every week. We have opened our world to the new experience of parenthood, and to the special gifts and responsibilities of an international adoption. We are part of a community here. We recently had an Ecuadoran picnic at our home, and families with children from Ecuador came. Mark and Jana brought Camila, who has become so verbal. Rafael, a toddler in Quito, was adopted by friends who live less than one mile from us. Another small boy, Carlitos, has learned English in just a few months and changed his obsession from bouncing rubber balls to ice hockey. And Paola, who is six, found a home with a family nearby and has a teenage sister who was adopted from Ecuador more than ten years ago.

As I watch Milagros thrive and grow, I am fascinated by how young children constantly push themselves, developing new skills and showing little fear with new situations. As adults, too often we lose that sense of self-development and seek to stay in zones of emotional comfort. In my mind, our infertility was a blessing. It forced us into an uncomfortable and awkward emotional space and made us grow, in the end, as people and parents.

♥

Waiting for Mei Mei

Bruce Covey

Last month, JingJing's friend Hannah Rose gave her a set of circular foam puzzles, each composed of three little shapes. Now the pieces turn up everywhere—two purple parallelograms in bed, red stars in the pockets of her pants, a blue triangle in the car. Usually very adept at puzzles, JingJing can take these apart but cannot put them back together. They continue to spread throughout the house like buttercups, things we wish for but can't control.

Waiting for Mei Mei (our nickname for our soon-to-be second daughter) seems so much easier, deceptively so. When we were waiting for JingJing, Kate and I always had some ritual to perform—going to a movie, driving around in the car, or when we really "missed" her, shopping for little dresses or T-shirts in some future size. We created a checklist of tasks—buying a rug for her room, painting the changing table, baby proofing, plus buying a carseat and a highchair and a stroller. I wondered whether I could properly engage in the elaborate chemistry of mixing formula, whether I could change a diaper, rock her to sleep.

We think every day about what Mei Mei will be like—what her laugh will sound like, what her favorite color will be, whether she'll wear dresses (JingJing won't go near them)—and how JingJing will react to a sister. One morning she tells her classmates in preschool, "I'm going to be a good big sister soon," right before she says, "Have you heard of Popsicles? They're amazing!" But the few necessary and practical tasks this time, such as buying a two-girl stroller and clearing additional space in the house, seem strangely simple. *Can we do them after we get the referral?* We're busy with daily things, less ritualistic than before—back and forth to work and school, dinner, cleaning up toys and puzzle pieces. *Are we overconfident now?*

It's too painful to think of Mei Mei waiting somewhere for us, not knowing our names, we not knowing hers. We know from our first experience that she's being treated well and is in a great space, but the red thread connecting us still seems infinitely long, too intricate a line to make a telephone call on. We play the name game to pass the time and distance, ponder over a multitude of possibilities, each beautiful but impossible to put a face to. We spent two years deciding that Violet would be the right name for our first, but we call her (and she calls herself) JingJing, from JiJing, her middle, given name. "Jing" means quiet and calm, which we all are trying to be during these slow months. *If we sit still enough, will Mei Mei come faster?*

JingJing plays the name game too, but she plays with us instead of her sister. Last week, with the kind of grand irony only a two-year-old can muster, she announced that her name was no longer JingJing, but "Telephone." She renamed me "Pig"—after Piglet in Pooh, I hope—but quickly changed it to "Turtle," perhaps observing my feigned dismay. She renamed Kate "Key." Yesterday, on the way home from school, she said my name was now "Mama" and Mama's name was now "Bruce Alan Covey." She is learning the full names of all eleven of her classmates. And she named her "baby," a realistic-looking Asian doll, Mei Mei. Today, she hunched her shoulders over a four-inch-by-four-inch square of paper and meticulously, one scratch at a time, tried to write her doll/sister's name with a red pen, an intricate set of swirls. We help JingJing differentiate between "Doll Mei Mei" and "Real Mei Mei," as if the concept of a sister-to-be could be real to a two-year-old, albeit a sharp one. "Do you want to give Doll Mei Mei some milk? Will you share your stroller with Real Mei Mei? Is she hungry or restless?"

So how can we make sense of it all? This wait, of course, isn't really any easier than it was for JingJing; we're just so much more adept at embracing distraction. And the joys of JingJing outnumber the raindrops pouring from the sky this morning like kitty cats and puppy dogs. We see, hear, feel flashes everywhere we go—like pieces of a puzzle, impossible to assemble. She hasn't come to me in my dreams. I see only the shapes, the concepts, nothing I can put a name to.

It's October now. Over the last four weeks we've celebrated the Autumn Moon festival, my birthday and our Family Day. I can't believe it's been two years. I send a note to our friend Zhu Li, one of our guides in Nanjing. Every day, JingJing says she "wants to talk about China," to hear a story. We saw a Hong Kong action film on TV tonight. Our Mandarin is getting better, able to sing some songs now. Like glaciers, we seem to be edging ever closer to our daughters' birthplace, the land we love.

Someone from one of our listservs writes to say she's heard that December referrals are definitely in the review room. Although, as experienced adoptive parents, we put no stock in rumors, our expectations rise like balloons. Even my metaphors draw together but still don't fit quite properly. *Is someone inscribing our names together, parents,* jie jie, *and second daughter? Are we almost close enough to call her on the telephone now, send her a letter? What do we call her now? What is her name?*

♥

Bringing Home Sara

Howard Cooper

Should we stay or should we go? Are we crazy?

I am driving in my car, battling traffic and internal dialogue. My wife, Jane, and I have been talking, for what seems an eternity, about getting on an airplane and traveling to Bogotá, Colombia, to adopt a baby girl. We can't wait to do so. We can't wait to bring her home. We want to go. We have decided to go. We will go. But. But Bogotá is the most dangerous city in South America. The State Department warns Americans not to travel there and tells us not to bother calling if we are kidnapped. The U.S. government doesn't negotiate with terrorists, we are told. *Are we nuts? Should we stay or should we go?* These are decisions that we shouldn't overanalyze, ones that have no clear answer. There are strong arguments for each side of the question, and no one can tell you what the right choice is.

It is evening. Jane and I and our five-year-old daughter, Hope, are having dinner. "Daddy, how long will you be in Colombia?" I answer: "Oh, not too long. Maybe a few weeks." "Is it dangerous there?" I don't answer directly. I avoid the question. Inside my head The Clash have begun to sing again. I think, *My life is great. I am relatively safe here at home. I love my wife and daughter. We have a good life. Do I want to take a chance of messing this up?* The questions don't leave my head until I fall asleep.

Later in the week I am watching television. Jane is at the computer. It is late. There is no song in my head. I start watching a movie. It is called *Proof of Life*. It looks interesting. I start watching. It is about an American captured by rebels in Colombia. The American, appropriately defiant but scared witless nevertheless, is extricated from his Saab (I drive a Saab) and marched through the mountains for a few months while being periodically tortured. I don't want to be tortured, separated from my family. I say to my wife, "Hey Jane, come watch this with me." She does.

Jane has to come with me the first week to start the adoption process in Colombia. We will travel by separate airplanes to Bogotá. She will come home after a week so that Hope is not without one of us for any longer than that. Jane turns to me and says, "Are we crazy? Is the risk worth it? Should we really go?" I can barely hear her. The music now pulsating is too loud in my head. I am getting sick of the song, but I cannot stop hearing it in my head over and over again. I wonder if I will have the guts or the savvy to escape from the rebels like the kidnapped American does in the movie. I also wonder if anyone will offer to pay any ransom for me if I am kidnapped.

I realize that the only family member I know who speaks Spanish is my five-year-old daughter, Hope. For a moment, I toy with the idea of suggesting to Jane that we bring her, just in case one of us gets kidnapped. As late as it is, this thought doesn't seem too strange. Thankfully for the sake of my marriage, I abandon it without ever opening my mouth.

Sometimes you have to make up your mind because time has run out. You're faced with a decision and there's no more time to consider options. It is now a matter of saying "yes" or "no." There's no option of "maybe." The time has come. *Will I stay or will I go?*

And then, leap of faith taken, caution thrown to the wind, we are there. We are in Colombia. We are at the orphanage in Bogotá. And we have just been handed our new baby daughter. We have named her Sara Julia after two of our grandmothers. She is beautiful. Jane is holding her. I am trying to take pictures so that we can show Hope later, so I can always remember the moment. I relive the feeling I had only one other time in my life: the moment the doctor handed me Hope. The moment is incredible. Our baby daughter is incredible. I am a new dad again. I look at Jane looking down in wonder. I look at Sara looking up at her new mother in wonder. I remember to snap a few more pictures. Then it is my turn to hold my new daughter. *How could I have even considered not being here?*

There are no questions in my head now as I gaze into my daughter's eyes. *Of course you go.* If I could have seen the face of my new daughter, I would have known instantly. Yet at this moment I am looking only at Sara, as she looks back up at me, and I know the voice of reason didn't help me get here—it was instinct or a higher power that brought me to Sara.

♥

A Letter to My Son on
His Twenty-Seventh Birthday

Dr. Timothy Johnson

D ear Son:

Your mother and I went to Indonesia for approximately three months during the summer of 1968 with the financial support of the Smith Kline fellowship program, which was designed to expose American medical students (and their spouses if they were in the medical field) to medical work in underdeveloped foreign countries. As part of the program, we had to pick a country and arrange our own medical supervision—that is, arrange for certified local physicians to supervise our work. (I was between my third and fourth years of medical school and therefore was not yet licensed as a doctor.) After a lot of discussion about many medical missionaries that Mother and I knew in various parts of the world, we decided on Indonesia, mostly because it was a part of the world we knew very little about, and because Dr. Phil Anderson, a Covenant missionary, enthusiastically agreed to be our sponsor.

So, in the late spring of 1968, we set off on what was to become not only a medical adventure, but a totally unexpected family adventure. We flew from New York City via Seattle to Tokyo, where we spent several delightful days as guests of Covenant missionaries in that city. Then we flew—with stops in Thailand and Malaysia—to Djakarta, the capital city of Indonesia, on the island of Java. (Indonesia is a country of thousands of islands scattered along the equator; it has the fourth-largest population of all the countries of this Earth.) While flying over Vietnam, during the height of the war, we could actually see the smoke from bomb explosions on the ground below us.

Arriving in Djakarta was true culture shock. As we departed from the airport, we drove along dirt roads with natives squatting along the side tending their lanterns and meager possessions. We soon found ourselves in the midst of a bustling city with people jamming the streets—and thousands crammed along the canals. We saw extreme poverty in the midst of obscene wealth, like nothing we had ever seen before. After an overnight at a missionary compound in the city, we were ready to board our flight to Monado, the capital city of the island of north Celebes (as the island was then known) at the northernmost tip of Indonesia, actually closer to the Philippine islands than to the southern islands of Indonesia. We had to arrive at the Djakarta airport at three in the morning for a flight that finally left many hours later. The plane was an old and rickety two-engine piston plane from World War II; it rattled and rocked and rolled, but in those days I wasn't afraid of flying so I considered it quite an adventure!

As we stepped off the plane in Monado, we quickly realized that we were in the middle of a very different climate and environment. The climate was considerably cooler because we were much farther north of the equator, and the surroundings were much more rural and much less hectic. We were met at the airport by the Andersons (Dr. Phil and Irene), and we soon started our approximately forty-five-minute journey, winding up the road into the small mountain village of Tomohon, where we were to spend the next several months. (On the way up, as Mother and I both vividly remember, Dr. Anderson joked about having a little boy all picked out for us; we didn't pay any attention to him because the idea of starting a family, even by adoption, was not at all on our minds.)

As we arrived in Tomohon, we found ourselves in still another very different environment. This was definitely a rural village, surrounded by farmland, with a very small-town feel. The hospital we were to work at—Bethesda Hospital—was right in the middle of town on the main (dirt) street. We were quickly introduced to Dr. Bert Supit, the Indonesian doctor in charge of the hospital, and then to our living quarters, which were a set of rooms in a hospital-owned building right across the street from the hospital. (The hospital was owned and operated by a church group that had been started in the days of the Dutch missionaries, then taken over by the natives when the Dutch left after World War II.) I could write for hours about our experiences at the hospital and in the country of Indonesia, but since this writing is focused on your adoption, I will now tell that story in more detail.

I met you for the first time the very next day when making my first rounds at the hospital with Dr. Anderson. You were a chubby, cute and outgoing little boy of eighteen months. You were in the spare pediatric ward of the hospital—dark with few windows, cement floor, wooden boards for a bed—because you had been found abandoned on the front porch of the hospital a few weeks before our arrival, suffering from some worm infestation and some mild lung problems. You were now doing much better, and you stood out from most of the children in the ward because of your personality. I started playing with you each day as I made my rounds, sometimes offering you chocolate as a bribe to play.

One day, several weeks after our arrival, Mother and I were going to a birthday party for one of the Indonesian nurses. As we were leaving the hospital, I noticed you playing in front of the hospital so I introduced you to Mother, and we decided we should bring you with us to the party. After the party, we decided to bring you back to our little apartment, mostly to give you a bath because you were quite dirty from playing without clothes (the kids in Tomohon at that time typically didn't start wearing clothes until closer to school age). That night, we gave you a bath, went to a little store nearby to buy you some shoes and a few clothes, and spent most of the night playing with you. We all had a wonderful time, and when it was time to take you back to the hospital, we decided you should sleep overnight with us—I would take you back in the morning when I went to work. (I remember that you didn't want us to take your shoes off, so you slept with them on that night.)

The next morning, as we sat having breakfast, we were all having such a good time that Mother and I looked at each other, started talking about what was going to happen to you (going into the orphanage associated with the hospital) and realized we didn't want that to happen—and then realized that meant we should adopt you, and we quickly decided that was exactly what we should do. So that's how it all began! From that moment on, you were our son just as surely as if you had been born to us. It was truly amazing how quickly we all bonded with each other!

We soon arranged for a crib in our bedroom (with mosquito netting over all the beds to protect against malaria) and for some simple toys and a high chair for you to eat in. (And did you ever eat—everything and anything!) You quickly became the focus of our lives, going everywhere with us, including to the hospital during the day when we worked. Then, one Sunday afternoon just a few weeks later, our happy lives were interrupted by a knock at the door from an Indonesian young lady about seventeen years old. Through an interpreter, we quickly learned that she was your biological mother. She proceeded to tell us that she had been in a common-law marriage when you were born and that your biological father had left shortly after your birth.

She had taken care of you until just a few months before, but when she could no longer breast-feed you, she had brought you to your father—who said he would take care of you but who instead left you on the hospital porch. She had just heard that you were in the hospital and had come to find out how you were.

Well, as you can imagine, we were in a state of shock. Our first thought and fear was that she would want you back. But when we explained what had happened and that we wanted to adopt you, she quickly agreed that would be the best for you. She was thrilled at the idea of your growing up in America. She came to visit most Sunday afternoons after that and was at the airport to say good-bye the day we left for Djakarta. I honestly believe that she cared very much for you and about you—and that her caring included the willingness to give you wider opportunities than she could. (Obviously, I cannot say the same about your biological father; I only met him once—very briefly—when we asked him to sign some papers that we thought we might need for your legal adoption when we returned to America.)

Now we had to start the legal process of getting you into the United States. Because there was no legal process at that time in Indonesia for adoption, we made up some papers on our own to be signed by your biological parents and the chief of the village where you were born. I then made a special trip to Djakarta to start the naturalization process with the U.S. Immigration Service through the American embassy in Djakarta. I discovered that I had to get some documents (such as a marriage license) from the States, so I had to call my father in Illinois, who in turn called Mother's father in Brockton, who then drove to our apartment in Albany to get the needed papers. (At that time, the only way to call the United States was via a so-called radio phone, which used radio waves and was available only for one hour each night at the embassy. I was very lucky to get through to my father the first night—and you can imagine how surprised they all were to hear of our plans!) I did not know it until we got back to the States, but my father also called our congressman at the time—John Anderson, who later ran for president—and he contacted the Immigration service on our behalf. That turned out to be critical because it ordinarily took many months to get approval from the immigration office, but we had it within several weeks, which really surprised the embassy in Djakarta. I then flew back to Tomohon.

As you can imagine, saying good-bye to all our friends in Tomohon was very difficult. We had really learned to love the people we worked with. Many of them came to the airport in Monado to say good-bye as we left for Djakarta. I can still remember two things about that flight. First, I remember how you grabbed me when the plane first lifted off the dirt runway. I think you thought the ground was falling away from us. Second, I remember how you chowed down the very spicy chicken they served on the plane, which was so hot that Mother and I couldn't eat it!

When we got to Djakarta, we had to go through the final stages of your immigration process, which included a physical exam and chest X-ray by an embassy physician. We thought it was going to be a routine matter, but the Chinese radiologist who read the X-ray said that you had active tuberculosis. Immigration regulations said that if a person seeking entrance to the United States had TB, they had to remain in their country of origin for two years to be treated—and then be reexamined to make sure the TB was inactive. We were in a state of panic, with plane reservations to leave in just a few days. We made arrangements for Mother to stay in Indonesia with you, for two years if necessary. But as I came to know the embassy doctor better, I finally said to him that it made no sense for you to stay there—that even if you had TB, which we both doubted, it would be best for you to receive treatment in America. Finally he agreed to fudge the record to say that you had "inactive TB," and we were able to leave the country. When that jet lifted off the runway at Djakarta, we were incredibly relieved! However, when we landed in Alaska and had to go through our first immigration check, the official in charge noticed your age and asked how you could have been treated for two years since you were only twenty-one months old? I told him what had happened, and he quickly agreed to let you in, even though it was technically illegal. So we flew on to Chicago, where we were met by Randy and Judy and infant Peter. The rest is history!

In fact, it is now a history of twenty-seven years, over twenty-five of them with us. And it has been a wonderful history of many joys and deep gratitude to God for you. I hope you will always know how much you are loved, and that you are a truly "chosen one."

♥

A Letter to My Daughter

Larry Kessler, The Sun Chronicle, *Attleboro, MA*

On the eve of Thanksgiving, the quintessential American holiday, a time when fewer people seem to care about the deep chasms that still divide people in this country, saluting immigrants seems appropriate.

Given the backlash by those Americans who have evidently forgotten their roots as immigrants—and who have forgotten the nation's historic role in welcoming people from foreign lands—Thanksgiving is an appropriate time to remind people that immigrants have always brought much to this country.

Despite the politically correct revisionists who believe that Thanksgiving is a sad reminder of the way the colonists conquered Native Americans, this holiday is the perfect time to emphasize the positive and show that people of different backgrounds can indeed unite as Americans regardless of their differences.

At this time, more than any other, the nation appears closer to the ideal of the melting pot. My parents, first-generation Americans, instilled the love of thanksgiving and pride in the United States in me, and now, as a parent myself, I am especially proud to be an American because my almost three-and-a-half-year-old daughter has become one of this nation's newest citizens.

Dear Arianna,

Someday, when you are celebrating Thanksgiving in school and are learning the story of the pilgrims and how they survived their first winter in the New World, I hope you, too, will feel the pride in becoming an immigrant. Tomorrow, when we have dinner with Grandfather Ike, it will mark the third Thanksgiving that you have shared with us, but the first since you became an American citizen in Boston on September 23.

That day, the first day of fall, was sunny and in the 60s. Your favorite part of the day was taking the commuter rail train from Attleboro into South Station before boarding the MBTA's Red and Green lines to go to the U.S. Immigration and Naturalization Services office in Boston's Government Center.

Since you're under fourteen, there was no public ceremony, per INS procedures—that event was held October 21 in Boston's Faneuil Hall—but we still took pictures of you afterward with an American flag just so you will have a pictorial record of an important milestone in your life.

We took one picture of you with a photograph of Ellis Island in New York in the background. One day you will learn the significance of that picture; millions of immigrants came through there in the early part of the twentieth century. America welcomed them, just as America welcomed you on September 27, 1997, when we landed in San Francisco after a long journey from China with all of your "Shen cousins"—the other little girls who lived with you at your home in China.

We were proud of you that day, and we were proud again two years later when you became a citizen. Why? Because despite all the complaining that grown-ups like to do about this country, the United States is still unequivocally the best place in the world to live.

This country allowed Mommy and Daddy's parents, their parents and their parents' parents to worship as they believed and to raise their families with a lot of blood, sweat, tears and hard work—and it continues to allow immigrants from across the world to put down roots and build new lives.

Citizenship carries with it many duties and responsibilities, including voting. Not enough people bother to vote, but perhaps you and your friends will become community-minded citizens and influence your generation to be good citizens.

Being a good citizen is not hard, but it starts with being a good person, following the Ten Commandments—a universal code of good conduct—and helping those who are less fortunate.

That's why we celebrate Thanksgiving each year; the Native Americans who were in Plymouth in 1620 and 1621 took pity on the Pilgrims and helped them survive the harsh winter. You'll learn more about Thanksgiving in the future, and one day we will visit Plymouth and its famous rock.

But for now, remember that you have become a citizen of a fine country, one that must continue to accept immigrants because, as this day reminds us all too well, everyone who is not a Native American came to this new world of America to flee persecution and enjoy the unique freedoms that this country offers.

Now, Arianna, you are an American and you, too, can enjoy that freedom.

As you grow up, I pray that you will use it wisely.

Love, Daddy

♥

CHAPTER SEVEN

Becoming Brothers and Sisters

The Big Decision

Matt Casey

As a kid, I always prided myself in being very deliberate when it came to making "important" decisions. When I went to McDonald's, it was always the Filet-o-Fish over the Happy Meal, which was a rare choice for a kid my age. I was a stickler for Converse high-tops instead of Nikes. And when it came time for my birthday party, I opted for Fun'N'Games Arcade over Canobie Lake Park. When you are young, the decisions you make are usually short-term, based on what you want at the time; they have no real effect on those around you. But at some point, this changes and you find yourself involved in making a grown-up decision, a decision that greatly impacts the rest of your life, the lives of your family and, in this case, someone whom I had never even met.

I was eleven years old when I unexpectedly become involved in such a decision. I had just spent eight weeks at sleepover camp in Casco, Maine. It was the first time that I had ever spent any significant time away from my parents and my sister Sarah, who was born two years after me.

Not too long after I returned home that summer, my parents told Sarah and me they wanted to have a family meeting. We were surprised, because to the best of our knowledge neither of us had done anything wrong, which was usually the precursor to a family meeting. Early that day, my parents told us that neither of us was in trouble, so we were relieved, although somewhat mystified. They mentioned they wanted to meet about an important family decision. Now I was looking forward to the conference in the living room that evening. When we met after dinner, my parents informed us that they were strongly considering adopting a three-year-old girl, which meant that Sarah and I would have a younger sister. My mother had founded and been the director of an adoption agency as long as I remember, so Sarah and I understood the concept of adoption. We had attended the agency summer picnics for years and had become accustomed to the concept of seeing parents with kids who had different hair color, skin color and features than their parents. However, knowing about adoption was one thing; having the dynamics of your family change so quickly was something else. Sarah and I were surprised and unaccustomed to having input in major decisions, and as I remember, we were very quiet at first. We were curious, scared and unsure of how to voice our questions and concerns. I think we were both excited about the prospect of having a baby sister, but concerned that the attention which we were accustomed to would shrink with the addition of a fresh young face. I could tell my parents were a bit nervous about how we would react. Seeing my parents exhibit any sense of trepidation or unease is rare, but the feeling was tangible this time.

We did not know it, but adopting a child had been something my parents had been considering for a long time. My parents had developed a close friendship with a woman who founded an orphanage in Bogotá, Colombia. They had expressed to her that they would like to adopt a two- or three-year-old child at some point, and when my father had visited her in Bogotá to assist in bringing a baby home for an adoptive family, he confirmed this desire to the orphanage director.

About six months later, the orphanage director called my mother and told her about a very special three-year-old girl named Catalina

Cuartas. She felt very close with this young girl and wanted her to become a member of the Casey family so that she could continue to know her and see her grow up after leaving Bogotá. My parents were excited and quickly agreed. All that was left to do was to discuss the concept with her future siblings.

After taking a few minutes to think about it, Sarah and I began to formulate questions. Sarah had one, which took my parents back initially. She softly inquired, "Is she going to be brown?" Sarah had obviously noticed that many of the adopted children from Colombia were darker-skinned than their siblings and parents. All of us, including me, sensed the nature of her concern. She wasn't really worried about the color of her sister's skin. Our parents had raised us not to let this affect our perceptions or feelings about others. Rather, Sarah was painfully shy and introverted at the time, and she immediately feared that she would have to answer questions from friends at school and elsewhere if her sister was adopted. She really did not want to have to answer any questions. My parents had a tiny photo, which showed that Marisa was fair-skinned, which was an immediate relief for Sarah.

My first question was, "Are we still going to be able to go on family vacations?" immediately followed by a more pointed, specific follow-up: "Are we still going to be able to go to Disney World?" For some reason I thought the family trips that I treasured may have to be put on hold until our new sister was older, but my parents assured me that was not the case. More questions followed, and after a little while, Sarah and I felt comfortable enough to give our blessing to the proposal. The meeting was adjourned with the decision to bring a new family member into our lives.

I went to bed that night excited about becoming a big brother again. I always was happy and proud of the fact that I had participated in such an important decision. I hoped that I would like my new sister and that she would get along with Sarah and me.

Twenty years later, Catalina Cuartas is now Marisa Catalina Casey, a beautiful, talented young photojournalist in New York City. More importantly, she is my sister, and I can't really imagine life without her. We may not have realized it at the time, but both Sarah and I now agree that our first "adult" decision was the best one we have ever made!

♥

My Baby Sister and Me

Stephen Phillip Policoff

All through the spring, Anna asks, "When when when is my baby sister coming from China?" Anna is six years old. Adopted from China herself at six months, she has been lobbying for a baby sister for more than a year; sometimes she even tells people she already has one.

"Well," my wife, Kate, reasons, "she does. We just don't know who she is yet."

After her best friend Alina's sister is born, we are required to buy baby bottles, pajamas and a package of diapers, just to satisfy Anna's deep craving for her own adventure to begin. They sit on Anna's dresser like mute witnesses to the glacial pace of the adoption process.

Several times over the summer, Anna bounds out of bed in the morning and says, "Hey! We forgot to buy a stroller for my baby sister!" Finally, in late September, Kate takes Anna shopping, and they choose a gleaming blue model. It sits in the middle of what will be their room. "That's for my baby sister. She's coming from China, like me," Anna announces to everyone—even the food delivery guys—who enters our Manhattan apartment.

As I help her dress for school each morning, Anna says, "How are you going to do this when there's two of us, Daddy?" Sometimes she launches into a chant: "You've forgotten how to diaper a baby, hold a baby, bathe a baby!"

"It's true," I say. "And there will be heck to pay when your sister arrives." She laughs hysterically whenever I say this.

In early October, we get the fax: Our second daughter will be waiting for us in Hefei, China, on November 19. We receive a photo of an adorable nine-month-old with huge eyes and wild hair. For months, Kate and I have been unable to decide on a name, but now Anna says, "Jane. I like Jane. Let's call her Jane." So we do.

Because Kate travels professionally and I am a notoriously bad traveler, it was long ago decided that I would stay home with Anna while Kate goes to China. Now, as the frenzy builds, Anna begins to realize what all of this means: Her beloved mommy will be gone for two weeks, and when she returns, nothing will be the same. "Mommy's going on a big trip," I overhear her informing one of her baby dolls. "When she comes back, she's bringing us a pal."

We are all quiet on the way to the airport. The disasters of September 11, two months before, weigh heavily on Kate and me. Anna is giddy in the terminal, especially when Kate tells her that she has left a note and present for every day she will be gone. But when it comes time for good-bye hugs, Anna sobs, causing Kate and me to well up too.

We joke her out of it; we reminisce about how she almost gave Mommy a heart attack by falling halfway down the airport escalator on their trip to Florida last spring. "It's okay, Mommy," she says finally, blowing kisses. "'Cause I've been wanting my baby sister for a long time!"

When we get home, Anna declares, "I need my first present now." It is a toy piano, which she instantly loves. She spends the evening playing discordant tunes and improvising nonsense lyrics. The words "mommy," "baby," "me" and "home" keep recurring in strange combinations.

The first few days alone, we are both jittery, and time is not our friend. With widely divergent anxieties, neither of us can sleep. We go out to Chinese restaurants and watch bad cartoons on television. Each night, we read Kate's note and cross a day off the calendar. We read the books Anna received at Jane's baby shower—books on the joys and duties of being a big sister, books on how your parents will always love you—over and over.

On the night of November 19, we have a long, ludicrously expensive conversation with Kate, who is in the Hefei Holiday Inn with baby Jane. Anna talks excitedly to Kate and shrieks joyfully when she hears her sister burbling in the background. Then her face contorts with sadness. She is listening to Kate coo to the baby, talking in the mommy voice to the new one, not to her. She hands the phone to me and bursts into tears. She cries off and on all night, and for the first time in ages won't let me leave her bedroom until she falls asleep.

I tell her again and again that we could never love anyone more than we love her. Yet I cannot help recalling a therapist's classic analogy: "Imagine that one day, your husband says, 'Honey, I'm bringing home another woman. She's going to sleep in your room and use all your stuff. But I'll always love you.' That's what your daughter will be going through."

Thanksgiving is long and lusterless without Kate. We spend it with cousins in the suburbs, where favorite aunts and uncles are a welcome distraction. The evening also features the first viewing of Anna's newborn cousin, a tiny, red-faced girl. When she arrives, Anna drops everything—including dessert—to check her out. When the baby shrieks piteously, Anna says, "My sister won't cry like that, will she?"

"She'll be older," I say, "but she'll cry a lot anyway." Anna sighs. "And there will be heck to pay."

On November 29, the two of us go out to the airport to meet Kate and Jane. Anna is strangely quiet. Of course, the plane is late, and we wander disconsolately through the American Airlines terminal, where we almost literally bump into our friends Meryl, Walter and Linda with their three daughters, all adopted from China and all there to greet Jane. The girls run around the terminal together, eating pizza, giggling. Anna seems tired and anxious, though. When the plane's arrival is finally announced, she grabs my hand so hard she leaves marks on my skin. We stand in a cluster, and Anna, who has almost preternaturally good eyesight, squeals, "Look! There's Jane! She looks just like a little doll!"

I squint and see Kate emerging from the crowd, carrying the petite Jane in a sling so that only her huge black eyes are visible. Anna runs headlong down the corridor and practically knocks Jane aside to leap into Kate's arms.

But Jane is so much more complicated than a doll, and for days she can't sleep, so none of us sleep, and Anna says, "That baby is driving me crazy."

Many nights, I end up on the couch in the living room while the jet-lagged Jane howls with Kate in our bed. Some nights, Anna creeps into the living room at dawn and snuggles with me on the couch, as if wishing to escape her new reality. "Heck to pay," we say together, and (sometimes) laugh.

What does Anna make of this squalling, demanding creature she has so yearned for? Will she ever feel truly connected to Jane? I want to ask her what she thinks, but she's very busy: She ricochets from following Jane around with a bottle to pointing out which toys she can't play with to yelping with delight at everything she does to muttering darkly, "If you don't stop crying, I'm going to kill you."

On one particularly bad night, vexed that Mommy is so busy with the baby, Anna shouts, "I hate Jane!" and weeps bitterly. A few minutes later, she is crawling around with her, murmuring, "I love you, Janie Janie Janie."

So I sit next to Anna on the floor, stroke her hand and ask, "Anna, how come a while ago you said you hated Jane, and now you say you love her?" Anna gives a look like I must be the most clueless parent on earth.

"Because," she shrugs, "she's my sister."

♥

Double Blessing

Lorraine Schuft

My world has been full of wonderful and unexpected gifts since my husband and I were referred twin girls from China. I've learned that surprises, big and small, can happen in many different and subtle ways. The innate closeness that our twin girls share amazes me on a daily basis. Of course I am surprised at how alike, yet how different, they are from one another. I am lifted by the degree to which my young adult stepchildren and our immediate families have embraced my daughters. I never could have imagined the sparkle I see in my own mother's eyes when she's with her newest grandchildren. The time that Nana and my daughters spend together is obviously pure delight.

When my husband, Chuck, and I made the decision to form our family through adoption, we always knew that we would like more than one child, so it was only natural to wish for siblings or twins. But wish is all we did. When we decided upon adopting from China, we were told that it was highly unlikely that we would be referred more than one child. Consequently, we proceeded with our adoption plan and requested a single child or *perhaps* siblings or twins, but realistically, for over a year, we never allowed ourselves to imagine the gift of more than one child.

What an incredible surprise the day we learned that twin girls were waiting for us in China! My first thought was to thank God, for this was certainly a double blessing for our family and sure to

bring happiness to our lives and theirs. I never could have anticipated how profoundly our daughters would affect our lives and our
relationships with one another and our extended family. Life will
truly never be the same.

As we anticipated our referral for what we thought would be a
single child, we agreed that our top two choices for our little girl's
name were Lily and Rose. We simply liked both names, not because
they're the names of flowers, but because we thought they were pretty
and sweet sounding. We didn't know then that we would use both
names at once, one flower for each of our nine-month-old girls. So, as
we are frequently asked about the origin of their names, we simply say
that we didn't intend to name our twin girls after flowers—because we
never expected twins.

We named our daughters Lily Xiaoshuang and Rose Xiaojue. As
it so happens, their names fit them perfectly, for they are lovely and
they grow more beautiful each day. Their Chinese names, Xiao
Shuang and Xiao Jue, also have very special meaning. We have been
told that *shuang* means double, and *jue* means two pieces of jade or
gems joined together.

I am constantly in awe of Lily and Rose. They have an irresistible
quality to them that I am unable to articulate. Of course they are
physically beautiful, but their personalities and approach to life are
simply delightful to observe. They find joy in the smallest details, and
they often belly laugh together in the way that completely uninhibited
two-year-olds can. A room they walk into is instantly brightened, for
no one can resist their gleeful eyes and their impish grins. They easily
win you over with their simple and endearing charm.

Lily and Rose are so alike, yet so different. Lily loves to be cuddled, to sing lullabies and to snuggle up with her favorite pink blanket. Rose uses her sweet demeanor and contagious giggle to capture

your heart. Watching the nature of their twinship emerge is remarkable, for they are obviously forever *entwined* with one another. How can you start your lives together more closely than sharing your birth mother's womb? Their trust in one another is so deep that when they are together, it's as if they share the same personal space, without any boundaries.

On a daily basis, I'm surprised at how Lily and Rose can anticipate each other's moods and behaviors in a way that no other human can. They are like two silver beads of mercury, separate and distinct, yet always drawn to merge. They intuitively know when to comfort one another, whether through the gift of a favorite toy or blanket, or simply touching each other. We observed this gentle concern since the day we met them. Even as we emerged from the airplane at Logan International Airport in Boston, they instantly reached out to touch one another, providing comfort at what must have been a frightening and confusing time for them. Before meeting my daughters, I would have thought such innate closeness beyond belief.

As we journey through our new life together, we commonly generate a lot of interest from those passing by. I'm still not sure to what I should attribute this fascination. Is it because I'm Caucasian and Lily and Rose are Asian? Is it because they are twins? Or is it simply because the girls are so charming? We are asked a lot of questions and are offered advice (some welcome and some unwelcome) wherever we go.

I sometimes get a knot in my stomach when I'm asked if Lily and Rose are identical or fraternal twins, because I do not know the answer to this question. It seems that as their mother, I should inherently know such a vital piece of information, yet I do not. Maybe one day we'll do genetic testing to determine the answer, so we can provide them with information that may be useful as they reach their own reproductive years. But for now, it's anyone's guess.

I often think about my daughters' birth mother. I can't begin to fathom the depth of the pain and loss she must have felt when she was faced with making such an overwhelming decision. I can only suppose that she is a strong and courageous woman. I hope that in some way, she'll know that her twin babies are in the care of loving and devoted parents. Without her, we would not be a family today.

So whether they are identical or fraternal twins really doesn't matter. They are Rose and Lily, and they are my daughters. Together, they inspire me to be a better person and appreciate life more each day. I consider it an honor and a privilege to be their mother, forever.

♥

The Rhythm of Five

Judy Collins

E very family has a rhythm, a faint musical beat that defines the pattern of its movements. Sometimes that rhythm speeds up to a frantic thrum, and other times it winds down to the slow thump of an elephant's heart. And when it gets like that, when you feel yourself rushing around like a maniac or moving in suspended molasses, sometimes you have to change something to make the rhythm right again.

I felt that our rhythm was off, with just my husband and me. I couldn't always tell, but there were times when I could feel the beat skip, like a record player, and I'd feel that same skip in my chest. Something felt missing. The needle would jump, and I'd get a sudden pang at the emptiness of the living room, the quietness of our house.

This was eleven years ago, right before we adopted Ashley and everything changed forever. She was four months old when she was placed in my arms, and the moment I held her I felt the shift in tempo. It was as though the needle lifted to stop time for a moment, before settling down into the light patter of a child's hands on the floor. It seemed too wonderful, like a dream that might come apart at the seams at any moment. I think my husband and I had doubted whether anything so incredible could ever happen to us.

Life with Ashley was delightful, filled with giggles and smiles and bows and clothes and endless hugs. For a while we just enjoyed our happiness, not even daring to consider if we should adopt again. But when Ashley was three, we started to wonder if we might be so fortunate again. There were many questions to consider: How would this change affect our family? We all seemed to fit together so perfectly; would another child fit the same way? How would a new child impact the rhythm we'd created together? And how would Ashley, my only baby, react to being a big sister?

These were questions of enormous importance to us, more crucial than how we would afford the cost of another adoption or the additional expense generated by another child. We felt those things would fall into place if and when we made the decision.

We finally decided to add another child to our already perfect family. The usual fears rattled around in my head. I was a good mother, but I'd never had to share myself with a second child. Ashley had me all to herself, something that she would never have again. I wondered if it would be possible to love another child with the volume and depth of my heart and soul, the way I loved Ashley. My friends all told me, "You don't split yourself, your capacity just grows! It's miraculous how your love multiplies with every child."

In September 1995, an angel came home to us from the East. Brittany was from China, and at ten and a half months, she was in our arms. It was incredible. The very second I laid eyes on her, and since I touched her soft cheeks and wispy hair, I knew what my friends said about loving was right. I loved her right away, as if I'd loved her my whole life. She was my daughter, as obvious as breathing. All my doubts and bouncing thoughts disintegrated into dust at her toothless smile.

Now we were a family of four, and the rhythm had definitely changed. It took longer to leave the house in the morning and to retire to bed in the evening, even though the beat was drumming faster. It was the sound of tiny feet running in the hall and small hands slapping the rungs of the crib, the sound of twin giggles in the bathroom and the shrieks of delight when we tickle them.

Ashley no longer had our undivided attention, but in return she was now the big sister and could show her little sister the rules of the house. She now had a little person to whom she was a goddess, and Ashley was perfectly fine with that. The girls developed an incredibly loving relationship and soon became best friends. Ashley was always ready with a blanket or doll or bottle whenever she felt her sister needed anything. Extremely protective of her little sister, Ashley took her big-sister role to heart. To think I'd been afraid that Brittany might not have enough attention from us seems absurd! I'm almost ashamed now that I didn't take into consideration the amount of love Ashley would in turn lavish upon this long-awaited member of our family.

Life was so joyous, and we had such renewed confidence, that it didn't take long to realize that we really wanted to be a family of five! We submitted our paperwork for another child from China, and on Mother's Day 1998, our daughter Madison became ours. She was a tiny baby, just six months old. Despite our enthusiasm, the ghosts of old doubts came back to haunt me. I wondered how Brittany would cope with being the middle child. Would she be impervious to the curse, or would she write a scathing book about us someday? Would this new baby be a fifth wheel? Had I disrupted the special relation-ship between my two daughters?

Again, these fears were allayed by the realization that my three children are happy, resilient and truly enjoy one another. Brittany is an easygoing child and is forgiving of me when I am forced to focus on Madison. I will admit that Brittany does have an uncanny ability to need me at the most inconvenient times! But she is patient nonetheless. And Madison is nobody's fifth wheel, which she makes clear on a daily basis. Ashley is my big helper and keeps her sisters busy and happy when I am giving someone a bath or rocking another to sleep.

Our family has found its rhythm again, although some days it may be hard to detect above the noise and giggles. But it's always there, beneath the clutter of toys, the laundry pile commemorating a playground day, the couch pillows in the living room strewn about during a playful fight or their mischievous smiles at each other from across the dinner table. I am a bit more tired, but couldn't be happier and more blessed. The old rhythms of three and four are now muted to an inaudible tap, and I can't imagine moving to any other dance beat than this. It's perfect . . . although . . . well . . . being a family of six does sound appealing!

♥

The Three-Part Fairy Tale

Monica, Paola and Alice Yerxa

God works in mysterious ways. But I think our story shows the magic in those mysteries and will hopefully inspire some families.

My name is Monica, and I am eighteen years old. God's plan for me was to be born to a mother who couldn't care for me properly. She made a difficult decision and put me up for adoption. I'm sure this decision is one of the hardest that a parent might ever make. God had given her the strength to let me go and allow others to care for me in a way that she couldn't. I was placed for adoption in Saint Vincent de Paul orphanage in Quito, Ecuador. In 1988, I was almost four years of age when the greatest people in the world adopted me. My mother, Sheila, and father, Lane, became my heroes.

I moved from the poorest surroundings to the richest. Following my adoption, we lived in Weymouth, Massachusetts, for about six years, and I was very content being the only child. My parents tried to adopt again in 1990 but were rejected because they were told they were too old. Personally, I was very content with that decision. I had many friends and my own family to keep me occupied, and I wasn't that interested in having a sibling anyway.

By the end of fourth grade, my parents decided to move to Walpole, Massachusetts, where I made new friends. I went through middle school and freshman year in high school still an only child. I was the average teenager. I had friends and family. I was athletic and responsible, but I wouldn't have considered myself a role model.

At that time, adoption laws were changing. My parents received great news from their adoption agency that they were no longer considered too old, and they were now eligible to adopt an older child. Before I knew it, in the spring of my sophomore year, my parents and I were on a plane heading back to Quito to adopt a younger sister for me named Paola. It was great that I was going to be able to identify with a sister coming from the same city where I was born. My desire to remain an only child had passed.

Paola was six years old when we met her. Unlike mine, Paola's story is somewhat more complicated than the average child's. She was abandoned as an infant and adopted in Quito by a young woman. When Paola was four years old, her mother, who was only forty-two, died of viral pneumonia. Paola was left alone with no family. She traveled from house to house, but kept getting rejected over and over, for no other reason than she just wasn't wanted. One day a taxi dropped her off at the door of an orphanage, carrying a small box containing her belongings. She lived there among little babies for a year, until God brought her to us.

She was absolutely beautiful, with big brown eyes and long black eyelashes. She spoke no English and would often watch the Spanish channel on television. How was I supposed to interact with her? I was fifteen, and I had no clue how I was going to get along with a six-year-old. I think it hit me when she would come into my bedroom in the mornings and play with my hair while singing in Spanish. This little girl was my sister, and I wanted her to know that no one could separate us.

I'd talk to her as if she understood me. That's the only way she was going to learn English, and eventually she was fluent. Now, I can't get her to stop talking. We learn from each other every day. She is so funny, very loving and such a caring sister. We do have our moments when we disagree, but the bottom line is that I love her and she is mine.

Even though we couldn't speak the same language, bonding with my new sister was instantaneous. When my parents received a picture of Paola, they had it enlarged and kept it on our refrigerator door until we brought her home. Each day that passed, she became closer and closer to me, until I felt that she truly was my sister, even before I'd met her. She is my Mini-Me. I cannot remember when it was just me, Mom and Dad. I have memories from the time when I was younger, but the best ones are my memories of being with Paola.

You'd think our story would end there, but it doesn't. My parents flew to China in September 2001 to adopt another sister for Paola and me. Her name is Alice, and she was abandoned when she was two years old. She was found in front of a store and brought to Xining Children's Home. Alice was born with a slight abnormality on her right hand: a sixth finger. It was successfully removed before she was abandoned. Other than the scar on her hand, she is absolutely normal. She is now nine years old, smart, energetic and very funny.

Alice's photograph was also taped to our refrigerator. Mom, Dad, Paola and I greeted her picture every day. The bonding began with the picture. Meeting her for the first time, I remember her as so small and cute. She barely talked to Paola and me because she didn't even know what a family was. She would say our names in English and that was all. She spoke Chinese, and Paola and I had no clue what she was talking about. It was the cycle beginning all over again. It wasn't new to me. We treated her like an instant member of the family and spoke to her as if she spoke English. She caught on quickly because she had a lot to say.

Alice is very energetic. She is the youngest, so she gets away with anything and everything. She is cute as a button and loves to tease.

Paola's and Alice's personalities are like night and day. Paola is passive while Alice is outspoken. Ten months apart, they get along very well. They share the same room, which means they giggle and play, and then get caught by Mom or Dad because they have not gone to sleep. They are inseparable, doing everything together. My role is the mother figure when Mom and Dad aren't around. I look out for them and make sure I take care of their needs. I take them here and there when necessary, especially to the mall and McDonald's. I am nine years older than Paola, and ten years older than Alice. It seems like quite a gap, but I think that age has nothing to do with it. Older children need love too, and children all over the world are not getting adopted simply because of their age.

God has given our family proof that older adoptions are successful and fulfilling. It takes work, but no more than any other adoptions, or even learning to love a newborn. Families do take work, but they are the greatest gift.

I guess I am now my sisters' role model, and they look up to me. We are a family. No race or age difference can change that. All three of us have different stories, but in the end we created our own fairy tale. Like the colored bracelets we make in my room, the threads start in separate directions at first, but eventually they are entwined into a single strand.

♥

Twin Peaks

Marianne Greeno

Moriah and Jackson look so much alike that we are often asked if they're brother and sister. Neither one of them looks like us, their parents, and that's probably what prompts the question in the first place. Of course, what people really want to know is if they are biological siblings, which they are not. But we always answer with a resounding yes, especially if asked in front of the kids. Besides, I can't imagine two children being more like brother and sister than they are.

Like the mountains for which they are named, Moriah and Jackson come from different ends of the world. Moriah was born in Shoaguan, China, on October 11, 1998, and Jackson was born in Coatepeque, Guatemala, on October 12, 2000. We take their physical resemblance and close birthdays to be part of that strange sense of fate running through so many adoption tales—that it was "meant to be."

People often ask why we did not return to China for our second child. Vinnie and I wish we had a simple answer, but it all comes down to a funny gut decision, as was going to China the first time. Going to Guatemala just felt right inside. I guess that is a simple answer, come to think of it.

When we seriously began the adoption process, we knew we were going to pursue a foreign rather than a domestic adoption. Our ages, the length of time for a child assignment to be made, the health of the children and the issues surrounding an open adoption policy were a few of the factors contributing to that decision. We were also influenced by the sweet adopted Korean child I used to babysit as a teenager and by our friends who had adopted from China and El Salvador.

The first time after attending the adoption agency's orientation meeting, we began to look into various adoption programs in South and Central America. We narrowed our focus to Guatemala, as the program was the best fit given our ages. However, at the time (1998), many unsettling issues existed with that country's adoption process, and it was undergoing many changes. We thought China was more predictable. Also, I'll admit that I was nervous about traveling alone to Guatemala, while I found the group trip to China very appealing.

The group trip was a wonderful experience for us, a ménage of single parents, couples, siblings, grandparents and friends. As a group, we adopted nine children, ranging in ages from ten months to four years. Two children were adopted by first-timers, six by second-timer China families, and one by a family on their third adoption trip to the country. The old pros took us neophytes under their wings. I am grateful to Bonnie for introducing me to the beautiful peasant paintings that now grace several rooms in our house. I am happy to have gone off with Mary to a tiny store she found on a previous trip to buy several gold charms for Moriah when she's older. Pat suggested I buy the red envelopes that we have used the past several years for Chinese New Year. I had not known of the old Chinese tradition and now enjoy the fact that our envelopes are unique and from Moriah's hometown. I am also thankful for the Asian dolls that I purchased at Julia's suggestion, for they indeed are hard to find here. And whenever I use Moriah's chops I always think of Joe and the adventure we had going to the store built on a staircase where he had found chops for his first daughter.

Collectively, the group seemed to have everything that anyone needed on the trip. There were also enough extra hands to take care of the children of parents busy with paperwork or to take photographs. Thanks to Tom, we have pictures of the very moment we met Moriah and when she was placed into our arms. I treasure these pictures and still cry when I look at them. Another member of our group was smart enough to get pictures of our children developed immediately so they could be e-mailed to our waiting families at home. And it seemed like it took the entire group to figure out how our baby Snugli worked. There was comfort in the fact that so many experienced parents, as well as a nurse, were in the group.

Although we traveled in the group, Vinnie, Moriah and I had plenty of time to ourselves. The ten-day trip allowed us to bond with our little girl in her world before bring her back to ours. My fondest memory of the trip was our visit to Moriah's orphanage. By that time we had had Moriah for almost five days. When it came time to enter the infant room, the other families left their children in the orphanage office to avoid confusing or frightening them. They didn't want the children to feel they were being given back. Had there been enough extra hands, I would have left Moriah too. As we entered the nursery, she was taken out of my arms and passed from one nanny to another. You could tell they were delighted to see her, everyone grinning and laughing to hold her again. But after a while Moriah made it very clear to all that she wanted to come back to me. She started to frown as if she might cry, and she held her splayed hands out to me. It made everything inside me swell to burst, and the nannies all laughed in delight and nodded approvingly.

Relatively soon after our return from China, we decided to adopt again. We reexamined the adoption situation in Guatemala and felt more comfortable this time around. Both the U.S. Immigration and Naturalization Service and the Guatemalan government had instituted new policies regarding adoptions that made us feel less at risk than we felt the previous year. In addition, the trip to China is a long one, especially if you have just been there. We were concerned about traveling that distance and for ten days, with or without Moriah.

Around the time we were starting to feel more confident about traveling by ourselves, we attended the adoption agency's summer picnic. There we met a family from our hometown that had adopted two children from Guatemala and were considering going back for a third. They spoke so highly of the experience, the beautiful country and their children. But the kicker was a photograph in the Sunday *Boston Globe* travel section of a boy celebrating Easter in Guatemala. Even grainy and in black and white, he looked exactly like Moriah.

The adoption paper trail in Guatemala was similar to that in China, but the actual referral and adoption process is quite different. We received our referral of Jackson within days of our papers arriving in Guatemala, whereas ten long months passed before it came for Moriah. With Jack, our wait came after the referral. They told us it would be six to eight months before we could travel to Guatemala to get him, and thank goodness it was only five in the end. The wait was shorter by far than for Moriah, but worse, so much worse, because of the picture. Jack's picture made him real to us, and I loved and missed him with a genuine sense of longing, rather than a wistful fantasy of the imagination.

At the end of our wait, we received a call on a Thursday telling us that we had to be in Guatemala by the following Wednesday. We decided quickly that Vinnie should go, and I would stay with Moriah. He flew out of Boston on a Wednesday morning and was back home in a flash on Friday night with Jack. All that Vinnie had to do in Guatemala was make a quick visit to the U.S. consulate, which took all of thirty minutes.

Vinnie stayed at La Casa Grande, where he became fast friends with the staff and night desk manager. There were numerous other adopting couples in the hotel using our agency. Vinnie even met Jack's foster family, whom he said could not have been more lovely.

One of the drawbacks of the short trip was the lack of bonding time Vinnie had with Jack in Guatemala before being thrust into the circle of family and friends at home. I found myself wishing I had gone with Vinnie, so I could have bonded with Jack at first, too. However, as the saying goes, watch what you wish for. Very soon Jack had become a real momma's boy. He is very hard pressed to go to anyone else—other than his sister, who would give anything to be big enough to pick him up. Unfortunately for her, she may never get that chance; although exactly two years younger than her, Jack weighs only three pounds less!

These stories tell how we became parents of Jack and Moriah, or more importantly how we became a family. From a cultural perspective, would it have made sense to go back to China? I don't think so. The way we see it, our family is not Chinese, not Guatemalan, but a hodgepodge of different cultures. Between Vinnie and me, we are Irish, French Canadian and Italian; first and foremost we are Americans. Together we will learn about all our cultures. Maybe Jack will learn to speak Italian, Moriah to Irish step-dance, Vinnie to speak Chinese, and I to weave bright and beautiful cloth reminiscent of the Mayans.

♥

Preparing for Number Two

Margaret Ronan Stack

When we were considering expanding the family, my husband and I were lucky enough to receive a huge amount of encouragement—but not all from the usual sources. When we were deciding to adopt, we received great support from our parents, siblings and close friends, but the greatest encouragement came from our first child, Tommy. After years of longing and patiently waiting for a sibling, Tommy's wish came true at age six when we traveled to Russia to bring home our new baby.

Our older son's desire for a little brother made the task of preparing him for the arrival of a sibling a little easier than it might have been. We were aware, however, that it was important to lay some groundwork in order to ensure his healthy acceptance of his new brother. We made sure that Tommy was fully informed and involved every step of the way in the adoption process. We discussed siblings whom we knew and directed his attention particularly to the fact that some of them got along well together, and others not so well. We discussed where the new baby would sleep (Tommy was all in favor of bunk beds in his room!), what foods he would like and if he would like the same toys that Tommy liked. We informed close friends and relatives about our decision to adopt and encouraged them to talk openly about the adoption, both in front of and with our older son. When we watched the videotape of the new baby, the excitement set in for real.

Although it had not been our original intention, we decided to take Tommy with us to Russia for our three-week stay after which we brought his new brother back home with us. We were permitted to visit the orphanage each day for two hours in order to become acquainted with the newest member of our family, Charles Dmitry.

That first visit to the orphanage had a dreamlike quality, and we were all fascinated and mesmerized by this tiny stranger who belonged to us. Subsequent visits, though still exciting for us, became boring for Tommy as we focused on the baby and our interpreter. This was Tommy's first taste of what it was like to no longer be the star attraction. After a few days, we brought a backpack of toys for Tommy and divided our attention between the two boys. This learning experience was intense for all of us. We allowed interaction between the two to happen more spontaneously, and Tommy's attitude toward and acceptance of his brother improved. Just as these small doses of interaction during the three weeks allowed Charlie to become accustomed to us gradually, so they gave Tommy a chance to adjust gradually to the reality of having a sibling.

After what seemed like ages, we finally returned home from Russia with a bigger family than we had when we left. When we arrived home, we noticed that Tommy disappeared for a few minutes. Just as we were beginning to wonder where he had gone, he returned, arms laden with stuffed animals! He plunked these most treasured possessions down in front of Charlie, exclaiming that he wanted to share them with his brother who he knew had no toys in Russia.

We can't say that life in the months since that time has always been so ideal. There have been the times when Tommy has given Charlie a push or reclaimed a toy as his rightful property, even though he'd given it negligible attention over the past five years. However, for the most part, the boys are the best of friends. Tommy always kisses

Charlie as he leaves for school or camp, and Charlie always greets Tommy's return with a broad smile.

We continue to work to promote this love and acceptance between the boys and within the family overall. We like to give each boy individual attention according to his particular needs, based on interests and maturity, so that they can each feel as treasured as they are. Tommy might be allowed a trip to the movies to see the latest children's release, while Charlie might spend an hour in the kiddie pool playing with his water toys. We also allow the boys their own time together, with a minimum of interruptions or parental directions, in the hopes they are able to develop a natural, loving relationship with one another in a setting where Tommy is able simply to relax and be with his brother, rather than feel like a watchdog. Most importantly, we try to spend as much time as possible together as a family. We feel that the preparation and continuing guidance with which we've provided the boys have played a major role in creating strong family bonds. We can't wait to add number three!

♥

CHAPTER EIGHT

Grandparenting an Adopted Child

Grandma Extraordinaire

Dale Azimow Wood

For the first twenty-three years of her life, her name was Anna Lavalle. She became Anna Lavalle Dartley when she married Dr. Seth Dartley. Her next title was Mother when she gave birth to Saideh, the first of her two children. But it wasn't until 1997 at the age of seventy-eight that she acquired the title she treasures more than any other: Grandma. With this title came two unexpected blessings she had never dreamed possible. Now she can't imagine life without them.

Today she is simply called Grandma, not just by her two loving and very different Chinese granddaughters, but by everyone who knows her. Anna Lavalle Dartley is Grandma to Anna Nicole Dartley, age ten, and Sara Ann Dartley, age six. They are the adoptive daughters of Saideh Dartley, Anna's firstborn child. And they both carry their grandma's name.

When you first meet Grandma, you see a sweet, frail, older lady, looking quite stylish with her perfectly coifed hair. She has difficulty hearing, but that is all she has difficulty with. One must not be fooled by her elderly looks. The cover of this book may appear somewhat worn, but inside you will find a story of incredible strength, courage and an indomitable spirit that has carried her through a life of painful challenges and led her to the greatest of all rewards.

Anna faced her first challenge when her husband died suddenly and left her with two small children, Saideh, age five, and Seth, age four. She was also left with the Herculean task of managing the building they lived in, which was also the location of her husband's medical practice. The building had other tenants, in addition to difficult maintenance requirements. Anna didn't even know how much rent the tenants paid. She had never written a check and had no idea how to manage or care for the property. But all the same Anna rolled up her sleeves, climbed back onto life's stairway and went to work. She was determined to learn everything, literally from the ground floor up. She took her children in hand and went from door to door, asking the tenants how much they paid in rent and wrote it down in a book. With trust in God, determination and courage she began her life as a single parent and a landlady.

In 1952, Anna battled cultural prejudices against single women. She became a pioneer of sorts, and even likes to call herself the first "women's libber." She struggled to get plumbers, electricians and carpenters to work for her. Despite their hesitance, in the end they finally came and stayed with her. As the years passed, Anna and her children grew together. Anna learned to operate in a man's world, and her children learned to live life armed with self-confidence, the power of positive thinking and the ability to be free thinkers. She taught them, and they taught her. This family of three created a bond as solid and strong as the building they called home.

Saideh and Seth grew up in the cultural playground of Boston, with museums and libraries as their favorite destinations. Anna had a passion for learning, and each school vacation always included a trip to a cultural event. Saideh and Seth were nourished not only with unconditional love, but also with unconditional support. She encouraged her children, with "You can do anything" as their mantra.

And that's just what happened to Saideh and Seth. They became exactly what they wanted. Seth's childhood dream of becoming a doctor was realized in 1972 when he graduated from Boston University

Medical School, and Saideh went on to become the elementary school teacher she had always aspired to be.

Then in 1972 life presented Anna with perhaps the most horrific challenge for a parent to survive. Her son died. While Seth was doing his residency at Emory University Hospital, he was diagnosed with the most aggressive type of leukemia. Seth called his sister Saideh to tell her he was coming home to die, and within two weeks Seth was gone. Saideh and Anna were devastated.

Brought even closer together in unbearable pain, Saideh and Anna once again rolled up their sleeves and climbed back on the stairway of life. Mother and daughter, each other's best friend, hand in hand, they began this new part of their life, forever changed, but forever determined.

Saideh continued with her teaching career in elementary education. For thirty-six years, Saideh focused her life on sharing the teachings and love that Anna had instilled within her. She remained single and accepting of the probability that she would never have children. Saideh had almost given up even the possibility of adopting children, but she pushed herself out of inaction, charged by her desire to be a mother, and she eventually found an adoption agency.

The seeds of adoption were planted on a hot day in August when Saideh came to an information meeting at the agency. With care and nurturing from the staff, Saideh began the journey that would lead her to motherhood and Anna to become a grandmother—two dreams come true for two women who had thought they were impossible.

Saideh first adopted Anna Nicole from China at age four and a half and then returned three years later, with Anna and Anna Nicole, and adopted Sara Ann at age three and a half. Anna adored China, finding that the Chinese culture so reveres the elderly that she never wanted to leave. "I felt so important there because I am so old," she says with pride. "But not too old to climb the Great Wall." For her it was easy. She has been climbing over walls for eighty years.

And so at the age of eighty-three, Anna has definitely reached the pinnacle of life with her new role as grandmother. "I can't imagine life without them," she says. Saideh gratefully adds, "And I couldn't have done it without my mother."

This woman, armed with a lifetime of wisdom, a heart full of love and devotion, and the belief that you can be anything you want to be, became "grandmother extraordinaire." She instills in Sara Ann and Anna Nicole the same doctrines of positive thinking that enabled her own daughter, Saideh, to be a teacher and mother.

From the beginning, the adoption of Anna Nicole and Sara Ann was a partnership in parenthood. Living together in the same building where their family started, Saideh and Anna can enjoy and participate in all the children's activities. The past five years have been filled with emotional ups and downs, tea parties, culture, and days of love and laughter. Every night the girls are tucked in and kissed goodnight by Grandma. Grandma is a part of everything they do, from baking cookies to Saturday night popcorn and video parties. The girls adore their grandmother. These four people are each other's best friends, and life is always a never-ending adventure anchored by Grandma, who is the "grandmother everybody wants to have."

Sara Ann and Anna Nicole have been blessed with the uncondi-tional love and adoration of two amazing women. These two young girls have been given a family and a foundation of love, courage, strength and determination, which is truly the gift of adoption.

The girls seem to realize the gift of family, too. One day when Saideh and the girls were riding a bus, Sara Ann yelled, spontaneously, "We are rich, we are so rich!" Saideh, thinking they would surely be mugged the minute they got off the bus, nervously said, "What do you mean, Sara Ann?" Looking at her mother in disbelief, Sara Ann turned to her and simply proclaimed, "We are rich and we are so lucky because we are a family."

♥

Waiting for Katherine

Kae Bowes

I had my first glimpse of her via a photograph sent from the orphanage in Bogotá, Colombia: a beautiful, serious little girl in a flowered dress standing in a sunny garden. Above the picture was "KATHERINE," her name . . . my name! I fell in love immediately with my new little granddaughter. Coincidence? No way. My Gaelic blood told me she had been destined to join our family.

Later, when my daughter and her husband went to Colombia to bring Katherine home to her brothers, PJ and Liam, I waited with the boys. It was an achingly long three weeks for all of us. I could not remember time stretching so endlessly before me, except when I was waiting to give birth. The anticipation—joyful but wearing—was the same.

How could we welcome her? We spent countless hours arranging her room. The boys saw that it was well supplied with Barbie dolls, Beanie Babies and bears. PJ drew a beautiful card and had all his teachers and classmates sign it. Liam was looking forward to asking her about CRAN, the orphanage she was coming from. Although he too had taken the long journey from Colombia to join our family, it had been ten years ago, when he was just four months old. Now he had the opportunity to get some firsthand information about CRAN. The boys wrote letters describing their house, school and friends. They talked to her on the phone and heard her say, "I love you, PJ," and "I love you, Liam." They couldn't wait. I looked forward to cherishing my little namesake and doing everything I could to make things as easy as possible for her.

The day finally arrived—Katherine was coming home! The boys were taken to the airport, carrying flowers and gifts to greet their sister, while I waited at her new home to welcome her. *She will be tired,* I thought, *and probably shy.* Such a big adventure for such a tiny person. And then the door flew open.

She swept into the house and into our lives. With a "Grandma Kae!" and a bear hug (around my knees) she was up the stairs, followed by her brothers, and into her room. Shy? Tired? Not then or any time since. In five short months she has mastered first grade and English (even idioms, "Oh man!" was her favorite for a while), danced in a recital, and been sought after for play dates. One thing she misses: She feels it was easier to make people laugh in Colombia, and Katherine loves to make people laugh.

At seven, Katherine can put into words how she feels and thinks, what she finds strange and what is familiar. Because she is seven, not only has she quickly become part of her new family but she has been able to take us along with her on this incredible journey. . . . The waiting for Katherine is over. Our new life with her has just begun.

♥

What Is Meant to Be Is Meant to Be: One Grandmother's Story

Joanne Cooper

One of the hardest feelings to cope with as a parent is the feeling that you can't do anything to help your child through a difficult time. You know your children are hurting, but they don't talk about it, so you don't ask. There's nothing you can say or do but sit back and wait for their cues. You pray a little and keep the faith that they'll sort things out, and when they're ready, come to you and include you in their decisions. So the night our eldest son stopped by and asked us how we would feel if he and his wife adopted a baby was one of those moments when, after working things out for themselves, our children came to us with their solution to their very personal situation. My husband and I in unison said, "That's the best news we've heard." Then he added, "You know, I just heard that Larry Bird adopted a baby." What else was there to say? After all, Larry Bird was our son's idol.

And so it began. Our kids were becoming parents, and we were about to be grandparents for the very first time. What was so wonderful about our first grandson's adoption was how special each member of the family felt as part of the process. When we received news that our grandson had been born, the two grandmas took the anxious mom to go layette shopping and order baby furniture and all the accessories. We grandmothers had the pleasure of setting up our grandson's room while his parents went to get him. We waited and waited to hear from them that momentous day, and when they finally did call, they were ecstatic; they couldn't believe it! They were the parents of the most beautiful and wonderful baby. They were overwhelmed with feelings of love at first sight. And so it was for all of us when they all finally came home.

Over the years our family grew, and soon there were six grandchildren—three girls and three boys, some adopted, some biological, each and every one of them a miracle. Our family has always had strong generational ties and a commitment to carry on the family name. Each one of my kids named a child for their dad who passed away several years ago. How he would have loved all of his grandchildren!

Despite all the good fortune in our lives, one of our other sons, Howard, and his wife, Jane, were hurting. They had a wonderful daughter named Hope, but they wanted a sibling for her. Hope would talk about wanting a baby sister, but it just didn't happen. Even though Howard's brother had experienced the same kind of difficulty building his family before finally deciding on adoption, Howard and Jane needed to figure things out for themselves, find their own path. Then Howard met a woman who ran an adoption agency and the wheels of adoption were set in motion in our family once again. Another miracle was in the making. Howard and Jane were going to adopt a baby girl from Colombia.

As thrilled as we were about the idea of having another granddaughter, we were worried for Howard's and Jane's safety. Colombia was not on our list of desirable places to go, given the political unrest and violence in the country. What were we supposed to say as concerned parents when our kids asked us our opinion as to whether or not they should go to this war-torn country to bring home their new daughter? My partner Bill and I had a long talk. Bill and his late wife had adopted a son over forty years ago, so he knew firsthand where the kids were coming from emotionally and the kind of determination they were feeling to make this adoption happen. He reminded me that Howard and Jane had gone the entire adoption route, not just the mountains of paperwork and the immigration process, but more importantly they had gone through the more difficult mental and emotional process. On the other hand, Howard and Jane had a great life here and a wonderful daughter. Was it so wrong of me to be worried about the danger?

I struggled to choose the right words, to show my support and to hide my worries as best I could. As any mother or father would experience, you know that whatever you say might very well be the wrong thing, so you ponder your response and ponder some more until you finally come to the conclusion that whatever they do will be the right thing for them. In the end, your children make their own decision, which is only theirs to make and which you know in your heart will be the right decision for them. If they end up going to Colombia or some other country that feels dangerous to you, you'll worry for sure. But as I learned in this process, that worry is my problem, not theirs, and to the degree I could hide it, Howard and Jane would never know my worries—well, not at least until they came home from Colombia.

So Howard and Jane went off to Colombia, and once again we waited as a family to hear about the newest addition to our clan. Howard's description of seeing Sara for the first time is one that only he and Jane could describe. I can tell you that when I first met Sara at the airport, it was once again love at first sight, just as it had been with each and every one of all my other grandchildren. Sara is named for my mother and Jane's grandmother, two amazing ladies. Sara reminds me of my mother because both have the same dark hair, dark eyes, chubby cheeks and beautiful smile. My mother would have loved her.

I have a picture of my mother when she was a little girl, which I'll give to Sara when she is old enough to appreciate it.

Grandchildren are just like our own children; no matter how many we have they are each special in our hearts, and we feel the same love for each one of them. Over all the years, each child's arrival has been its own unique miracle, and I will never forget the utter joy in my heart when I met and held each of them for the first time.

As I look at my family, I am so grateful—grateful to have each and every one of my children and grandchildren. I am so fortunate to be able to watch my children raise their families, to watch my wonderful grandchildren learn and grow. How lucky we are to have them all. Having traveled the adoption path with my children a few times now, I do believe that in life, what's meant to be is meant to be.

♥

Like Being Young Again

Grandma Mary

*S*he's *crazy,* I thought to myself. *She's completely crazy. It'll never work.*

My daughter Linda was still smiling, her face wet from the rain, waiting for my reaction. I tried to keep my face calm, staring past her face at the rain hitting the window. *What am I supposed to say?*

Ten seconds before, my daughter had come through my door and announced that she was going to adopt a child from Guatemala. Initially, I felt a shiver pass through my body. That faded, and now I didn't quite know what to feel. *Think of something to say!* I ordered myself. *Think of something fast, before she thinks you've turned to stone.* I kept staring at the rain patterns on the glass.

"Mom?" Linda said. "Hello?"

Just smile, I told myself. *Smile, and say, "That's wonderful, honey, I'm here for you all the way." It's easy, just open your mouth and say it.* Of course I was there for her, and I wanted to make her happy, but deep down I felt anxiety building.

"You're a single woman," I blurted the words out before I could stop myself. *Nice going,* I thought.

"So . . . ," Linda said.

It was too late now. I had to continue to explain my reservations. "So," I said, "you'd be a single mom in her forties, working full time. Maybe it's too much responsibility and too much of a financial burden. How will you have time to take care of her? I mean, let's say you have to go to the store. Will you always take your baby along? And you never know. I mean, let's say there's something wrong with the child? You don't know anything about the child, anything about their situation. Anything could go wrong!"

My daughter was looking at me with that look of infinite patience. It was one of her sweetest and most infuriating gestures. "Are you done, Mom?" she said, smiling.

"Sorry," I said. "But I worry. I don't want to be negative. And I'm not saying you shouldn't do it. I just want you to consider everything, you know? Weigh the pros and cons."

"I will, Mom," she said. "Don't worry so much."

But I did worry. During the whole eight-month process I worried—sitting at home, doing housework, before falling asleep—thinking about all of the possible negative outcomes as the adoption grew closer. But my daughter didn't feel my anxiety at all, as though she were wearing some impervious Teflon covering that my anxieties bounced off like raindrops. "Don't worry so much, Mom," she kept saying. Although her calm demeanor should have helped, it only made me worry for both of us, given that she didn't seem to worry at all.

Toward the end I was so worried I could barely stand it. Now, it was the plane trip that frightened me, for I've always been afraid of flying. My other daughter, Sue, was going to Guatemala with Linda, and the thought of my two girls together on a plane made me shudder. When the opportunity arose for them to make the trip a month earlier than was planned, I didn't know what to say.

On the one hand, it would get the whole thing over and done with quicker. But on the other hand, their departure date would now be September 11, 2002. I figured no one would be flying then, so it would probably be safer than ever, but I couldn't get the horrible flashback images of the prior September 11 out of my brain.

With an air of resignation, I said, "Go. Just go, and let's hope all will turn out okay."

Incredibly, three days later, they were back, on Friday the thirteenth no less. I was at the airport waiting for their return, and I felt a strange calm settling over me. Maybe it was merely a sigh of relief from my worrisome inner self. *At least they are back safe now.* But maybe there was something else, too. Perhaps I was starting to realize that it was all going to be all right.

I saw my daughters right away as they stepped from the terminal gate, along with a peek of a tiny face resting on Linda's shoulder. All at once I became quite excited, and felt as though my daughters were walking in slow motion toward me. "C'mon," I mumbled. "C'mon. Get over here with my granddaughter!"

Little Sarah was so beautiful, it stole my breath away. I knew she would be, of course, from Sue's phone call from Guatemala. "She's so beautiful!" Sue had said, two days ago, after having first seen Sarah. "You won't believe it, Mom!" Sue had never exactly been a baby person. I think she always just wanted a dog instead. So for her to say those words, I knew my granddaughter must be a real star.

Sarah was five months old when she came home, and now she is nearly one. She exudes a magic charm that makes everyone fall in love with her at first sight. Everything around her seems softer and brighter. She is smart, animated and so happy, and I know that she was loved and cared for in Guatemala.

The experience of being a grandmother is like nothing else on Earth. I cannot describe it. It is the purest joy imaginable. Especially for me, with two unmarried daughters, who never thought I would feel that joy. When my husband was alive, we would talk in hushed tones of hope about grandchildren, but never thought it would happen. Sometimes when I hold Sarah, I feel a twinge, as I think how my husband would have loved her.

Sarah now goes to day care four days a week, and I care for her on Fridays. She's reached the stage when she cries forlornly whenever her mother leaves the room. Even when she's left with me, Sarah's eyes well up, and she makes it clear she is not happy with her mother's departure. I know it's just a stage, but it makes me unhappy to see her so, crying when left with her grandma. But clever me, I found the trick. I just distract her with a toy or with tickles until her mother leaves the room, and Sarah barely notices she's gone.

I do have an illness, one that has made me weaker with age. Before Sarah was even an idea, I remember thinking, *This will all be over soon.* But when the suggestion of a granddaughter seemed to be possible, I began to think, *All right, let me just hold on until I see her.* And the more time I spend with my granddaughter, the more hopelessly I fall in love, the more I keep upping the ante. *Let me see her reach the age of one . . . her first step . . . first word . . . the age of five. Please God,* I think now, *just let me hold on for another five or ten years, as long as I can.* It's as though I've suddenly been given something to live for. It's like being young again, almost like being a child. Time no longer passes in one long streak, each day a blur, blending into the next. My life is now broken into a series of wonderful moments, each distinct as bits of colored glass, and each one made painfully sweet with anticipation. *One more day, one more day until I see Sarah. My God, how am I going to make it through one whole day before I can hold my granddaughter? I can't wait.*

♥

CHAPTER NINE

Encountering Shadows of the Past

Shadows of Adoption

Stephen K. Mackowitz

As far back as I can remember, I have known that I was adopted. For all of my fifty-three years, "being adopted" has seemed normal to me. Some people are right-handed, some people are left-handed, and some people are adopted. My cousin, who was my surrogate brother, also was adopted. Being adopted was no big deal to me.

I had no reservations about telling anyone I was an adopted child. In fact, during my dating years, telling a girl that I was adopted could even score a few points! "Being adopted" also got me out of a couple of ninth-grade biology parent survey, hereditary homework assignments.

My adoptive parents never spoke about my birth parents or the situation that brought me to the adoption agency. My only curiosity was wondering what time I was born. I remember my parents saying that they tried to find out, but a fire had destroyed my birth records. I don't know if this statement was just a ruse to quell my curiosity about my birth history.

In retrospect, it is odd that my cousin and I never discussed any issues about our adoption. I have heard about adoptees who had a strong, primordial desire to search for their birth mother, feeling they could not be whole unless they uncover their roots. I never felt that way.

I don't recall even once really wondering about my birth parents. I never asked myself, *What were the circumstances of my conception?*

How did my mother feel giving me up for adoption? What role did my birth father take? How did they feel afterwards? Do they ever think of me?

Once in a while, though, I would fantasize about them. A recurring fantasy was that one day I would receive a call from a lawyer asking me to come to his office. When we met, he would say, "I have been your birth father's lawyer for many years. Your father always watched you from afar. He followed your athletic achievements and your career. He was proud of you. However, I am sorry to tell you he recently passed away. And by the way, he left you $25 million." I guess that is not much different than people dreaming of their "long-lost millionaire uncle." Later I was to find out that my birth father was a bus driver from New York City, and now all I can picture is that Ralph Kramden was my father. It's a bit of a letdown, I'll admit.

I have no idea why my adoptive parents did not give me more information. Were they afraid I would leave them if I found my birth parents? In the late 1990s my mother came up with a strange theory about my cousin's and my trip to Europe on 1969 college summer break. Both my mother and his mother, knowing that our birth mothers were in Europe, thought we were really on a search for our birth family. Frankly, nothing was further from our teenage minds.

On the evening of May 29, 2002, I sat down to read the paper after being away for a couple of days on business. Noreen, my wife, and Andrea, my sixteen-year-old daughter, came into the room. Noreen sat down next to me and took my hand. Her touch, so light yet so heavy with apprehension, gave me a chill of foreboding. Noreen said, "Andrea is pregnant."

One can imagine the emotions that erupted, the questions that were asked and the answers that were given. From that moment our family's world changed. Within thirty seconds of dropping the three-word bomb, Noreen said, "Andrea and I think adoption may be the best answer." I had already started to ask myself, *Could we raise another baby?* The word "adoption" struck me like a lightning bolt. It seemed incredible to me that we would give a baby to someone else! But then I was adopted. Why couldn't it work here? All of these thoughts raged like a storm in my head, but I think my love for my daughter cleared my brain, and I began to search for the right answer. I did feel betrayed, hurt, angry and dumbfounded, but I tried to push those feelings aside.

Over the next days and weeks my own adoption came more and more to the forefront of my thoughts. *Is this what happened to my birth mother and father? How did each one react? Did they tell their parents? Did their parents even know? What went through their minds?* I started to ask all the questions that I had not even thought about during the first fifty-two years of my life. Not only was I dealing with the emotions of our current family situation, I also felt rising to the surface unresolved issues from my adoption.

During Andrea's pregnancy, we felt it was important that she receive counseling. We found an excellent counselor with extensive adoption experience, who was, in fact, also adopted herself. Mary Ellen was extremely helpful to Andrea. We were very concerned that the adoption alternative was Noreen's and my solution, but that deep down it might not be Andrea's choice. Mary Ellen did, however, confirm that Andrea felt that adoption was not only best for her but also for the baby.

Eventually, I started to feel that I could use Mary Ellen's counseling as well. We talked about the emotional aspects for the adoptive baby, and I learned that negative feelings experienced during adoption may manifest themselves later as depression, loneliness and anger. I realized that I have experienced these emotions and wondered if they related to my adoption.

Mary Ellen explained that adoptive children often suffer low self-esteem and feel unwanted. The child often feels "there must be something drastically wrong with me, because my own mother did not want me!" Another by-product is the child becoming afraid to form new relationships. The child, and later the adult, believes that if a relationship is started, then abandonment is right around the corner; thus, it is better to avoid being hurt by never entering into a relationship in the first place.

Mary Ellen and I talked about how my parents might have felt and how I had felt. I was in a foster home for nine months before I went to my new home, which must have been a lonely and confusing time for me. I must have thought, *There is something very wrong with me, nobody wants me.* Mary Ellen had a great cure for this troubling feeling. She made me picture myself as an infant and I, as an adult, holding that infant. She encouraged me to talk to him and enjoy him. When doing this exercise, it was impossible to think of that infant as bad in any way. The infant was an infant; he was pure, he was full of new life, he was happy. Concentrating on this picture and thinking of the feelings of my birth parents gave me a wonderfully new positive perspective on my adoption.

From that counseling session in May until the birth of Andrew on September 28, I relived my adoption, both from my birth parents' point of view and from mine. During that whole time I felt like I was preparing to give myself away. Whenever I spoke about the adoption, I cried. The process was difficult. In my own way, I became attached to Andrea's unborn child. At times, I thought that unborn child was me. I often questioned whether adoption was the right thing for the baby. Should we change our minds for the sake of the baby? Eventually, I concluded that adoption was still the best alternative for the baby and us, especially in the light of the adoption options available today.

The adoption process now is quite different from what it was in 1950. Today we have options, from the closed process to complete open adoptions. Like *The Bachelorette* or *Joe Millionaire*, we can set the criteria for the adoptive parents, interview prospective candidates, choose parents with alternate lifestyles and establish visiting rights. The birth mother (and her parents!) can be choosy.

After reviewing a number of prospective families, Andrea found a family she thought might be a good fit. Doug and Paula were looking to adopt a second child. Andrea felt that this young professional couple possessed many of the values and attributes that she felt were important.

When we met them at a brunch we arranged, I felt like I was interviewing a job applicant. I asked questions, listened to answers, watched their mannerisms and how they interacted with their daughter and with Andrea, scrutinized how they were dressed, and tried to determine their value system. I also observed how Andrea was reacting to them. Was there chemistry? One of the key issues for Andrea was having future interaction with the baby and the adoptive parents. I wanted to make sure that as often as possible the baby would feel Andrea's heartbeat and hear her voice. We had to determine if the young couple would be open to having Andrea be a small part of their family.

Andrea, Noreen and I left the brunch all with the same thought: Doug and Paula would be great parents for Andrea's baby. We were so impressed with their sincerity and character. (My only reservation was that Doug was a New York Mets groupie, which didn't sit well for this Red Sox fan. Hopefully I will be able to have some influence on the child!) We all felt that if we could have designed a couple, we could not have come up with better parents than Doug and Paula, and I thank God for sending them into our lives. Later on, our feelings were bolstered when Doug and Paula said they would name the baby Andrew, after Andrea and Doug's father.

Andrew was born on September 28. What a joy it was for me being in the delivery room coaching Andrea through the delivery. (I was at her head, with Noreen closer to the doctor!) But I was in fact the first person, besides the nurses, to hold Andrew. It was heaven. We spent two days with him. We enjoyed every second. He is a beautiful child.

During those forty-eight hours, I often held Drew, privately talking to him about his adoption and my adoption. I often cried. Oh, how I wanted him to know that Andrea loved him and would always love him. I wanted him to know everything was right about him. I wanted him to feel loved and wanted. I needed him to know he could call on Andrea, Noreen or me at any time.

In forty-eight short hours, I was completely in love with Andrew. We all were. The hardest event of our lives was actually handing him to Doug and Paula. When Andrea was ready to be discharged from the hospital, she dressed and packed her bags. Noreen and Andrea dressed Andrew. We then all said good-bye to him, and each of us held him one more time. We all gave him a kiss. With Drew in Andrea's arms, we all headed down the hall to a room where Doug and Paula were waiting. I thought this must be just how a prisoner feels going to his execution.

Doug and Paula were so gracious. They were so empathic and concerned about our feelings. I greatly respect how they handled this heart-wrenching moment. Everyone was crying. The only words I could speak were to Doug. I asked him to make sure that Andrew would never forget Andrea. We left the hospital empty-handed and with a hole in our hearts.

That was five months ago. Doug and Paula have been incredible. We have been together three or four times. They invited us to their home at Christmas. They send and e-mail pictures of Andrew. They have Andrea's picture in Andrew's room. I truly believe Doug and Paula love Andrea. Andrew is thriving. Every time we see him he is happy. He has a wonderful disposition. I am so grateful to Doug and Paula. They are wonderful, caring people. I deeply feel that Andrew will be fine and have a happy life.

Noreen was a pillar of strength during this crisis. She was so instrumental in keeping us all on track. She was wonderful with Andrea, rubbing her back, allaying her fears, taking her to the doctor and helping her find prospective parents.

Andrea, my beautiful daughter, was outstanding. She went to school until the day before Andrew's birth. She was strong, she had a great attitude, and she made the right choice. I love them both.

This has been a cathartic experience for me. I have been able to unleash some repressed emotions surrounding my own adoption. I have been able to see my adoption in a new positive light.

But I do miss Andrew.

♥

A Story for Ancient Moon

Adam Schwartz

Today is September 4, 1996, the first day of Rosh Hashanah, a time when Jewish people celebrate the New Year, a time when we think about new beginnings. Today's date is also an occasion for me to think about my daughter's beginnings. Almost a year ago, on September 16, 1995, my daughter Annie was found on the steps of a middle school in Wuhan, China. She was five months old and had probably been left by her birth mother, almost certainly because she was a girl. China's one-child-per-family policy imposes brutal economic penalties for couples who have more than one child. Because sons are more highly valued than daughters, many thousands of baby girls are abandoned in China every year.

I have other dates to celebrate my daughter's beginnings; her birthday, of course—April 26, 1995; and the date she was placed in our arms—April 15, 1996. So why would September 16, 1995, the day she was abandoned, also be sacred to me?

Baby girls adopted from China come to their adoptive parents with virtually no history. The orphanage provides a birth date, which may or may not be accurate, and a name, which may or may not be the one given by the birth parents. About the only real information you receive is the certificate of abandonment, a document stating where and when the child was abandoned. I already knew many people who had adopted babies from China, and I was surprised to hear some of them tell me that they had very little curiosity about their daughters' lives before the adoption. One woman said to me that she felt her daughter's life began the moment she was placed in her arms. I was dumbfounded by this attitude. Perhaps I was projecting my concerns onto the daughter I had not yet met, but it struck me as unbearably sad that she would never be able to contact her birth mother if she wanted to, that she would never be able to ask questions of the woman who gave birth to her and then abandoned her. Would this missing knowledge, these unanswered questions, keep her from feeling whole?

Before we left for China, we knew our daughter's birthday, April 26, 1995, and her Chinese name, Wu Guyue, which means "ancient moon." We also had a black-and-white, passport-size photo of her. She looked exactly like her name: a high moonscape of a forehead, and eyes like a pair of shiny black pearls. Her eyes stared calmly back at the camera, a look so clear and knowing that she truly did have an ancient countenance. Her eyes were exactly like the "ancient, glittering eyes" of the Chinamen in Yeats's poem "Lapis Lazuli." We showed her name to some Chinese friends, all of whom said it was unique, not like the generic names commonly used by the orphanage. Between this information and her photograph, I was sure my daughter had been named by someone who knew and loved her.

We arrived in Wuhan on Sunday night, April 14, and at 10:30 the next morning, in a dim, dilapidated government office, our daughter, who we named Annie, was handed to us. She cried nonstop for an hour. Then she fell asleep, and when she woke up later that afternoon in our hotel room she smiled and laughed with my wife and me as if she had known us all twelve months of her life. In the hotel restaurant the next evening, she cried when I left the table to retrieve something from our room; I looked back, and my daughter was reaching out to me with her doll-sized hands.

After two days with Annie, I could better understand the woman who felt that her daughter's life began at the moment they met. The love I felt for Annie was so completely transforming, so shockingly powerful, and the bond between us so deep and immediate, that I believed in every cell of my body that we were meant to be together. I couldn't imagine another fate for either of us. Of course, I knew she existed because sometime in July 1994 a man and a woman in China made love and conceived a child. But this fact was—and still is—as remote to me as the idea that God created the world in seven days, or any other creation myth.

On our third day in China, officials from the orphanage came by our hotel room with some documents, among them the certificate of abandonment:

> This is to certify that Wu Guyue, female, born on April 26, 1995, was found to be abandoned at the Xingou Middle School, Dongxihu District, Wuhan City, Hubei Province, on September 16, 1995. She was sent to our court by the People's Government of Xingou Town, Dongxihy District, Wuhan City, Hubei Province, on September 16, 1995. Her innate parents couldn't be found.

My blood pounded as I read this. Perhaps it was the official, unsentimental account of a heart-shattering act; perhaps it was a reminder that my daughter did indeed have a history, but a history she would never know. Then I noticed the date again. Her birth mother had kept her for nearly five months. I know that most of the babies are abandoned after only a couple of days or weeks at the most. The more I looked at this date—September 16, 1995—the more it looked like a sliver of light, a small fragment of evidence that Annie's birth mother wanted desperately to keep her.

Very soon that sliver of light turned into a small window; only fifteen minutes after I had read the certificate of abandonment, my wife and I found another document, this one unofficial and completely unexpected. Two days earlier, when Annie was handed to us, she, like all the babies in our group, was swaddled in many layers of clothing, even though it was the middle of April and warm in Wuhan. After we brought her back to our hotel room, it took us about twenty minutes to peel off all the layers of clothing. We wanted to keep the clothes of course, and sent them to the hotel laundry. The clothing was delivered to our room just before the orphanage officials came by. As my wife was putting the clothes away, she noticed a red cloth stitched over the heart of the innermost garment. She looked closer and saw that this red cloth had writing on it. We called our translator. He examined the cloth, told us it was a letter from her foster mother and then read it to us:

> To Guyue's parents: Greetings to you. I am Guyue's foster mother. Baby Guyue was brought from the orphanage to my house to be in my foster care more than half a year ago, and now she is adopted by you two kindhearted people. I feel happy for her, but at the same time it is hard to accept that she is leaving me to cross the ocean to the other shore. I would like to ask you to take good care of baby Guyue, and on her birthday every year, please send back some pictures to relieve my longing for her.

As the translator read this letter, I was holding Annie in my arms, my eyes damp with tears. I was crying, I think, because I realized we had come upon something very valuable for my daughter. She would have a personal and direct connection to her homeland; she would have more than a certificate of abandonment to account for her origins; she would know, without question, that she had been deeply loved before she was adopted.

When I heard this letter, I couldn't help but think of Annie's birth mother, who had cared for her for nearly the same amount of time as the foster mother. I couldn't imagine the depth of her grief and longing. Or perhaps I could, and the mystery was not the abandonment itself but how she, or any parent, could bear such a terrible loss. I asked our translator why her birth mother would have waited five months before giving her up. He clearly wasn't comfortable with my curiosity and questions, but finally he said that the husband has all the power in a marriage and very possibly Annie's mother tried to keep her for as long as possible. I thanked him very much; that was exactly the answer I was hoping for.

Not long after we returned to the United States, I had a dream about Annie's birth mother. In my dream, I was crossing a wide, traffic-choked avenue in Wuhan. Coming toward me was a woman with the dazed look of someone recovering from a long illness. In the middle of the avenue our eyes met; I think she sensed something familiar about me, knew that we were connected in some way, but could only offer me a pained, perplexed gaze. I wanted to tell her who I was, wanted to let her know that her daughter was safe and loved, but I didn't have the language to communicate with her. I reached out to touch her, but she was suddenly pulled back into the tide of people crossing the street, one woman among millions.

I thought of her constantly, always imagining her looking just over my shoulder, wondering what she would think as I played with Annie at the park, fed her lunch or sang her to sleep. Perhaps I couldn't quite accept the fact that we would never meet, that I could never let her know that her daughter was safe and loved, that her longing would never be relieved with the photographs and letters we could send to the foster mother. Perhaps I was driven by the same impulse as anyone who invents and tells stories, a desire for connection and solace with something that's been lost—a mother, a place, a history.

I continued to ask questions whenever I could. We had a Chinese babysitter name Li Li. She had been in the country for only three years; in Beijing, she had been a math professor. Li Li told me that the shape of Annie's eyes was considered very beautiful in China. I had actually heard the same comment from other Chinese women. Before we left for China to adopt Annie, I passed her picture around to my classes, and all the Chinese students remarked upon the beautiful shape of her eyes. Li Li explained that no woman in China would want to give up a daughter with such rare and beautiful eyes, and that no doubt the birth father gave the orders. Li Li said all this without a trace of conjecture; she knew my daughter's eyes, and she knew China. Li Li told me that her grandfather had ten sons, and when his eleventh child turned out to be a girl he was bitterly disappointed. "He have ten boy," Li Li exclaimed, "and he still upset about girl!"

In the meantime, we had written to Annie's foster mother. We thanked her for loving our daughter and expressed our hope that she would always be part of Annie's life. We asked her to tell us anything she could about Annie before we adopted her. Her reply stunned us. "When she came to my house," the foster mother wrote, "she was so skinny that she was like a skin-wrapped skeleton. She had bronchitis. The hospital issued a notice of critical illness, stating that the child's condition was fatal." The foster mother tramped from one hospital to the next with Annie, and at every one the doctors said they could do nothing to save the child's life. But Annie did live, of course. Her foster mother wrote that Annie's life was "snatched back from the hand of the God of Death." That's one explanation. But I know my strong-minded, iron-willed little girl, and I think that she had a resolve to live that no doctor could have guessed at as they looked at her frail, skeletal body.

The letter from Annie's foster mother enabled me to complete the story I had been trying to construct about her abandonment—the first of many stories I hope to tell my daughter. I believe that Annie was given up because her birth parents did not have the means to care for such a sickly and malnourished child. Her birth mother left her on the steps of the school because she wanted to give her a chance at life. Perhaps she hoped that Guyue would be cared for by someone like her goodhearted foster mother; I doubt she imagined that in a year's time her daughter would be on the other side of the world, celebrating the Jewish New Year.

I hope my daughter keeps the God of Death at arm's length for another 120 years and that she leaves behind many daughters and granddaughters and great-granddaughters, some of whom might trace their roots to the predawn hours of September 16, 1995, in a Chinese city of eight million, when a woman left her small bundle on the steps of a school and then hurried away into the darkness.

♥

Not for Me

Jennifer M. Kimball

It's pretty sad when a person takes a look at one's own life and skims over all of the good things accomplished. They look past the two wonderful kids, the loving husband, the beautiful home and the supportive family until their world is reduced to hollows and shadows, and they begin to imagine that something is missing at the core. You can call it a midlife crisis, a sense of unfulfillment, a panic attack or whatever you will. Some people dye their hair and others buy a sports car. I guess that same motivation drove me toward wanting to adopt a child.

I was adopted as an infant into a loving, supportive and sometimes crazy home. During my teens I struggled with my being adopted, as I imagine many adolescents do. Even back then I always assumed that I, too, would adopt when I grew older, so that I could give a child the same opportunity for a family that I'd received. I was blessed with a loving home, and I felt that I should do the same for a child somewhere, that it was my responsibility. My husband and I already had two biological children, but I still felt the weight of that duty. Of course, a sense of duty is not a good reason for a person to adopt a child, but for me it was quite a strong one.

I also knew that I would be able to give a wonderful home to someone, and that our shared adoption status would be a uniting point. Adopted children are often plagued with questions that spin around and around inside their heads, many times without answers.

Do I look like my birth mom? Why was I given up? Are my birth parents alive? Do they think of me on my birthday? What's my medical history? Will I die of some genetic disease? I knew that I might not be able to answer all of these questions for my child, but at least I could sympathize with the scary, unnerving and sometimes overwhelming feelings. I could say, "I know, sweetie, I wonder about that, too." I so loved the thought of being able to reassure a child. I thought my being adopted would connect me with this child in a way that non-adopted parents may not be able to. That is not to say, of course, that people who weren't adopted themselves aren't wonderful parents to adopted kids, but it would be one less hurdle to deal with for our family and our child.

The adoption process is not for the faint of heart. It is a long and arduous journey that often requires much courage and even more patience and steel nerves. In domestic cases, you and your family are presented to birth mothers, your life compressed into a small photo album that attempts to summarize who you are. And if you are not chosen by the birth mother, rejection sets in, the feeling that you have presented your whole life and it still wasn't good enough. The international route presents a great deal of travel to foreign countries, time spent away from home, reams of paperwork, the fickleness of foreign bureaucracy and uncertainty about the child's background. You must be willing to let go and free-fall, your stomach in your mouth and your heart strung out on a wire, and live with that feeling for months at a time.

With my family behind me, I plunged into the process. I cannot possibly describe the year-long spiral of people we met, children we were shown, snippets of conversation with social workers, bad dreams, good dreams, dreams and love for children we had never even met. The only image I can think of for that year was a flip book whirring along at full speed, with flashes of soft baby faces and blurred faces and patches of darkness and strange cries and sighs, and yet always with me in the center. I became like the one image on every page that stays the same, swaying and moving her hands slightly, but with the rest of the world changing frantically around her.

You see, my adoption search was all about me, and it never should have been in the first place. I was trying to fill something in my life, something that I imagined to be missing, and I hoped that adoption would change that, that it would somehow change me and my life into something better. Of course, I had the desire to give a child a family and a home, and to love them completely. But even my desire to be that perfect mom, that perfect family with an understanding and adopted mother and her adopted child, was a selfish one. It was as though I wanted to be that perfect mom for me, not for my child.

I don't know if the process changed me, or if it simply lifted the veil from my eyes. But I know that it was a whirling storm of emotions and memories and feelings about my childhood and my family's, and in the process everything was shaken up. When everything began to settle, I saw how naive I'd been. I was dreaming about the perfect family, and yet I already had it. Maybe I just needed that violent jolt, that shake like the snowstorm in a souvenir glass bubble, to recognize that I was so happy, complete and fulfilled in my life, in my beautiful family.

At the end of that year-long process, there was a little boy in Florida who was almost ready for us. But when I was speaking on the phone with our social worker, I felt a strange quietness inside, as though something were amiss. Sensing my fear, the social worker said, "Are you sure you're ready to do this? Are you ready to be a parent again?" And I knew that it was all wrong, that I was doing it all for the wrong reasons. The little boy was asthmatic, and I realized that all my thoughts were on the wrong track. *Will he keep everyone up late at night coughing? Will I have time to look after my other children if he is sick? Will we be able to go on vacations?* I think maybe I realized then that this little boy, as wonderful as he was, couldn't make my life complete. And I knew I would only ruin his in the process.

For the readers who think that I am against adoption or the difficulty involved is not worth it, you couldn't be more wrong. Adoption is one of the most selfless, beautiful and loving acts of which we are capable. Nothing greater exists in the world than giving a child a home. But I would like people to know that if you decide your journey won't end with you welcoming a child into your home, it's okay. More importantly, adoption is not about the adoptive parents, and it's not about saving yourself or becoming a hero. It's about a child who needs a home and a family that is willing to give everything of themselves to make it so.

I am so grateful that I was adopted into a loving family, even if it has burdened me with questions I cannot answer. I do think about my birth parents from time to time, but in a way the mystery is almost a gift. I can make my birth parents anything I want them to be. I can imagine that they are alive and living out their days happily. It makes me feel warm to think they are happy and that someone loves them very much.

♥

Interpreting Lucy

Marilyn Sides

On July 4, 1997, I brought my fourteen-month-old daughter, Lucy Mariana, a lively, charming child, home from Romania. At first, she could not even crawl, but within days she began to move around on her knees, and by October she was walking. She has been incredibly physically active ever since. As my father says, "She seems to be making up for lost time." She also has a quick intelligence to match her physical capabilities. In brief, she is a healthy child, smart and loving.

Still, even in this best-case scenario, I find the question that most haunts me whenever any discussion comes up about my daughter's development—physical and emotional—to be a subtle question of interpretation: Which characteristics belong to her as an individual and which were shaped by her preadoption experience? Last year in kindergarten and this year in first grade, Lucy's physical and personal exuberance have started to take on more complex meanings. It is very hard for Lucy to sit still, especially at moments like quiet time or waiting in lines to go somewhere; she is likely to start goofing around. She seems to be very demanding of the teacher's attention, always hovering nearby or not following instructions, requiring the teacher to stop and pay more attention to her. This, understandably, distracts and frustrates the teacher and the other children from the tasks at hand. I have had many conferences about how to get Lucy to be less impulsive, to help her redirect her energies.

These may seem like the usual rough edges that need polishing for any young child adjusting to new routines in school. Many books are available that try to address the joys and problems of raising a "spirited" child whose profile seems to match Lucy's. But I find myself constantly worrying if these behaviors are something else. Are they somehow tied to Lucy's experience in the orphanage before she was adopted? I began to read articles and talk to therapists who have seen many children adopted from Eastern Europe. They often bring up the diagnosis of post-traumatic stress disorder; the constant physical activity and the absolute need for attention are symptoms of anxiety, an inability to relax, let go and trust in the environment. They speak of possible abuse and the consequences of neglect. Suddenly Lucy's rough edges seem the traces of a painful early childhood experience, which I can't ever fix or even come to grips with by having a clear picture of what may have happened.

That sends me straight to the sadness that often lies near the heart of the adoption experience, a mourning for not being there at every moment in your child's life to protect them, know them, somehow be able to account for the texture of their existence from its very first moment. I know that sadness, and I know the temptation of letting it have too much power. I know the idealized fantasy of total control that no one, not even parents of biological children, could possibly have. So I say to myself, *Well, all right, Lucy may just be an exuberant child who will take a little longer to master all the energies she has been given so abundantly. Maybe she does have anxiety left over from her past. Probably both.*

In the end, as always, the question of interpretation settles itself by the need to move forward, to help her in whatever way possible to be both her exuberant self and a richly contributing member of a social group. That seems real, very much about the present—an interpretation that allows me to act.

♥

Our Story

Donna Marie Harris

I was an adopted child. Before I had even met my husband Jack, I knew that I wanted to adopt. I had known since I was a young girl that when I grew up I would adopt, whether I was able to have children or not. Because my feelings about adoption were so strong, I knew that the man I married had to be willing to adopt as well.

My husband Jack and I married in June 1996. After a year and a half of marriage, we began the process of becoming adoptive parents. Jack does case work for the Department of Social Services, so he felt compelled to go through the state to adopt. The preplacement process involved attending ten weeks of parenting classes with the Department of Social Services with a home study to follow. In a home study, nothing is secret. Every aspect of your life is uncovered. After six months, we had completed everything the state required of us to adopt a child.

After waiting some time, I was beginning to wonder if we were at the bottom of the list of parents waiting to adopt. Then one afternoon the phone rang. A woman from a private adoption agency (one with whom we were not even registered) was calling to see if we were interested in a specific little girl. Curiosity got the best of me, and I asked her where she had found our name. Her reply surprised me because our name had come from the regional director of the D.S.S. At our meeting we discovered that the little girl we were so interested in adopting had an extremely rare medical condition, so rare that she is the only one in the world with her genetic disorder. No doctor could tell us what would be in the future for this little girl.

After leaving our meeting I was both mad and heartbroken, mad at the state and the agency for not being able to place this child because of her medical condition, and heartbroken for this little girl and her uncertain future. Our names came up (both for the state and the private agency) as potential adoptive parents for this child because of our backgrounds in social services and education. Jack is the chairman for the Commission on Disabilities, and I am a former special education teacher. Most importantly, we were willing to adopt a special-needs child. Given our backgrounds and experience, everyone involved thought we were a perfect match for this little girl.

Once I understood the medical information about this little girl, my mind was made up. I wanted to adopt her even before I had had a chance to meet or hold her. Jack thought we needed to spend some time thinking about the challenges ahead and how our "new family" would impact all of our lives. I just knew in my heart that God had sent us this special child, and I was ready to meet her. I think Jack knew my mind was made up; he could see in my determination that we were meant to parent this child.

Just a week had passed since our meeting with the agency, but to me, the week seemed like a month. Soon, we were on our way to see our daughter. When I first laid eyes on her, her eyes locked into mine; we touched noses, and she cooed. I held her close and sang to her, "You are my sunshine, my only sunshine." She smiled and cooed even louder. A tear came to my eye, something I had never expected. I had already fallen in love.

A couple of weeks passed. We spent every available waking moment with her in her foster home. One day, I had a phone call after returning home from a visit with our daughter, a call with news I had never expected. I was pregnant. Despite the news, it never crossed either of our minds not to follow through with the adoption. The only thought that had entered my mind was what it would feel like to have two children so close in age.

Finally, the day came for us to bring our daughter, who we decided to name Emily Rose, home. She took to her new environment. Emily's arrival was the easy part; unfortunately, I experienced complications with my pregnancy. I was around fifteen weeks pregnant when the doctor informed me that the baby was not growing. Not too long after receiving this news, we lost our baby. While difficult, the loss of our baby was easier to handle because we felt so blessed to have Emily. She really helped us get through our loss.

Emily is beginning to blossom with the help of Early Intervention Services. She is globally delayed, due to her genetic imbalance. Moreover, she had to have hip surgery at the age of twelve weeks and stay in a body cast for three months. All of these factors have contributed to her delays. Emily is going to be leaving Early Intervention at the age of three to move on to pre-K, and her therapists are preparing us for this transition. Having worked with them for three years, they have become a part of our family.

One afternoon, Emily's occupational therapist told us about another little girl she was working with who was up for adoption. She asked us if we were considering another child. She felt this little girl would fit right into our family and would blossom just as Emily had. We were quite surprised by her compliment, and, of course, we wanted to know as much as we could about this new little girl. We also laughed at ourselves because, if we adopted this little girl, then we would continue to have contact with the therapist from Early Intervention, a person we had grown attached to and didn't want to see leave our collective life.

Within a few days I contacted the agency about this little girl, whose name was Kate. Kate is very similar to Emily in that they both have rare chromosomal imbalances. As attracted as we were to the idea of adopting Kate, we really needed to think about what kind of impact caring for two disabled children would have on our lives. We wanted to be sure that each child was going to receive the attention she needed. We knew that we wanted a sibling for Emily, but we still needed to think through the decision. The more we discussed the idea of adopting a second daughter, the more we thought the new family arrangement would be the best option for both girls. Our main thought on the matter was that the girls would be ideal siblings because they would have a common bond and would always be able to relate to each other. Ideally, they would have each other to lean on when life was challenging.

Now that we had pretty much made our decision, we needed to address the specifics of the adoption process. We needed to learn the requirements for the private agency placing Kate. We met with Kate's social worker. He was very forthcoming with information on her. We felt a special connection to him. He had been a social worker for D.S.S. before working for the private adoption agency. He updated our home study and came to know us as a family. One concern I had was how Emily would adjust to a new baby in the house. He agreed to let us see the baby frequently in her foster home so that we could all get acquainted. Emily was quite taken with Kate from the start. I think she thought Kate was a doll!

The two girls' adoptions were different in many ways. Emily's parents were from out of state and not involved with her placement. Kate's parents, whom we actually met, were involved. They had a say in the placement of their biological daughter. We have a semi-open adoption with Kate's parents. Emily's adoption is closed. As adoptive parents we feel an obligation not only to these special children but also to their biological parents. We want to make sure these girls get the best physical, emotional and medical care possible.

Having two disabled children has made an impact on all of our lives. Balancing the busy, structured daily life of medical appointments, therapies and family quality time is a juggling act for us, but we wouldn't change our situation in the least. Jack's and my professional background and general knowledge of what it takes to raise special-needs children has made it easier for us to give our daughters everything they need.

♥

The Gift of Two Perspectives

Brenda M. Cotter

I am the parent of two girls, ages eight and seven, both of whom were born in China. My daughters and I have something important in common. We share the experience of joining a family through adoption. While I never expected to become an adoptive parent, I have come to realize that it is an incredible benefit and gift to have this experience in common with my children.

I was adopted by my parents in 1956 when I was five months old. During that time, adoption was not openly discussed, and the recognition of the importance of birth parents and genetic connections to adoptees was only just appearing on the horizon. While I always knew that I was adopted and my parents expressed very positive feelings about that fact, I always sensed that my parents could not comfortably discuss it.

As I grew into my early teens and beyond, I started to actively wonder about my birth parents. I was very curious about the physical similarities so evident in my friends' nonadoptive families: Oh, he looks just like his grandfather did when he was young; she has the same hair as her mom. Those similarities, which my friends took for granted, were fascinating to me. Over time, I began to shift from mere curiosity to a much more intense yearning for information about my genetic heritage. These feelings were often quite painful because I believed that I would never know the answers to my questions.

I also found little support for my questions and feelings. In light of that, I viewed my own feelings as negative, and I tried, with little success, to forget about them and move on. In retrospect, I see that my parents were frightened by my questions, worried that it meant they had done something wrong or they would lose me.

In my early twenties, I made some connections to others who had been adopted and also read a book that changed my life. *Lost and Found* by Betty Jean Lifton described the experiences of adoptees who shared so many of the feelings that I had. I realized for the first time that the very deep yearning I felt was not at all uncommon among adoptees. And in my midtwenties, I searched for and found my birth mother. I learned that my birth father was dead, but I looked for his family all the same.

Two quite profound effects resulted from meeting my birth mother and other genetic relatives. First, it was deeply satisfying, essentially filling what felt like a gap or space in my most essential self. Second, it made me realize how grateful and glad I was that my life had gone exactly the way that it had. While I certainly liked my birth family and it was pretty neat to look into that genetic mirror—my mother with that same gap between her front teeth—I had a sudden epiphany that if my life had been any different, I would not be who I am. I would not be connected to all of the people, including my parents, who I love so much. Despite their fears, my parents had been supportive of my search for my birth parents. My parents were quite relieved to see that my quest for the essentials of my own identity had nothing to do with, and did not diminish or threaten, our family.

All my life, I had always loved kids and planned to be a mom. I was sure of one thing, however: I wanted to have biological kids. I wanted the experience of having a family with whom I had a genetic connection. I wanted to experience those same genetic touchstones that I had envied in my friends' families when I was growing up. But when the time came in my midthirties and I tried to have a child, I found that it just wasn't working. I tried fertility treatments, and it still wasn't working. When my partner suggested that maybe we could consider adoption, I was adamantly opposed. Not only did I want that biological connection with my child, I did not want my child to feel the painful yearning I had felt as a child. I wanted no part of adoption.

Well, as I have learned and relearned in my life: Never say never. I was absolutely committed to becoming a parent and, over time, my mind started to open to the idea of adoption. At some point, I realized that my heart was starting to follow my mind. I knew better than many that the family connection forged by adoption was as true and deep as that made by biology. Love was not the issue. The only requirement was that I let go of my desire to experience a biological connection to my child. I started to realize that I could. In fact, I began to realize that my hope for that biological connection was a very minor element of my desire to be a parent. I wanted to love and care for a child, not to gaze at myself in her face and fingers. And my need to love intensified as the adoption process drew out, expanding like a flame, and finally becoming clear and sharp around the edges, until the moment my five-month-old daughter was placed in my arms in China. I loved her instantly and completely. Everything was meant to be just exactly the way it was and is.

I realize now that life has led me to this place (albeit sometimes kicking and screaming) because I was meant to be here. I cannot believe how lucky I am to be the parent of my daughters. I have found that my experience of being adopted is an incredible resource in being a parent to my children. Among other things I've learned:

- There is no substitute for having the experience yourself. You can read about what being adopted is like (just as you can with any other human characteristic or condition), but the truth is that you cannot truly understand how it feels unless you have had the experience. While my children and I have different histories, and they will have their own feelings about adoption, undoubtedly different from mine, they will know that I understand how it feels to be adopted.

- I will not be particularly threatened when my children are furious at me as teenagers and scream, "You are not my real mother! I wish you had never adopted me!" I thought and said those things to my parents, and I know they reflect nothing more than teenage angst.

- I will understand the deep existential longing my daughters may feel for their genetic and cultural heritage, and support them in expressing that in whatever way their hearts lead them.

- I feel comfortable with adoption and with talking about adoption. While I love to explore all of the resources available in books and articles on the subject of adoption, I trust and rely most on my own gut instincts on this subject.

- Most importantly, just the fact of my own adoption makes my children feel good. They like that we have that in common. A few mornings ago, I told my daughters that I was asked to write an article about being both a person who was adopted and an adoptive parent. I asked them how they felt about the fact that I was adopted too. "Happy," said my six-year-old. My eight-year-old pondered for a moment and said, "Connected." I am so grateful for all that has brought me to this place.

♥

Encounters on the Path

Jonathan Scott

If you venture off the main road in Jamaica Plain's Arnold Arboretum, there is a long ribbon of a path meandering through a fairytale forest of conifers. Each tree is an inspiration, a rare jewel and a unique species. Every one is an amazing and lovely being. Majestic as a king, sacred as a newborn.

Stroll deeper, and the beguiling trees envelop you like a beautiful love poem, like dancers in a Degas paining, or like an illustration in an antique children's book of some enchanted emerald woods that lure you deep inside the page. Even their names lull you into a kind of magical trance: silver fir and white scrub pine; blue atlas cedar and dawn redwood; purple cone and dragon spruce. There are the weeping hemlocks and the English yews; the Hinoki cypress and the Japanese larch; and the great tree of all—the giant sequoia.

Along this path, early last fall, on a sleepy sunrise of a September morning, the most unexpected encounter happened to my six-month-old son Luis. It was an occurrence of the most amazing and strangest order. Some would call it an encounter of fate or destiny. Others would say just plain luck or serendipity. Either way, it is an encounter along the path that is now and forever a part of the life story that belongs to Luis.

Luis is my adopted son. He was born in March 2003 in the small mountain village of Saquisili, Ecuador. During the month I lived with him in a hilltop orphanage in Quito, when he was barely three months old, we came to know each other in a land defined by the mystery and supreme beauty of Mother Earth. Every morning with Luis in my arms, we'd watch from our balcony the misty sunrise over the snow-capped peak of the Cotopaxi volcano. And every night before Luis fell to sleep, we'd gaze at the twinkling blanket of a million city lights. We'd imagine all the stars had fallen to Earth and landed in the valley of Quito. I'd whisper to him *"Toca el cielo"* (touch the sky), and wave his hands into the night.

The first thing everyone notices about Luis is his hair. It is a shiny, black rainbow, soft as velvet. It feels like a bouquet of feathers against your cheek, and it smells as fresh and crisp as clean linen or a teaspoonful of vanilla. His eyes are two big, sparkling droplets of wet indigo ink on bright, clean white paper. When his gaze catches yours, everyone exclaims, *"Ay, que lindo!"* (How beautiful!). One woman at the orphanage called him *"mi amor escondito"* (my hidden love).

His ears remind me of seashells. Perfect. Round. Mysterious. And his hazelnut skin has just enough adobe highlights in his cheeks. When he's wet in your arms he's a slippery *lobo marina papi* (seal pup), and when he's dry, he's a warm loaf of soft, fresh bread. He's a quiet little guy, except after naps in his crib when you can hear him talking to himself, making the gawking and cawing sounds of an exotic parrot.

Even at three months old, Luis was an unmistakably brave and self-confident boy. He seemed at once to be independent, resourceful and very social. Luis is the kind of popular, fun-loving person I surmise many during his whole life will proudly claim as their friend. He also likes a good party and dressing in very fine clothes, especially bright bold colors. Few others can get away with wearing neon pumpkin the way Luis can.

On the particular morning of Luis's encounter, it was nearly a month after we'd made the long, harrowing odyssey from his birth country Ecuador back to Luis's new home in Massachusetts. I was pushing Luis in his efficient blue ultra-terrain mountain stroller down the pebbly, evergreen-lined forest path. This walk had become our customary morning ritual. It was, after all, our favorite hidden spot to unleash our dogs and let them run free. As we turned the bend near a grove of short leaf pines, I noticed farther down the trail three men heading in our direction.

In the middle was an older man, clearly of Asian heritage. Two young and sturdy fellows flanked him. They were gently holding the older man's arms to guide him along the way. Although I was hardly paying much attention, I do remember pausing when I heard the sound of chanting coming from their direction. I recognized it as similar to the unmistakable chanting I heard in a Buddhist monastery I visited many years earlier on a Himalayan trek through Nepal. To see three men walking with linked arms at sunrise on this path was certainly an uncommon sight, but to hear three Buddhist monks chanting on the path was a first for me. I stopped the stroller to let them pass.

A few feet in front of us, the older man dressed in plain gray monk's walking clothes, ceased his chanting. His companions became quiet as well. They pointed to Luis. They smiled and nodded. The old man bent over the stroller and murmured a few words, unrecognizable to me. Then he made a sweeping gesture in the air with his hand over Luis as if drawing a perfect circle. The gesture seemed like a blessing, or the punctuation at the end of a special prayer to honor this little boy.

Only then did the old man look up and his eyes met mine. Then I recognized him. In the filtered morning light of that evergreen forest, I witnessed a moment I can only describe as amazing. I wasn't certain at first because he didn't have on his glasses, nor was he wearing his formal flowing maroon robes, but it was unmistakably him. It was His Holiness—the Dalai Lama.

Could it really be that one of the world's greatest living spiritual leaders was in Jamaica Plain, of all places? Could it be His Holiness walking on a discreet path through the woods in the early morning and then bending over to bless my son as he passes by—my son Luis, a little boy orphaned at birth, but strong and willful enough to survive? He was an infant with hope and strength enough to make the long journey to his new home and a new beginning. Was it an accident that Luis arrived here just at this moment to find this encounter? Or was it destiny for Luis to have this encounter find him?

Later that morning I read the *Boston Globe's* coverage of the Dalai Lama's visit to Cambridge and Brookline. In the article, he described himself as a simple monk, and told the audience made up mostly of Harvard students that, "Intelligence alone is no guarantee of a happy life. . . . While you are making progress in your education, pay equal attention about the development of your healthy person."

Early one morning, somewhere underneath a rare blue Spanish fir, to the left of a grove of towering red cedars, a prayer was whispered into the heart of my son. What was said exactly, I may never know. Yet somehow I am certain that Luis is blessed all the days of his life.

♥

About the Alliance
for Children Foundation

A portion of the proceeds of this book will go to The Alliance for Children Foundation, Inc., a nonprofit international relief organization devoted to alleviating the suffering of vulnerable children living in orphanages throughout the world. The Foundation's goal is to provide these children with the nutrition, shelter, medical care and enrichment they need to become healthy and eligible for adoption.

The Foundation's mission is to rebuild the lives of children who are often invisible to all but a few caregivers within their own institutions. Ideally, the Foundation's work will physically and emotionally strengthen these children so that they become known to prospective adoptive parents, either in their own country or abroad, who will give them a full, rich, and loving family life.

While adoption is the best solution for orphaned and abandoned children, the Foundation also seeks social justice and nurturance for children who will remain in orphanage care. For these children, the Foundation's focus goes beyond the essentials of life to include enrichment and skill-building opportunities that will enable them to become successful, independent adults with a strong sense of self-worth.

For more information, contact:

The Alliance for Children Foundation
55 William St.
Suite G-10
Wellesley, MA 02481
Phone: (781) 431-7270